school
programs
in
speech-language:
organization
and
management

school programs in speech-language: organization and management

Elizabeth A. Neidecker

Prentice-Hall, Inc., Englewood Cliffs, N.J. 07632

Library of Congress Cataloging in Publication Data

Neidecker, Elizabeth A
  School programs in speech-language.

  Bibliography: p.
  Includes index.
    1. Speech therapy.   2. Speech, Disorders of.
I. Title.
LB3454.N44   371.9'14   79-26643
ISBN 0-13-794321-0

Printed in the United States of America

10   9   8   7   6   5   4   3   2   1

Editorial/production supervision
  and interior design by: Barbara Kelly
Cover design: Jorge Hernandez
Manufacturing buyer: Harry P. Baisley

Prentice-Hall International, Inc., *London*
Prentice-Hall of Australia Pty. Limited, *Sydney*
Prentice-Hall of Canada, Ltd., *Toronto*
Prentice-Hall of India Private Limited, *New Delhi*
Prentice-Hall of Japan, Inc., *Tokyo*
Prentice-Hall of Southeast Asia Pte. Ltd., *Singapore*
Whitehall Books Limited, Wellington, *New Zealand*

In memory of my family ...
Fred, Alpha, John, Nancy

contents

2

the school clinician as a professional person   14

3

new directions for school programs   27

4

the first steps in establishing programs   44

5

applying management techniques to speech-language programs   55

6

essentials of the program   63

7

case finding, case selection, and the individualized educational program   81

8

scheduling and implementing therapy   108

9

working with others in the school   128

10

special categories of programs   148

11

program maintenance and professional responsibilities   169

12

taking the first step—student teaching   188

preface

This book is about programs for speech, language, and hearing handicapped pupils in the educational environment. Written primarily for undergraduate and graduate students preparing for positions as speech-language pathologists in the schools, it could also serve as a source of information for school superintendents, school principals, directors of special education programs, as well as for individuals already working in schools as speech-language specialists.

The school speech-language pathologist is called upon to plan and implement programs and to make decisions in regard to the programs. This person must be able to work cooperatively and effectively with educators, medical personnel, rehabilitation specialists, and parents. I have attempted to present information which I hope will help the school clinician in planning and carrying out the programs, and will help that individual in making the many decisions necessary to the process.

In many situations there is no one "right" answer to a problem. There may be, however, a "best" answer, and this "best" answer would depend upon the school clinician's ability to assess the situation and then apply the most appropriate alternatives or options. This is a roundabout way of saying that this book is not a "cookbook" and does not contain "recipes." It contains information which the school clinician may be able to utilize in program organization and management.

The first three chapters provide a background of information including the early history and growth of school speech and hearing programs, the basis of professionalism, and the changes that have culuminated in a new direction for speech, language, and audiology programs in the schools.

Chapters Four, Five, Six, and Seven contain information on starting a program, establishing goals and applying management techniques, and planning and implementing the essential elements of a program. Case finding, case selection, and the individualized educational program, are the subjects of chapter Seven.

Scheduling pupils for therapy and implementing therapy programs for pupils, are the topics discussed in Chapter Eight.

Chapter Nine deals with working with school personnel; including principals, classroom teachers, special teachers, the school nurse, psychologists, guidance counselors, social workers, and reading specialists. The chapter also discusses the roles of the physical and occupational therapists, and physicians. The role and supervision of the communication aide are also treated. The importance of a good community information program is stressed.

Chapter Ten includes information on speech-language improvement programs, high school programs, vocational school programs, and summer programs. Examples of programs in Arizona, California, Delaware, and Ohio are included.

Program maintenance, record and report systems, accountability practices, and research by school clinicians are topics included in chapter Eleven, along with professional organizations, teachers organizations, continuing education, and publications and resources.

Student teaching is speech-language pathology and audiology is the subject of chapter Twelve. The roles and responsibilities of the student clinician, the cooperating clinician in the schools, and the university supervisor, are outlined.

The Appendixes contain a list of organizations of interest to the school speech-language and hearing specialist, a list of commercial materials and equipment with their estimated prices, and the publishers. Some sample record and report forms are also included. The Code of Ethics of the American Speech-Language-Hearing Association is given, as well as the requirements for the Certificate of Clinical Competence of the American Speech-Language-Hearing Association.

The advent of Public Law 94-142 (The Education of All Handicapped Children Act) has brought about many changes in the education of handicapped children. The intent of the law is good. The implementation of it is sometimes difficult. Many school clinicians have been carrying out the intent of the law long before it was in effect. In implementing the law in speech, language, and hearing programs, it is good to keep in mind that the law was never meant to supplant common sense, and the criterion for making decisions subsequent to it must always be. "What is best for the child?"

That segment of the speech-language and audiology profession working in the schools is a dedicated, competent, conscientious, hard-working group. They are the front-line of the profession. The challenges they are facing, and will continue to face, are many. It is my sincere hope that this book will meet some of the needs of present and future school clinicians and will assist them in their day-to-day professional activities.

I am indebted to many persons in the preparation of this book: to my students at Bowling Green State University who gave me the opportunity to try out ideas; to friends and colleagues who offered advice, answered questions, and provided encouragement and moral support; and to the many individuals who so graciously allowed me to quote from their works.

I am especially grateful to the reviewers of this book whose comments and suggestions helped immeasurably in the preparation of the manuscript. They are: Jean L. Anderson, Speech and Hearing Center, Indiana University; Margaret C. Byrne, Division of Speech Pathology and Audiology, University of Kansas; Margaret Hatton, School of Speech, Kent State University; Elizabeth Lambert Johns, Institute for Educational Leadership, The Geroge Washington University; and Derek A. Sanders, Speech and Hearing Clinic, State University of New York at Buffalo.

My colleagues at Bowling Green State University, whose expertise I borrowed, helped me with particular sections of the book. They include Faith Jackson, Ruth and Glenn Varney, Marie Hodge, and Herbert and Bonita Greenberg.

Barbara DeWeese, William Freitag, Ruth Terry, and Polly Young, all school speech-language pathologists, provided me with valuable information about their various programs For their generosity and time I am very appreciative.

I would also like to acknowledge the contribution of the school clinicians with whom I have worked over the years in the student teaching programs at Bowling Green State University and Case-Western Reserve University. They have provided me with many of the ideas I have incorporated in this book.

It would not be possible to write a book and not have errors creep in. For any errors that may occur I will assume responsibility.

Elizabeth A. Neidecker

Speech Class
(for Joe)

We were outcasts—
you with your stutters,
me with my slurring—
and that was plenty for a friendship.

When we left class to go to the therapist
we hoped they wouldn't laugh—
took turns reminding the teacher:
"Me and Joe have to go to shpeesh clash now,"
or "M-m-me and J-Jim ha-have to go to s-s-speech now."

Mrs. Clark, therapist, was also god, friend, mother.
Once she took us to the zoo on a field trip:
"Aw, ya gonna go look at the monkeys?"
"Maybe they'll teach you how to talk."
We clenched teeth and went
and felt the sun and fed the animals
and we were a family of broken words.

For years we both tried so hard
and I finally learned
where to put my tongue and how to make the sounds
and graduated,
but the first time you left class without me
I felt that punch in the gut—
I felt like a deserter
and wanted you
to have my voice.

> Jim Daniels
> Bowling Green, Ohio

1 | the growth and development of the profession in the schools

INTRODUCTION

This chapter provides an historical background of the profession of speech, language, and hearing, and the development of programs within the schools of the United States. The philosophy of education in the United States which invited speech, language, and hearing programs into the schools is described. Also discussed is the expansion of school programs, both professionally and geographically. The chapter points out the role of the school pathologists in the early days and the changes in that role, as well as the factors which influenced those changes. It also considers the prevailing philosophy and legislation mandating equal educational opportunities for all handicapped children, and the implications of this for both the programs of the future, and the roles and responsibilities of the school pathologist of the future.

EARLY HISTORY

Although speech, language, and hearing problems have been with us since the early history of mankind, rehabilitative services for children with communication handicaps were not realized until the early part of the twentieth century. The growth of the profession and the establishment of the American Academy of Speech in 1925 reflect the realization of the needs and special problems of the speech and hearing handicapped population.

According to Paul Moore and Dorothy Kester (1953), the educational philosophy which invited speech correction into the schools was expressed in the preface to a teacher's manual published in 1897 which contained John Dewey's "My Pedagogic Creed." The preface, written by Samuel T. Dutton, superintendent of schools, Brookline, Massachusetts, stated:

> The isolation of the teacher is a thing of the past. The processes of education have come to be recognized as fundamental and vital in any attempt to improve human conditions and elevate society.
>
> The missionary and the social reformer have long been looking to education for counsel and aid in their most difficult undertakings. They have viewed with interest and pleasure the broadening of pedagogy so as to make it include not only experimental physiology and child study, but the problems of motor training, physical culture, hygiene, and the treatment of defectives and delinquents of every class.
>
> The schoolmaster, always conservative, has not found it easy to enter this large field; for he has often failed to realize how rich and fruitful the result of such researches are; but remarkable progress has been made, and a changed attitude on the part of the educators is the result.

Moore and Kester (1953) have suggested that child labor laws influenced the growth of speech programs in the schools. Barring children from work forced both the atypical and the normal child to remain in school, and teachers soon asked for help with the exceptional children. A few got help, including assistance with children having speech defects.

According to Moore and Kester, it was in 1910 that the Chicago public schools started a program of speech correction. Ella Flagg Young, the superintendent of schools, in her annual report in 1910 said:

> Immediately after my entrance upon the duties of superintendent, letters began to arrive filled with complaints and petitions by parents of stammering children—complaints that the schools did nothing to help children handicapped by stammering to overcome their speech difficulty, but left them to lag behind and finally drop out of the schools; and petitions that something be done for those children. It was somewhat peculiar and also suggestive that these letters were followed by others from people who had given much attention to the study of stammering and wished to undertake the correction of that defect in stammerers attending the public schools. Soon after the schools were opened in the fall, I sent out a note, requesting each principal to report

the number of stammerers in the school. It was surprising to find upon receiving the replies that there were recognized as stammerers 1,287 children. A recommendation was made to the committee on school management to the effect that the head of the department of oral expression in the Chicago Teachers' College be authorized to select ten of the members of the graduating class who showed special ability in the training given at the college in that particular subject and should be further empowered to give additional training of these students preparatory to their undertaking, under the direction of the department, the correction of the speech defects of these 1,287 children. The Board appropriated $3,000.00 toward the payment of these students who should begin their work after graduation at the rate of $65 a month during a period extending from February 1 to June 30.

Instead of gathering the children into one building or into classes to be treated for their troubles, a plan was adopted of assigning to the young teacher a circuit and having her travel from school to school during the day. The object of this plan was to protect the young teacher from the depression of spirit and low physical condition that often ensue from continued confinement in one room for several successive hours at work upon abnormal conditions. It was soon found that the term "stammering" had been assumed to be very general in its application and many children who had been reported as stammerers had not the particular defect reported but some other form of speech defect. (1953, pp. 49.)

The superintendent of schools in New York City in 1909 requested an investigation of the need for speech training in the schools, and two years later the following recommendations were presented to the board of education: First, the number of speech handicapped children was to be ascertained and case histories were to be obtained on them; second, speech centers were to be established providing daily lessons of from 30 to 60 minutes; third, English teachers were to be given further training and utilized as instructors; and fourth, a department for training teachers was to be established. It was not until four years later, however, that a Director of Speech Improvement was appointed to carry out the recommendations (Moore and Kester, 1953).

EARLY GROWTH

During this same decade there was an increasing number of public school systems employing speech clinicians. Among them were Detroit, Grand Rapids, Cleveland, Boston, Cincinnati, and San Francisco (Paden, 1970). In 1918, Dr. Walter B. Swift of Cleveland wrote an article entitled, "How to Begin Speech Correction in the Public Schools." (The article was reprinted in *Language, Speech and Hearing Services in Schools*, April 1972.)

To the state of Wisconsin goes the credit for establishing at the University of Wisconsin the first training program for prospective specialists in the field, and for granting the first Doctor of Philosophy degree in the area of speech disorders to Sara M. Stinchfield in 1921. Wisconsin was also the first state to enact enabling legislation for public school speech services and to appoint in 1923 a state supervisor of speech correction, Pauline Camp. Meanwhile, other universities throughout the United States were developing curricula in the area of speech disorders. Until 1940, however, only eight additional states added similar laws to their statute books (Irwin, 1959). By 1963, a study by Haines (1965) indicated that forty-five of the states had passed legislation placing speech and hearing programs in the public schools. These laws provided for financial help to school districts maintaining approved programs, supervision by the state, responsibility for administering the law, and the establishment of standards. The laws described minimum standards which the programs were expected to exceed (Haines, 1965).

The first state supervisors, in cooperation with the school clinicians in their respective states, did a remarkably far-sighted job in establishing state-wide programs in regard to the organizational aspects. With no precedents to follow, they established program standards that have retained merit through many years. The Vermont program (Dunn, 1949), providing speech and hearing services to children in rural areas, and the Ohio plan (Irwin, 1949) furnish two such examples. They addressed themselves to such topics as: finding children who need the services, diagnostic services, caseload, the scheduling of group and individual therapy sessions, rooms for the therapist, equipment and supplies, coordination day, summer residence programs, in-service training of parents and teachers, and periodic rechecks of children.

A PERIOD OF EXPANSION

The decades of the 1940s and the 1950s were times of growth and beginnings for all aspects of the profession. In 1943 the American Medical Association requested that a list of ethical speech correction schools and clinics be provided for distribution to physicians. During World War II the entire membership was listed in the National Roster of Scientific Personnel. The organization which started life in 1926 as The American Academy of Speech Correction with twenty-five dedicated and determined individuals changed its name in 1948 to The American Speech and Hearing Association and in 1979 to The American Speech-Language-Hearing Association. Its membership had increased to 1,144 persons in 1948 (Paden, 1970), and in 1978 the membership was reported to be 27,642.

It was also during these decades that the public school programs increased and expanded, both professionally and geographically. School clinicians found themselves wearing many hats. In addition to selling the idea of such a program to the school system and the community, the clinician had to:

devise a set of forms to be used for record-keeping and reporting,
locate the children with speech and hearing handicaps,
schedule them for therapy after talking with their teachers as to the most convenient time for all concerned,

provide the diagnosis and the therapy,

work with the school nurse on locating the children with hearing losses,

counsel the parents,

answer hundreds of questions from teachers who were often totally unfamiliar with such a program,

keep the school administration informed of what was going on,

confer with persons in other professional disciplines,

and, at the same time, remain healthy, well groomed, trustworthy, modest, friendly, cheerful, courteous, patient, enthusiastic, tolerant, cooperative, businesslike, dependable, prompt, creative, interesting, and unflappable.

Furthermore, the clinician had to keep one eye on the clock and the calendar and the other eye on state standards.

development of programs
for the hearing impaired

The concern for the hearing handicapped has long been an issue both with the families of those individuals and with professionals. The history of the education of the deaf had its beginning in Europe in the sixteenth century. Educational programs for the deaf were first established in the United States in 1817 with the founding of the American School for the Deaf at Hartford, Connecticut (Bender, 1960).

Initially, programs in this country were designed for deaf children and the needs of the hard-of-hearing child were for the most part neglected. Deaf children were educated in residential schools or institutions until the establishment of classrooms in regular schools. More recently, hearing-impaired children as well as profoundly deaf children have been helped in preschool classes, special classrooms, and regular classrooms as well as in residential schools. The educational programs are individualized and, wherever appropriate, mainstreaming is the case. The program for the hearing-impaired child is bolstered by the co-ordinated efforts of parents, classroom teachers, otologists, educational audiologists, psychologists, and speech-language pathologists.

speech improvement

School programs designed to help all children develop the ability to communicate effectively in acceptable speech, voice, and language patterns have been historically called *speech improvement* programs. Such programs were usually carried out by the classroom teacher with the speech-language clinician serving as a consultant and doing demonstration teaching in the classroom. Many such programs were initiated in the 1920s, 1930s, and 1940s and were concentrated on the kindergarten and first-grade levels. One of the purposes was to reduce the number of minor speech problems.

The programs were not considered part of the school clinician's regular duties in many states. However, in some cities, speech improvement programs were carried out successfully despite lack of state subsidies. According to Garrison (1961), the communities of Arlington County, Virginia; Brea, California; Des Moines, Iowa; Hartford, Connecticut; Hingham, Massachusetts; New York, New York; Wauwatosa, Wisconsin; Wichita, Kansas; and Youngstown, Ohio, were recognized as having well-organized speech improvement programs.

In recent years the philosophy of the speech, language, and hearing profession has expanded to include prevention of problems. As a result, many school clinicians are incorporating speech improvement programs into their activities. They may be carried out on the kindergarten and the primary-grade level or on the high-school level. They are usually planned and implemented cooperatively with the classroom teacher. A more apt term for such programs might be *speech-language development programs*.

programs for language
disordered pupils

Although school clinicians have been dealing with language problems in schools for many years, awareness of language difficulties in children has been heightened during the last decade. During the 1940s, 1950s, and early 1960s, there was considerable interest among professionals in articulation and speech sounds. The focus changed in the late 1960s and early 1970s to an interest in syntactic structures and sentence forms.

Along with this growing awareness of language problems has been the realization that the school clinician has a commitment to the student whose language is disordered or delayed. This may include students who are hearing-impaired, mentally retarded, learning-disabled, physically handicapped, emotionally disturbed, or environmentally disadvantaged. These children may have communication difficulties ranging from mild to severe, or they may have multiple handicaps.

INCIDENCE
OF COMMUNICATION PROBLEMS

The problem of attempting to ascertain the numbers of school-age children with speech and hearing handicaps was a huge one in the early days of school programs. As Milisen (1971) stated, "Early workers had to demonstrate the number of people who had disabling speech handicaps before superintendents would hire clinicians and before college presidents would allow courses in speech pathology to be listed in their curricula." Milisen further suggested that once the need for speech rehabilitation was established by incidence figures, the study of incidence could then be directed toward the solutions of other problems.

Unfortunately, determining the number of speech disordered individuals is not simply a matter of taking a head count. The complicating factors which were present in the early days of the profession are still with us today and have become even more complex.

Johnson (1959), in a report issued by the Office of Education, Department of Health, Education and Welfare, stated that 4 percent of school-age children have severe speech and hearing impairments. His report stated that the figures were based on a total estimate of 40 million school children (5-17 years of age inclusive) in the United States as of October, 1957. He cautiously advised that this was probably an underestimate but that he felt it better to be conservative in view of the fact that the data currently available were not adequate to support precise estimates.

In a study prepared by the Committee on Legislation of the American Speech and Hearing Association (1959), it was estimated that 5 percent of school-age children and 1.3 percent of children under five have speech problems. In addition, 0.7 percent of school-age children and 0.3 percent of preschool-age children were estimated to have handicapping hearing problems. These populations did not include Alaska, Hawaii, or Puerto Rico.

TABLE 1-1.   ESTIMATED NUMBER OF SCHOOL-AGE CHILDREN PER 10,000 WITH EACH TYPE OF SPEECH AND HEARING PROBLEM

	Percent of Children With Serious Problems	Children With Serious Problems
Articulation	3.0	300
Stuttering	1.0	100
Voice	0.1	10
Cleft Palate Speech	0.1	10
Cerebral Palsy Speech	0.1	10
Retarded Speech Development	0.2	20
Speech Problems Due to Impaired Hearing	0.5	50
Total	5.0	500

The committee stated, "The above estimates are believed to be conservative, and in each instance err on the side of underestimating the number of children with speech and hearing problems. For example, it should be noted that only children with significant or handicapping hearing losses are included above. An additional one million school children have non-handicapping reductions in hearing acuity."

A national study of disorders among school-age children has been reported (Hull, 1969). This survey included 40,000 pupils and was based on a random demographic sample. It covered overall speech patterns, articulation, voice, fluency, and hearing, and was also broken down by grade levels. Despite some limitations this survey has provided us with important information about the communication disorders in public schools. (See Table 1-2.)

In regard to the incidence of language problems, Jones and Healey (1973) observed, "The incidence and prevalence of language and language learning problems are not known. Only recently has there been increased awareness of the

TABLE 1-2.

Degree and Type of Deviation	Percent
Acceptable overall speech pattern	34.8
Mild overall speech deviation	53.1
Moderate overall speech deviation	10.6
Extreme overall speech deviation	1.5
Acceptable articulation	66.4
Moderate articulation deviation	31.6
Extreme articulation deviation	2.0
Acceptable voice	50.1
Moderate voice deviation	46.8
Extreme voice deviation	3.1
Acceptable fluency	99.2
Dysfluent	.8
Normal bilateral hearing	88.8
Reduced hearing	11.2

problems many children have in using linguistic symbols in comprehension, transformation and/or expression for communication."

The difficulty in ascertaining the incidence of children with language delay and language deviances continues to be a problem, not only for speech, language, and hearing clinicians, but for all workers in the field of special education. As indicated earlier the number is probably larger than we suspect.

summary of incidence

Reports on incidence and prevalence of speech and hearing handicaps among school-age pupils have not been complete for several reasons. Sometimes the data were based on too few children, and sometimes the surveys were based on the reports of persons with little or no training in identifying speech problems. Often bilingual children, institutionalized children, children in special classes, and school dropouts were not included in the survey. Because of wide discrepancies in obtaining language samples, very little if any information was obtained on the incidence of language problems. Many children who might have died at birth are today being saved through improved medical care, and this points to an increase in communication problems.

Despite the difficulties in obtaining incidence figures, it is safe to assume that while speech, language, and hearing problems have always been with us, the prevalence of them is increasing in both the preschool and the school-age population.

Jones and Healey (1973) stated, "Estimates of the number of children with communicative problems and needs vary, but present information available indicates that the number of children of all ages with all kinds and degrees of communication disorders exceeds three million."

IMPROVEMENT IN QUALITY

The growth in numbers of clinicians serving the schools was steady during the 1950s and the 1960s. That era concentrated on the improvement of quality as well as quantity by emphasizing increased training for clinicians through advanced certification set by the American Speech and Hearing Association.

A major project geared toward improving speech and hearing services to children in the schools was undertaken by the United States Office of Education, Purdue University, and the Research Committee of the American Speech and Hearing Association (Steer et al, 1961). The major objectives were to provide authoritative information about current practices in the public schools and to identify unresolved problems. On the basis of these findings, priorities were established for identification of urgently needed research. With the cooperation of hundreds of clinicians, supervisors, classroom teachers, and training institution personnel, a list of topics for further study and research was distilled by the work groups. Given highest priority were the following topics: the collection of longitudinal data on speech; comparative studies of program organization (with special attention to the frequency, duration, and intensity of therapy); and comparative studies of the use of different remedial procedures with children of various ages presenting different speech, voice, and language problems.

Six additional topics were also identified and assigned a high priority: the development of standardized tests of speech, voice, and language; the development of criteria for selection of primary grade children for inclusion in remedial programs; comparative studies of speech improvement and clinical programs; comparative studies of group, individual, and combined group and individual therapy programs; studies of the adjustment of children and their language usage in relation to changes in speech accomplished during participation in therapy programs; and comparative studies of different curricula and clinical training programs for prospective public school speech and hearing personnel.

The study also addressed itself to such topics as the professional roles and relationships of the school clinician, the supervision of programs, diagnosis and measurement, and the recruitment of professional personnel to meet the growing needs of the communicatively handicapped in the schools.

THE QUIET REVOLUTION

Things were changing rapidly in the late 1960s and early 1970s for the school clinicians and the "quiet revolution" referred to by O'Toole and Zaslow (1969) became less quiet as the school clinicians talked about breaking the cycle of mediocrity, lowering caseloads, giving highest priority to the most severe cases, scheduling on intensive cycles rather than intermittently, extending programs throughout the summer, utilizing diagnostic teams, and many other issues. The emphasis had shifted, slowly but surely, from quantity to quality.

The appointment in 1969 by the American Speech and Hearing Association of a full-time staff member to serve as Associate Secretary for School/Clinic Affairs; the publication in 1971 of *Language, Speech and Hearing Services in Schools*; and the appointment by ASHA of a standing committee on Language, Speech and Hearing Services in Schools all attest to the recognition of the public school clinician as a large and important part of the profession.

It was not the professional organization's thinking alone that brought about the many changes. There were outside influences—mainly the changes in the philosophy and conditions surrounding the American educational system—which began to effect changes in the profession. Increased populations, tightened school budgets, focus on the lack of reading skills in the elementary school, more attention to special populations such as the mentally retarded and the socially and economically disadvantaged child, all had an impact.

FEDERAL LEGISLATION

In 1954 the United States Supreme Court's decision in the case of *Brown* vs. *Board of Education* set into motion a new era and struck down the doctrine of segregated education. This decision sparked such issues as women's rights, the right to education and treatment for the handicapped, as well as the intrinsic rights of individuals, including blacks and minority groups (Martin, 1975).

Parent organizations have long been a catalyst in bringing about change, and in the case of handicapped children they were certainly no exception. According to Reynolds and Rosen:

> Parents of handicapped children began to organize about thirty years ago to obtain educational facilities for their offspring and to act as watchdogs of the institutions serving them. At first, the organizations concentrated on political action; since 1970, however, they have turned to the courts. This fact may be more important than any other in accounting for the changes in special education that are occurring now and are likely to occur in the near future (1976, p. 444).

An extension of the Brown vs. Board of Education decision, according to Reynolds and Rosen (1976), was the consent decree established in the case of the Pennsylvania Association for Retarded Children, which stated that no matter how seriously handicapped the child may be he or she has the right to education. The PARC case established the right of parents to become involved in making decisions concerning their child, and stipulated that education must be based on programs that are appropriate to the needs and capacities of each individual child.

One of the unexpected aftermaths of the PARC case was to place the stamp of judicial approval on *mainstreaming*. According to Reynolds and Rosen:

> Mainstreaming is a set or general predisposition to arrange for the education of children with handicaps or learning problems within the environment provided for all other children—the regular school and normal home and community environment—whenever feasible. (1976, p. 558.)

Mainstreaming has special implications for the regular classroom teacher as well as other personnel involved in the education of children with handicaps. Reynolds and Rosen have this to say on that topic:

> Obviously, mainstreaming makes new demands on both regular classroom and special education teachers. In the past, a regular education teacher was expected to know enough about handicapping conditions to be able to identify children with such problems for referral out of the classroom into special education settings. At the same time, special education teachers were trained to work directly with the children with certain specific handicaps (as in the days of residential schools) in separate special settings.
>
> Under mainstreaming, different roles are demanded for both kinds of teachers. The trend for training special education teachers for indirect resource teacher roles rather than narrow specialists is well established in many preparation centers. Concurrently, programs are underway to provide regular education teachers with training in the identification of learning problems. At the local school level, regular and special education teachers in mainstreamed programs are no longer isolated in separate classrooms. They work together in teams to share knowledge, skills, observations, and experiences to enhance the programs for children with special problems, whether the children are permanently or temporarily handicapped. Thus, it has become essential for special teachers to learn the skills of consultation and for both teachers to learn techniques of observation as well as communication. (1976, pp. 557-58.)

implications of legislation
for the school clinician

In 1967 the U.S. Congress created the Bureau of Education for the Handicapped and began a program of grants to speed the development of educational programs (Martin, 1975). The mandatory legislation (the Education for All Handicapped Children Act), which has been adopted in most states, extends coverage beyond the school-age individual and includes preschool handicapped children, as well as eventual coverage to age twenty-one. Full implementation is to be achieved by 1980.

Of what import is this legislation to the speech, language, or hearing handicapped child and his parents? And what are the implications for the speech-language pathologist working in the schools?

Let us consider the word *handicap*. According to the dictionary, a handicap is something that hampers a person, hinders, or impedes. The child with a communication handicap, then, is a child whose opportunities for taking full advantage of the education offered in the school are considerably diminished. For example, the child who cannot hear will not be able to follow directions from the teacher; and the child who cannot process language may have considerable trouble learning to read, a skill which involves a high level of language facility. Likewise, the child with a stuttering problem may never have an opportunity to participate in classroom discussions, school plays, or the debate team.

Are we integrating our roles as speech and hearing specialists in the educational system? In 1974, Edwin W. Martin (Director of the Bureau of Education for the Handicapped), in an address to the members of the American Speech and Hearing Association, stated that he did not feel that we were doing so successfully. He pointed out that there have been some historical divisions between speech and hearing specialists and special educators, probably rooted in traditional rivalry between arts and science colleges and colleges of education. Martin urged that speech, language, and hearing pathologists must be actively involved in interdisciplinary efforts with parents, with learning disability specialists, with administrators, with guidance counselors, with classroom teachers, and with all of their educational colleagues in an effort to alleviate communication handicaps among children.

According to Martin, who is presently Associate Commissioner of the Bureau of Education:

> Today, 3.5 million handicapped children are enrolled in special education programs; many of them are children with speech and hearing disorders receiving assistance from our profession. But, we have a long way to go, for there is an equal number of children, including many children five years old and younger, for whom no services are presently being offered. For the most part the school-age children are in schools, but unfortunately are receiving no specialized assistance and so their schooling is frequently marked by failures, frustration, self-doubt, and ultimately, high rates of dropping out. It is perhaps more accurate to see this as being forced out. (1975, p. 385.)

Perhaps we can summarize the state of affairs by saying that we've come a long way, but we've a long way yet to go.

Traditionally in the United States, the preponderance of speech, language, and hearing services for children has been offered as a part of the school program, and the bulk of the profession has been employed in the schools. While in this country we have followed the *educational model*, speech, language, and hearing professionals in other countries have followed the *medical model* and have provided services through health and medical facilities. This is not to say that there are not numerous health, medical, and community agencies throughout the United States providing excellent speech, language, and hearing services. It is undoubtedly a reflection of our democratic philosophy of education that children have a right to education and that our function in the schools is to prevent, remove, and alleviate handicapping communicative barriers that interfere with the child's ability to profit from the education offered.

CONCLUSION

This chapter is a look back into the early history of our profession and particularly that part of it involved in the schools. Why is it important today that we look backward? The most obvious answer and perhaps the most meaningful one is that by reexamining the past we are able to gain our perspective for the present, and to plan better for the future. Someone once said that if we don't understand the past we are destined to reinvent the wheel every year.

Knight (1970), a school clinician, in an article originally presented as a paper at an ASHA Regional Workshop for School Specialists, indicated that in reality we have come a long way in our young profession, and that the questions raised can serve as guidelines for improvement. On a confident note for the future she stated:

But I have faith in the resilience of the school clinician. I am confident, also, that if we keep our work child-centered instead of clinician-centered, if we capitalize on the elements of our setting which are assets rather than wasting our energies in complaining about those which are liabilities, and if we demonstrate that we are clinically competent by the excellence of our performance rather than by our insistence on the trappings, we shall continue to improve status both for ourselves and for our profession.

2

the school clinician as a professional person

INTRODUCTION

The titles which we have applied to ourselves over the years have changed along with changes in our professional responsibilities and roles. The changing roles are examined in this chapter, along with our present and projected responsibilities.

The school pathologist affiliates with some professional organizations and knows about many others. A discussion of organizations is included in this chapter.

The Code of Ethics defines our accountability to our colleagues, our clients, and to ourselves A discussion of the Code of Ethics of the American Speech-Language-Hearing Association is included here, and the code is included in the appendix.

Accreditation is required for speech, language, and hearing practitioners in many areas of the profession. What are the various forms of accreditation and which agencies grant accreditation? These questions are dealt with in this chapter.

TERMINOLOGY

At this point it might be helpful to clarify the terms by which we call ourselves. In reading and in listening to professionals in the field you have undoubtedly heard the following designations: speech and hearing therapist, speech and language clinician, hearing clinician, speech correctionist, speech teacher, communications disorder specialist, communicologist, and others. Unfortunately, none of these designations adequately describes all of the workers in this professional discipline, but realistically they probably reflect the growing pains of a young profession. As our professional horizons continue to expand and widen, terminology is modified to accommodate these changes. It does not mean that the earliest writers and workers in this field were careless in their choice of terms; it simply means that not one of them owned a crystal ball by which they could foretell the future. Nor does anyone today.

The United States Department of Labor uses the title, *speech pathologist* as its official designation. The American Speech and Hearing Association, in a preference survey in 1977, discovered that the terminology most acceptable was *speech-language pathologist*. In this book we shall use the terms *pathologist* and *clinician*.

THE CHANGING ROLE
OF THE SCHOOL PATHOLOGIST

The changes in descriptive terminology are but a reflection of the changing role of the school pathologist; and indeed, they also reflect the perceptions of the school pathologist's role as viewed by others in the profession.

Ainsworth examined two possible roles of the school pathologist—participant and separatist. He described the separatist role as one which:

> looks upon the speech specialist as an independent professional person who is responsible for diagnosing and treating the speech disorders of children in public schools. This point of view assumes that the responsibilities of the specialist are fulfilled when he successfully carries out the clinical activities for which he has been trained. (1965, p. 495.)

Regarding the participant's role he stated:

> This concept is similar to the first in that it views the role of the speech specialist to be that of an independent professional who provides a remedial and therapeutic service to the children in the schools. However, it conceives of additional responsibilities which can be summarized by saying that the speech specialist is obligated to make a direct contribution to, and thus be an integral part of, the on-going educational program. In addition to conducting himself appropriately as a speech pathologist, this specialist is obligated to carry out this work in such a way that it will reinforce and, in turn, be reinforced by appropriate educational activities in the total school program. (1965, p. 495.)

Ainsworth, after examining both roles, felt that it was neither desirable nor possible for the school clinician to maintain a separatist position, and that the child who would be treated as part of the school program would receive better quality care if therapy were integrated into the educational process. Indeed, he felt that an entirely new concept of funding speech therapy would need to be developed if the separatist role were to be the school pathologist's role.

Ainsworth explained that through the years the clinical speech program (under a variety of designations) has been enthusiastically welcomed into the public school setting on the basis that it contributed substantially to the total program. He further pointed out that even before the profession emerged as such, public schools were employing such specialists because alleviation of disorders of communication was vital if the child was to be able to take advantage of educational opportunities.

Ainsworth's participant versus separatist article was written in response to two position statements issued by the American Speech and Hearing Association. The first article, issued in April, 1962, described the basic services and functions of the school clinician and differentiated this individual from the instructional, curriculum personnel, such as the classroom teacher. The second article, issued in June, 1964, also dealt with basic responsibilities. It delineated the speech clinician's role in respect to speech improvement and the broad language-arts skills as being in a consultative relationship with the classroom teacher.

These articles seemed to be directed more to the world outside the profession; hence, Ainsworth felt it appropriate and crucial for the profession as a whole, the pathologists in the schools, and the major professional organization, to look more deeply into the roles and the responsibilities of the speech specialist in the schools.

Van Hattum (1966), in his article entitled, "The Defensive Speech Clinicians in the Schools," posed the question, Are speech clinicians working in the schools defensive or are their present and past concerns valid? He summarized the concerns as follows:

> Their training, in respect to program management and therapeutic practice, is not appropriate.
>
> Some of their training was inadequate.
>
> They do not get research help or practical advice to help them solve their professional problems.
>
> They feel that the association they support does not meet their needs.
>
> They feel their professional colleagues do not respect them, even the colleges that trained them.

Van Hattum suggested a number of actions to alleviate the plight, and further, pointed out encouraging things that were happening, such as an ASHA sponsored conference on research needs for public school clinicians, more articles of value and interest to the school clinician in the *Journal of Speech and Hearing Dis-*

orders, and increased activity by the ASHA Committee on Speech and Hearing Services in the Schools.

THE ROLE OF THE
SCHOOL PATHOLOGIST NOW

It is probably safe to say that pathologists in the schools often have been viewed as itinerant workers dealing mainly with functional articulation problems and working with children in groups rather than individually because of high maximum caseload requirements set by state law. Unfortunately, this stereotype has persisted and it is now time to exorcise the ghost. The school pathologist's role is continually changing. Let us look at the roles and responsibilities of the school speech, language, and hearing specialist

The school pathologist plans, directs, and provides diagnostic and remediation services to communicatively handicapped children and youth. The pathologist works with children with articulation problems, language problems, voice disorders, disfluency (stuttering) problems, hearing impairments; as well as speech, language, and hearing problems associated with such conditions as cleft palate, cerebral palsy, intellectual impairment, visual impairment, emotional and behavioral disturbances, autistic behavior, and aphasia.

An important aspect of the school pathologist's duties is cooperation with other school and health specialists including audiologists, nurses, social workers, physicians, dentists, special education teachers, psychologists, and guidance counselors. Cooperative planning with these individuals on a periodic basis results in effective diagnostic, habilitative, and educational programs for children with communication problems.

The school pathologist works with classroom teachers and resource room teachers in an effort to implement and generalize remediation procedures for the handicapped child. Working with parents to help them alleviate and understand problems is also a part of the pathologist's function. School administrators are often the key to good educational programming for children, and the school pathologist works with both building principals and superintendents toward that end.

The school pathologist may also be a community resource person, providing public information about communication problems and the availability of services for parents and families and for the personnel in both public and voluntary community agencies.

Many school pathologists are engaged in research related to program organization and management, clinical procedures, and professional responsibility. The field of language, speech, and hearing is constantly broadening, and the school pathologist must keep abreast of new information by reading professional journals and publications, attending seminars and conventions, enrolling in continuing education programs, and by sharing information and ideas with colleagues through state, local, and national professional organizations.

Frequently school pathologists are asked to share in the training of university students by serving as supervisors of student teaching experiences and by providing observational opportunities for students-in-training. The supervision of paraprofessionals and volunteers in school programs is also the responsibility of the school pathologist.

Because the school pathologist is considered an important part of the total educational program, the size, the need, and the structure of the local school district will have much to do with the program organizational model used as well as the nature of the services provided. Many school pathologists work as itinerant persons. Some will be assigned to a single building while others may work in special classes, resource rooms, or self-contained classrooms. Often the school pathologist will be either a full- or part-time member of the pupil evaluation team, or may serve as a resource consultant to teachers, administrators, or other school staff members. Many school pathologists are employed as supervisors or administrators of speech and language programs.

Many other services are provided by the school speech-language and hearing pathologist. These include service to: high-risk infants in school-operated child development centers; preschoolers in Head Start programs; severely handicapped children in special schools, centers, classes, or home-settings, multiply handicapped students in special schools; and elementary, middle, and secondary-school pupils.

The role of the school pathologist is changing from that of an itinerant clinician who, because of heavy caseload requirements, worked with large numbers of children with articulatory problems, to that of the specialist in communication disorders. The consultative role is becoming more and more important, and more is required of the school clinician in the way of diagnosis of speech, language, and hearing problems. Classroom teachers, special teachers, and personnel in other specialized fields will depend on the school pathologist to provide diagnostic, assessment, and treatment information.

Some school clinicians may be sensitive about the term *specialist.* Freeman (1969) pointed out in "The Speech Clinician—As a Consultant," that the term *special* should not be equated with *superior* as it implies no superiority over the other school personnel. The school clinician is a professional specialist in the school, whose role is similar to that of the speech, language, and hearing clinician in the hospital setting or the community agency.

The roles of the school clinician as a consultant or a resource person have been described by various persons. Articles describing some of these programs have appeared in the publication *Language, Speech & Hearing Services in Schools.* It is not possible to list all of them, however a few are described in the following paragraphs.

Northcott (1972) described the role of the speech clinician as an interdisciplinary team member in regard to the hearing-impaired child. The term *hearing-impaired* was used to include every child with a hearing loss that was developmentally and educationally handicapping. The importance of early intervention was stressed. Northcott describes the school clinician's role as: (1) providing appropriate components of supplemental services directly to hearing-impaired children; (2) serving as a hearing consultant to teachers, administrators, and resource specialists, helping them make reasonable accommodations to meet the special needs of the hearing-impaired child in the integrated class setting; and (3) serving as a member of an interdisciplinary team developing new components of comprehensive hearing services within the school district.

Crabtree (1974), through a case study, described the role of the speech pathologist as a resource teacher for the child with the language-learning disability. She stressed the idea that the speech pathologist, in order to function successfully as a communication specialist, must have a theoretical background in language development, must be able to identify and develop prescriptive techniques for problems related to phonology, syntax, and semantics, and should be able to relate these aspects of linguistics to all levels of oral and written language. In addition, according to Crabtree, the speech pathologist must be a generalist as well as a specialist. In other words, the speech pathologist must know how academic learning is developed and the effect of sensory deprivation, from any cause, on learning.

Simon (1977) described a program in which the speech-language pathologist worked closely with the learning disabilities teacher in a developmental program in expressive language. The essentials of the program involved cooperation, communication, and programming. The speech-language pathologist and the learning disabilities teacher focused on how they could best combine their talents, expertise, and schedules to increase the linguistic sophistication of the children in the program.

Freeman and Lukens (1962) reported on a program of speech and language training for educable mentally-handicapped children in Oakland County, Michigan. In the program, the teachers, the speech clinicians, and the county consultants formulated an interdisciplinary program which could be carried on in the schools. The speech clinician was responsible for the diagnosis of the speech and language problems and for formulating a plan for improving communicative skills. The speech clinician also treated any children whose speech and language problems were not attributable to depressed intellectual function. The speech and language skills were part of the regular classroom curriculum. The classroom teachers were responsible for cooperating in the formulation and execution of the oral communication program.

There are other articles describing the working relationships between clinicians and special teachers in the schools. Most school clinicians learn by doing in the area of establishing working relationships with other specialized personnel. Specialists must learn to work together, respect one another's disciplines, draw on one another's knowledge and experience. Why? Because without this kind of cooperation the child suffers.

While it is important to provide a job description and to enumerate the various roles and responsibilities of the school pathologist, it is equally important to be constantly aware of the major focus of this profession—namely, that whatever is done, is done in the best interests of the child. Speech pathologists must keep in mind that they are on the children's side and that they speak for children who cannot speak for themselves.

THE FUTURE ROLE
OF THE SCHOOL PATHOLOGIST

What is the future role of the speech-language pathologist in the schools? According to Edwin W. Martin:

> It seems to me, however, that the speech and hearing profession must do more than simply claim competence in language development and language disorders. We must delineate a role for speech and hearing specialists, perhaps several roles, and document our abilities to meet such roles. Will the speech and hearing specialist offer advice and counsel on language to the teacher of learning-disabled children? Will the speech and hearing specialist actually be the main professional person working with one child or with a small group of such children; in other words, be their "teacher" or perhaps the basic resource specialist to supplement their regular education program? Will speech and hearing specialists provide language instruction according to set curricular objectives or objectives designed to reach certain competencies equivalent to the goals of regular education for children of a given age or grade? What about the written aspects of language training: spelling, writing, and reading? Will speech and hearing specialists accept responsibility in these activity areas? (1965, p. 386.)

The future roles and responsibilities of the school pathologist are linked closely with the entire profession of speech, language, and hearing pathology. What strengthens one arm of the profession also strengthens the other arm. The ultimate aim and focus of the entire field is to help people with communication difficulties, and all efforts should be bent toward this goal. The profession must be responsible to the needs of an ever-changing world, a world segmented with the problems of overpopulation, hunger, disease, energy shortages, human conflict, and human isolation. Perhaps communication is the "glue" that will ultimately hold it all together.

The excitement and challenge of being part of a profession that deals with human communication can never be measured. It is as exciting today as it was for the early members of the profession because, in a sense, we are still in the pioneering stage. As Alvin Toffler (1970) warns in his provocative book, *Future Shock*, we are in the midst of an educational revolution and rather than trying to refine the existing educational machinery under the heading of *change*, we must transform the basic structure of the educational system; we must revolutionize the curriculum; and we must encourage a future-focused orientation.

As we attempt to analyze the roles of the school pathologist, many of the problems that present themselves today have to do with utilization of time. Time is our most valuable commodity and it is becoming increasingly apparent that the school pathologist cannot function effectively under the artificial time constraints imposed by state departments of education and by school systems. For example, the child with a language problem may need daily intervention rather than two half-hour periods per week. Unfortunately, many of the decisions that are made regarding the question of how the school pathologist's time is to be utilized are based on surveys which yield information on "how most of the pathologists are scheduling today" rather than "what are the needs of the children with handicapping conditions?" Too often the quick answer is given, "We need another pathologist in our school," before anyone has studied the priorities of the program to determine whether or not more help is really needed, and, if so, what kind of help.

ORGANIZATIONS

One of the chief agents of change and growth in the profession has been The American Speech-Language-Hearing Association. The appointment of a full-time director of school-clinic affairs and the publication of the quarterly journal, *Language, Speech and Hearing Services in Schools*, have been concrete evidence of the organization's concern for this sector of its membership. The increasing number of convention programs directly related to school affairs, the encouragement of research performed by school pathologists, and the publication of guidelines for school programs, help to inform school pathologists, as well as all ASHA members, of recent and current issues.

Students-in-training are encouraged to affiliate with the National Student Speech and Hearing Association (NSSHA) which is an affiliate of the American Speech-Language-Hearing Association. The student group affords many opportunities not otherwise available to individuals in training. For example, it keeps students informed about matters of legislation and accreditation as well as providing special programs and publications for students.

Every state has its professional organization which holds conventions, publishes journals, sponsors continuing education programs, and offers short courses. The state organizations also publish directories with members' names and professional addresses listed. A listing in a professional directory authenticates the member.

In addition to the state organizations, the state may contain regional organizations. Affiliation with the regional group provides an invaluable opportunity for exchange of information and offers support to individual members. Involvement in such groups is both rewarding and enjoyable.

There are a number of other professional organizations with which the school clinician may wish to become affiliated. As a matter of fact, membership in other professional groups provides opportunities for valuable exchanges of information and enhances cooperation and understanding. Some of these organizations with which you may wish to affiliate or to know about are included in the appendix of this book.

One of the first tasks of the American Speech and Hearing Association was the establishment of a Code of Ethics. Mindful of the fact that there were unscrupulous individuals who would take advantage of persons with handicapping conditions by making rash promises of cures and by charging exorbitant fees, the earliest members of the profession felt it necessary to maintain professional integrity and encourage high standards by formulating a Code of Ethics. As may be expected, it was a difficult task and throughout the history of the organization the code has been periodically updated to meet current problems; however, it has remained substantially the same. The code outlines the ASHA member's professional responsibilities to the patient, to the member's co-workers, and to society. Thus, it might be said that accountability has always been one of the profession's highest priorities.

Most of the state and regional organizations have adopted a Code of Ethics as well. (The Code of Ethics of the American Speech-Language-Hearing Association is printed in this publication in Appendix 1.)

accreditation and the accrediting agencies

Understanding the various forms of accreditation in speech-language pathology and audiology is part of each person's professional responsibility to himself. To the neophyte pathologist the task of understanding accreditation may seem to be a formidable one; however, some basic information may help clarify the situation.

Prerequisite to understanding accreditation is a knowledge of the types of agencies in the United States and their roles in relation to the profession of speech-language pathology and audiology.

The Voluntary Agency. One of the types of agencies is the voluntary agency. Voluntary agencies have developed in countries which have a democratic form of government. The voluntary agency is more clearly identified with the United States than with any other nation, and has usually evolved out of an unmet need and a concern with one's fellow men. The unmet need may be one related to social issues, to leisure time and recreation, or to health. Voluntary health agencies may be related to specific diseases or handicapping conditions. Usually the membership of voluntary agencies is made up of both lay persons (in many cases, parents) and professionals. Examples of voluntary health agencies are the Society for Crippled Children and Adults, the United Cerebral Palsy Association, and the National Multiple Sclerosis Society.

Voluntary agencies are not accrediting agencies in the usual sense of the word, however they perform extremely vital functions for the handicapped individual.

The Official Agency. Another type of agency is the official agency. This agency is tax-supported and may be on the city, county, regional, state, state-federal, or federal level. Official agencies cover a myriad of categories, including health, education, welfare, vocational, recreational, emotional, and social. In the area of official health-related agencies, interests are in the prevention of problems, in research, and in the specific disease category. Examples of official agencies are the city or county health department, the Office of Vocational Rehabilitation, and the State Department of Education. The public school is an example of an official agency. Some official agencies may be accrediting bodies. An example would be a state department of education.

The Professional Organization. In addition to official and voluntary agencies there are also *professional organizations.* These, as the name implies, are made up of individuals sharing the same profession. Their goals are the establishment and maintenance of high professional standards, research, recruitment of others into the field, the sharing of professional information, and accreditation. Examples of the professional agencies are the American Speech-Language-Hearing Association, the American Medical Association, and the American Dental Association.

These various types of agencies often work together in a unique fashion, sometimes motivating each other to carry out specific tasks, often supporting each other financially and in other ways, frequently exchanging services and information, and often preventing duplication of services. The official agencies and the professional organizations are often accrediting bodies in addition to their other functions. The voluntary agencies usually are not.

state certification

What are the various types of accreditation offered by these groups and how is this related to the school pathologist?

In the case of the speech-language pathologist who chooses to be employed in the schools, certification is issued by the state department of education in each of the states. The qualifying standards are set by each state and include following a prescribed course of study and fulfilling the practicum requirements. The practicum requirements include both clinical practice in the university clinic or one of its satellites under qualified supervision, and student teaching done in a school under the supervision of the cooperating school pathologist and the university supervisor. The certification is awarded at the master's level in an increasing number of states and at the bachelor's level in the remainder. Each state has various levels of certification, and moving from one level to another requires additional experience and course work. Information on the certification requirements of each state can be obtained by writing to the office of the state's commissioner of education or its equivalent.

Where requirements are the same, there is reciprocity among the states in regard to certification, and individuals may move from one state to another with a minimum of difficulty.

licensing

Another type of accreditation that is required in some states is licensing. Just as attorneys, physicians, nurses, real estate agents, and beauticians must be licensed to practice within the geographical boundaries of a state, so must speech-language and hearing specialists. Licensing came about to protect the public from unqualified and sometimes unscrupulous persons. The public may identify the license holder as a person who has met experience and academic qualifications and has, in addition, passed a state examination. Usually a licensing board is appointed in the state where licensing has become established by law. The board sets the standards and procedures for obtaining and retaining a license in the area of speech-language pathology, or audiology. The licensee must display the license at the place where he or she practices. The board may deny, suspend, or revoke the license of an applicant or a licensee for violations or for unprofessional conduct. Usually a fee is charged for the license.

A license is necessary within any state in which it is required to practice the profession of speech-language pathology or audiology. The licensing laws are not uniform among the states at this writing; therefore it is best to write to the state's department of commerce to find out the requirements for obtaining a license in that particular state.

accreditation by the professional organization

Another type of accreditation is that issued by the American Speech-Language-Hearing Association. Unlike licensing and state certification, it has no legal status, but nevertheless it is recognized by various states and by other professions as authenticating the holder as a qualified practitioner or supervisor. ASHA certification is known as the *Certificate of Clinical Competence* and can be obtained by persons who meet specific requirements in academic preparation and supervised clinical experiences, and who pass a national comprehensive examination. It may be granted in speech pathology or audiology and some individuals hold certification in both areas. It permits the holder to provide services in the appropriate area and also to supervise the clinical practice of student trainees and clinicians who do not hold certification. According to ASHA, the Certificate of Clinical Competence is held by more than 11,000 of its members who provide services in schools, universities, hearing and speech centers, hospitals, clinics, and other programs throughout the United States, Canada, and many foreign countries.

Information on how to apply for ASHA certification may be obtained by writing to: American Speech-Language-Hearing Association, 10801 Rockville Pike, Rockville, Maryland, 20852. (ASHA certification requirements are listed in Appendix 2.)

summary of accreditation
and general considerations

Briefly, those are the three types of certification which directly affect the profession. Certification of one type does not preclude certification in the other two. In fact, many individuals hold several types of accreditation.

In looking at the academic, clinical practicum, and experience requirements of all three types of accrediting agencies you will note that they are almost identical. The academic requirements follow the same pattern and specific courses can be utilized to fulfill requirements in several types of accreditation. For example, a course in articulatory problems can fulfill the requirement for ASHA's Certificate of Clinical Competence as well as the state's department of education requirements for school certification and for the state's board of speech pathology and audiology's requirements for a state license.

Table 2-1 may help to clarify information about the various forms of accreditation in speech-language pathology, and audiology.

TABLE 2-1.   ACCREDITATION AND ACCREDITING AGENCIES

Accrediting Agency	Form of Accreditation	Possible Holder
State of _____ Department of Education	Certificate to practice in the schools of _____	Person who wishes employment in the State of_____, as a speech-language pathologist in an educational facility.
State of _____ Board of Speech-Language Pathology and Audiology	License to provide speech, language, hearing services in the State of _____	Person wishing to practice in a voluntary or official agency (except specifically named educational facilities), or do private practice in the State of_____.
American Speech-Language-Hearing Association	Certificate of Clinical Competence (in Speech Pathology and/or Audiology)	Anyone who wishes to be identified by the American Speech-Language-Hearing Association as a qualified practitioner and, or, supervisor in speech-language and/or audiology.

CONCLUSION

Ainsworth's participant versus separatist article, written in 1965, challenged the profession, and particularly that segment of it employed in the schools, to carefully examine roles and objectives. This marked the beginning of more attention to the roles and responsibilities of the school clinician by the national organization and by individuals in the schools.

Changes have been brought about by internal as well as external pressures.

Currently, we are experiencing "future shock" and an understanding of the forces that are shaping the profession will better enable us to plan for the future. Attention must be given to legislation, to professional organizations and their statements of ethical responsibility, to the various forms of accreditation, and to the needs of the communicatively handicapped children both within the schools and outside them.

3 | *new directions for school programs*

INTRODUCTION

This chapter presents definitions of professional terms which are basic to an understanding of the "Continuum of Language, Speech and Hearing Services for Children and Youth" model developed by the American Speech-Language-Hearing Association.

That part of the continuum-of-services model which describes the various options for providing the service is referred to as the *delivery-of-services* model, thus presenting a model within a model.

In this chapter we will consider various aspects of Public Law 94-142, the Education for All Handicapped Children Act, and its implications for the present and the future in respect to speech, language, and hearing services in the schools.

The growing concern for the hearing-impaired child in the educational environment has resulted in an increased demand for audiological services in the public school system. The functions of the educational audiologist will be presented in this chapter.

DEFINITIONS OF TERMS

Students in training and other users of this book have undoubtedly been provided with good definitions of the various types of communication disorders as a part of their academic course work. In the future, these same individuals may find themselves in the position of defining and interpreting communication disorders to other persons such as parents of handicapped children, teachers, medical personnel, and legislators. With this in mind, the classification schema as developed in the publication, *Comprehensive Assessment and Service Evaluation Information System for Language, Speech and Hearing Programs in Schools* (NEEDS Project II, American Speech and Hearing Association, Anita Pikus, Project Director, September, 1976), is presented:

I. Communication Disorders - refer to impairments in articulation, language, voice, or fluency. Hearing impairment may be classified as a communication disorder when it impedes the development, performance, or maintenance of articulation, language, voice, or fluency. A communication disorder may range from a mild to severe developmental or nonmaturational deficit. These impairments may also occur in any combination, thereby constituting a multiple communication disorder. Individuals with multiple handicaps may have any combination of communication disorders with concomitant physical, intellectual, or emotional problems. Any individual with a communication disorder, regardless of degree or type, may require services from language, speech and hearing personnel.

   A. *Articulation Disorder* is defined as the abnormal production of one or more phonemes (speech sounds). There are four basic types of abnormal productions: omission of phonemes, substitution of one phoneme for another, phonemic distortions, and the inappropriate addition of a phoneme.

   B. *Language Disorder* is defined as the abnormal acquisition, comprehension, or use (including all receptive and expressive language skills) of spoken or written language. The disorder may involve all, one, or some combination of phonologic, morphologic, semantic, or syntactic components of the linguistic system. Individuals with a language disorder frequently have problems in sentence processing or in abstracting information meaningfully for storage and retrieval from short and long-term memory.

   For the purposes of this classification system, the following definitions are operational:

   Phonological disorder involves the sound system of a language: the particular sounds that comprise the sound system and the ways in which the rules of a language permit them to be combined to form larger units of a language such as words.

   Morphologic disorder involves the structure of words and the construction of word forms from the basic elements of meaning: morphemes. Inflectional suffixes indicating plurality and tense are examples of morphologic units.

Semantic disorder involves the meaning of individual words and the combination of word meanings to form the meaning of a sentence.

Syntactic disorder involves the rules governing the order and combination of morphemes in the formation of sentences and the relationships among the elements within a sentence or between two or more sentences.

C. *Voice Disorder* is defined as the absence or abnormal production of voice characterized by defective vocal quality, pitch, and/or loudness.

D. *Fluency Disorder* is defined as the abnormal flow of verbal expression, including rate and rhythm.

E. *Hearing Impairment* is defined as abnormal hearing sensitivity and/or damage to the integrity of the physiological auditory system. An individual with a hearing impairment has a communication disorder when the abnormality in the physiological auditory system prevents or impedes normal development, comprehension, use or maintenance of effective communication behaviors.

II. Communication Differences - refer to maturational or cultural/ethnic linguistic variations that are not considered communication disorders. However, these differences may require services provided by language, speech, and hearing personnel.

MODELS IN GENERAL

Before a comprehensive speech, language, and hearing program is organized in Anytown, U.S.A. by the pathologist employed by the Anytown School District, some basis must be established for implementing such a program. We call this basis a *model*.

What is a model for? In his book, *An Analysis of Clinical Behavior in Speech and Hearing,* Schultz has this to say:

There are several kinds of models. One type is a representation of something, altered in size, such as a scale model of a house or a greatly enlarged model of a complex molecule. Other models represent ideal forms, as a model political order, model law, or model constitution, none of which is necessarily attainable in the world of practical politics. A moment's reflection will make most of us aware that mathematics tends to be the base of most of the models we use in the everyday world because it allows us to deal with complex relationships in a condensed manner.

Consider some common examples. We need not build an actual house to see if the walls will support the roof; we build a mathematical model. We quickly, and without physical effort, experiment to learn "what would happen (to the roof) if . . . . " We calculate from still another model based on weather reports, geography, soil conditions, etc. what the expected snow loads or wind velocities will be; we estimate the weight and thrust the roof must bear and whatever else concerns the architect. Each consideration of roof design brings some advantages and some disadvantages, and one must evaluate each in consideration with the others to reach his decisions on design and lumber needs. But all of it is decided by using models, not buildings.

One more example may help our understanding of the nature of models. What takes place when one considers whether to go from Chicago to San Francisco by the northern or the southern route? We can easily trace the alternatives in a road atlas (another model), determine the advantages and disadvantages of each alternative, and reach a decision. If we find, after driving too long one day, that there is a hundred-mile detour before the next gas station, we might be upset with the model maker even though we know a model does not necessarily contain everything in the original. If it were to have everything, we would no longer have a model, but an exact duplicate.

A model should include all considerations important to the decisions one expects to have based upon it and should exclude all the minor factors that could obscure the issue. Of course it may be an arbitrary decision as to what is of major and minor importance in the process or state of nature being modeled, so a model may be neither ideal nor even adequate in what it includes and excludes. A model may also be adequate for some purposes and not for others. (1972, pp. 4-5.)

A model, then, is an approximation of the real world and is meant to be used, manipulated, changed, added to, diminished, and expanded. The speech-language pathologist in the Anytown School District is the decision maker who must take into account all the information available in the situation and, using the model as a guide, construct the program in speech, language, and hearing for that particular educational community.

We are going to consider two basic models, one of which is imbedded in the other, which should be of help to the school pathologist in constructing a program. Let us first consider the continuum-of-services model.

CONTINUUM-OF-SERVICES MODEL

The American Speech-Language-Hearing Association has developed a continuum model which can be used as a framework to assist the school pathologist in planning a program that will meet the needs of the communicatively handicapped in Anytown School District. This model defines the population served and the program goals in respect to various segments of the population. Further, it helps the pathologist in planning the program, in carrying out the program, in evaluating the program, and in providing ideas for future directions of the program. The model is shown in Table 3-1.

The children included in the communicative disorders component include those with severe to moderately severe problems in language, voice, articulation, fluency, or hearing. These are the children who would require intensive individual or small group intervention by the pathologist in addition to services by other specialists. Also involved in the habilitation of these children would be the parents and the classroom teacher. Some of these children would be those who had never acquired language for causes unknown, and some with serious language delay would be children with other handicapping conditions such as profound hearing loss, mental retardation, or serious emotional disturbances.

Those individuals in the communicative deviations section of the continuum would include children with somewhat less severe but significantly handicapping problems in communication such as nonmaturational misarticulations, mild language delays, or mild hearing losses. Children with developmental lags, and mild intellectual retardation conditions would also be included.

The intervention would include less intensified direct or indirect services by speech-language pathologists as well as parents, teachers, aides, counselors, psychologists, physicians, nurses, social workers, psychiatrists, and dentists.

The communicative development component has two major goals. One is the prevention of communication problems in young children. The other is the enrichment of the total use of language for children who may be proficient in the use of a dialect or language other than English.

The communicative development program is primarily the responsibility of the classroom teacher to carry out, while the role of the language, speech, and hearing clinician is that of consultant who works closely with the teacher in such areas as:

1. Providing information on normal speech and language development
2. Screening or developing screening procedures to be used by others to determine specific needs or class groups and individual pupils
3. Helping teachers to define goals, plan activities, and select materials appropriate for groups of children
4. Demonstrating procedures and techniques for teacher use
5. Planning, providing, and evaluating in-service programs for teachers, administrators, parents, and others who will be expected to participate in the program.

the uses of the continuum-of-services model

Does the continuum model suggest guidelines for the future for speech, language, and hearing programs in the schools? Would the school specialist be able to utilize it as a workable base for planning, implementing, and evaluating programs? Can it be used for the present and for the future as well?

The American Speech-Language-Hearing Association, and particularly the School Services Program, has provided practical suggestions for the school pathologist. The continuum-of-services model is not intended to answer all questions, however, and this becomes obvious as the model is carefully examined. The major ingredient in the model is the school pathologist who must become the information processor and the decision maker. The model, or portions of it, may be applied to the Anytown School District and utilized appropriately. But the appropriateness can best be determined by Polly Pathologist, Clancy Clinician and their colleagues in the Anytown Schools.

TABLE 3-1   THE CONTINUUM OF LANGUAGE, SPEECH, AND HEARING SERVICES FOR CHILDREN AND YOUTH

| | Continuum Components | | |
	Communicative Disorders	*Deviations*	*Development*
Population Served	Pupils with severe language, voice, fluency, articulation, or hearing disorders.	Pupils with mild - moderate developmental or nonmaturational deviations in language, voice, fluency, articulation, and those with mild hearing loss requiring minimal aural rehabilitation procedures.	All pupils in regular or special education classes.
Program Goals	1. Provide direct, intensive, individualized clinical-educational services to effect positive change in communication behavior of pupils with handicapping disorders. 2. Provide information and assistance to other participants.	Provide direct and/or indirect clinical-educational services to stimulate and/or improve pupils' communication skills and competencies.	Provide prevention-oriented, sequenced curricular activities to help pupils develop communicative behaviors in appropriate social, educational, and cultural contexts.
Services Provided by Language, Speech, or Hearing Specialists	1. Identification 2. Comprehensive Assessment (diagnostic evaluation) 3. Referral (for additional services) 4. Parent Counseling and Instruction 5. Pupil Counseling and Placement 6. Teacher Counseling and in-service orientation/Instruction 7. Direct Clinical-Educational Management	Assessment and Evaluation of Communicative Skills. Direct or Indirect Clinical-Educational Management.	Demonstration Lessons.

TABLE 3-1 (continued)

	Continuum Components		
	Communicative Disorders	*Deviations*	*Development*

Program Types and Alternatives	8. Program Evaluation
	9. Pupil Re-assessment
	10. Dismissal and Follow-up
	11. Research
	
	1. Diagnostic center placement
	2. Special class placement
	3. Regular classroom placement with:
	  a. Itinerant services
	  b. Resource room services (emphasis on individual—small group)
	4. Home or hospital services
	5. Parent/Infant Instruction
	6. Residential placement
	(Transportation, Purchased services - May be required to facilitate provision of a service continuum.)
		Regular classroom placement with:
		  a. Itinerant services
		  b. Resource room services (emphasis on group services).
			Consultation (for individual pupils or groups).
			
			Regular classroom placement with:
			  a. Supportive services from other participants.

Other Participants (most common)	Parents, teachers, administrators, aides, counselors, psychologists, physicians, psychiatrists, social workers, nurses, occupational therapists, physical therapists, dentists.	Parents, teachers, administrators, aides, counselors, psychologists, physicians, psychiatrists, social workers, nurses, dentists.	Parents, teachers, administrators, aides, counselors, curriculum specialists.

As was mentioned earlier, this model is contained within the continuum-of-services model. Because of its importance to the school clinician we need to consider it carefully.

The Council for Exceptional Children (1971) issued a policy statement on some of the major principles on which a special education program should be organized and administered. The statement included recommendations on *delivery models* for all handicapped children. Utilizing this as a basis, ASHA described a delivery-of-service model for communicatively handicapped children. The model includes a variety of options and covers the range of communication handicaps from severe disorders to developmental problems. It also makes provision for the prevention of communication problems.

The reasons for presenting a number of options for the delivery-of-services are compelling. First of all, the number of children needing services and not receiving them is high. According to Weintraub (1971), a breakdown of services available supports this idea (see Table 3-2).

TABLE 3-2. COMMUNICATIVELY IMPAIRED CHILDREN
RECEIVING EDUCATIONAL SERVICES

	Deaf	Speech Impaired	Hard of Hearing	Language Impaired
Estimated number of children	45,681	2,145,647	260,981	not given
Number of children receiving services	20,771	1,122,232	44,430	not given
Percentage of children receiving services	45	52	17	not given

Traditionally, speech and language services have been provided on an itinerant basis and have been based on state regulations that define caseload, number of child-contact hours per week, and ratio of clinicians to school populations. Historically, the hearing-impaired and the deaf have received treatment in residential or day schools and special classes in regular schools. By providing more options for the delivery-of-services instead of relying solely on the itinerant model, more children who need help can be reached. This does not imply that the itinerant model is not a good model when it is used in the appropriate circumstances; however, it does mean that the speech, language, and hearing profession must break the habit of thinking of it as the only option.

Delivery-of-Services Options. In the publication, *Project Upgrade: Model Regulations for School Language, Speech and Hearing Programs and Services* (1975), the following recommendations for delivery-of-service options for school speech, language, and hearing programs, are presented:

Recommendations: The following types of options constitute component parts of a continuum model appropriate for pupils with communicative disorders, deviations or needs:

I. Diagnostic center placement. This option may be employed to provide thorough diagnostic assessments and appropriate educational plans for pupils enrolled in the center on a short-term basis. Services are given by speech pathologists, audiologists, teachers of the hearing impaired and other support personnel in a inter-disciplinary team approach. Such centers may operate on either a local, cooperative or regional basis.

II. Special classroom placement. This option should be considered when the diagnostic assessment indicates that the pupil's needs cannot be met by placement in the general education program. The special classroom program should be designed to serve small groupings of pupils with severe communicative disorders. In some instances, these classes may be housed in special schools. When the classrooms are located in or near regular school facilities, pupils may be programmed into regular classes and activities for part of their instruction and related services as they demonstrate potential for successful performance.

III. Regular classroom placement with supportive services. This option may be used for pupils with communicative development needs. Supportive services provided by language, speech, and hearing specialists include:

A. Direct/indirect services to pupils enrolled in regular or special classrooms from a language, speech, or hearing specialist and/or a team operating on:
1. Itinerant basis - the specialist provides continuous, on-going services to pupils in more than one school or center. Scheduling options for this type of service include: intermittent sessions on a regular basis, or intensive cycling, which provides daily service in a particular school or center for a specified block of time. Flexibility of operation and scheduling is desirable in itinerant programming in order to provide for the varying needs of individual pupils.
2. Single building basis - the specialist is assigned full-time to one building or center. Services may be provided by either intermittent or intensive scheduling.

B. Direct/indirect service to pupils provided through a resource room within a school staffed with language, speech, and hearing program personnel. Pupils remain in regular or special classrooms for the major part of the day, but are scheduled into the resource room for one or more periods of individualized instruction.

C. Consultative services to regular or special classroom teachers, curriculum specialists, parents, etc., to provide them with information on communicative skill development, specialized materials and procedures, demonstration sessions and other activities organized to help pupils develop appropriate communicative behaviors in social, educational, and cultural contexts.

IV. Home and/or Hospital Services. Language, speech and hearing specialists may use this option to serve pupils who are unable to attend school because of confinement to their homes or to a hospital setting.

V. Parent/Infant Instruction Services. In this option, parents are provided with guidance and instruction for assisting infants and pre-schoolers to develop appropriate communicative behaviors and skills. The guidance and instruction provided by language, speech and hearing specialists may be given in schools, centers, homes or other approved facilities as appropriate. This model is considered most applicable for children who, because of organic, behavioral, or other symptoms, are determined to be actually or potentially handicapped in developing necessary communicative skills.

VI. Residential Placement. This option is usually reserved for pupils with severe disorders. Education and specialized services are provided in addition to residential care.

The delivery-of-services model allows implementation of all of the preceding options and tends to discourage the sole use of the itinerant model or any other single method for delivering language, speech, and hearing services. The provision of service commensurate with pupil need and adaptive behavior should be the primary concern in establishing intervention programs. Organizational models used to deliver services should allow adequate frequency and intensity of help for optimum pupil progress.

Examples of various delivery-of-service models can be found throughout the United States. Some models are described in the publication, *Language, Speech and Hearing Services in Schools*, and some descriptions are found in the journals published by the various state associations. As the impact of Public Law 94-142 is being felt on the state and local levels, programs are changing to better meet the needs of handicapped students.

PUBLIC LAW 94-142, MANDATORY LEGISLATION

Public Law 94-142, the Education for All Handicapped Children Act, which triggered mandatory legislation in each of the states, assures every child, including the handicapped child, of the right to an educational program suitable to his or her needs. The law stipulates that a free, appropriate education shall be made available to all handicapped children between the ages of three and eighteen, beginning September, 1978, and all those between ages three and twenty-one by September, 1980. It does not apply, however, to those between three and five and between eighteen and twenty-one in states where the requirement is in conflict with state law and practices, or court orders.

The implications of Public Law 94-142 are far-reaching. These changes can be seen at the present time but many of them are contemplated for both the near and the distant future. Let us look at some of the changes that have occurred, are occurring, and some that may occur.

Mainstreaming. The mandatory legislation carries with it the obligation of each local school system to provide a plan for the delivery-of-services to the handicapped child. These services must provide for instruction as well as habilitation and must be coordinated with the regular educational system in such a way that the child is able to move across administrative lines for whatever periods of time are necessary to meet changing needs. This type of arrangement, previously described in Chapter 1, is known as mainstreaming.

Mainstreaming may be compared to regular care, intensive care, and long-term care in a hospital. A patient who is critically ill will be in intensive care until such time as his or her condition is improved and he or she is moved to regular care. Eventually, when completely recovered, the patient is dismissed. Some patients never completely recover, and they are placed in long-term care. The patient in a hospital, then, is involved in mainstreaming.

Mainstreaming may mean that the handicapped child attends the same school or the same classes as other children. Or mainstreaming may be social in that the handicapped child interacts with, uses the same facilities as, and intermingles with, other children.

Another aspect of mainstreaming is on the instructional level. Exceptional children may be instructed by the same teachers as the rest of the children. Depending on the type and degree of handicapping condition they may not necessarily be recipients of the same information. The heart of the Education for all Handicapped Children Act is the written Individualized Educational Program. It is the I.E.P. which becomes the link between the handicapped child and the special education he or she requires and is appropriate to his or her special needs. Furthermore, the I.E.P. sets forth the way in which the special education is actually delivered and monitored.

More Personnel Needed. Earlier in this chapter it was pointed out that only 50 percent of the needs of the communicatively handicapped children were being met. With the mandate to service preacademic children and youth beyond school age, as well as children in nonpublic schools, there is an obvious need for more trained personnel in the field. In addition to the qualified speech, language, and hearing specialists, there will also be an increasing need for trained aides and trained volunteers in the school speech-language and hearing program. The use of trained aides and volunteers implies that someone will have to train them and when they are employed, someone will have to supervise them. That someone may well be the speech-language pathologist in the schools.

Preventive Programs. The intervention with preacademic children as well as early academic children is largely preventive in nature and the utilization by teachers of the speech-language pathologist as a consultant is increasing. In this particular role the speech-language pathologist provides materials and suggestions and often demonstration teaching so that the classroom teacher may implement strategies in the classroom for the children with marginal communication deficits. Thus, the school pathologist will need to spend time in developing and assisting in the implementation of programs to prevent potentially serious problems from developing.

Older Students Need Help. In the opinion of numerous school pathologists, one of the neglected areas of service is the high school. There are several reasons for this. One is the difficulty in scheduling students and another is the problem of adolescent motivation. It is possible that in many instances the school pathologist attempted to modify the approaches used successfully with the elementary school child, and imposed them on the secondary school student. This resulted in programs that were not very effective on the secondary-school level.

With the mandate that handicapped students up to the age of twenty-one be serviced by 1980, the school pathologist will need to develop ways of working with this age bracket.

The proliferation of technical and vocational training centers and high schools presents a challenge to the school speech, language, and hearing specialist to provide meaningful services. In these settings, motivation for changing speech and language behavior and enhancing hearing capacities may be related to vocational choice to provide more incentive for the student.

Knowledge of Community Resources Needed. The school pathologist's knowledge of community, state, and national social service agencies serving the communicatively handicapped will need to be broadened. In a school district which does not employ a social worker, the responsibility of referral may very well rest with the school pathologist. A knowledge of agencies, both voluntary and public, is essential. In many communities there is a community agency council which furnishes information on various agencies and their policies regarding referral, service, cost, and other matters.

Team Approach Emphasized. The school pathologist will also be working with other professionals in a team approach framework. The *placement team* which periodically evaluates handicapped children almost invariably includes the school pathologist. Decisions are made by the placement team, or its equivalent, regarding the child's academic and habilitative future. The parents of the handicapped child and in some cases the child as well, will participate in decisions regarding his/her individualized program.

Diagnosis and Assessment. An increased awareness and knowledge of diagnostic and assessment information will become a part of the pathologist's responsibility. The knowledge of diagnostic and testing procedures, testing instruments, evaluative observation, and the interpretation of all of these aspects of diagnosis must not only be understood and utilized, but must be committed to paper as well, in a clear, precise, and orderly manner.

Accountability. The school pathologist is accountable to the local school administration and board of education, the parents and the community, professional colleagues on the school staff and colleagues in the speech, language, and hearing profession. The school pathologist is also accountable to the state and federal governments who may provide financial support for the program as well as administrative guidelines, standards, and constraints. Most important of all, the school pathologist is accountable to the child with the communication handicap.

The phenomenon of accountability, the need for a uniform data system on case management and program management, and the need to collect and eventually retrieve information on which future programs may be built, indicates a need for an accountability system. The American Speech-Language-Hearing Association has developed a data-systems approach to record keeping in language, speech, and hearing programs and some school systems have developed their own systems.

Litigation. Local school districts have no choice but to meet the explicit provisions of Public Law 94-142 or be subject to prosecution for violating the handicapped child's civil rights. The Education for All Handicapped Children Act protects the rights of handicapped children by setting up a due process procedure. This procedure assures the parents or the parent surrogates that the law really works and that the handicapped child gets the education he or she needs. This is a part of the constitutional heritage of our country and protects the rights of all citizens.

Under due process the parents are entitled to the following procedures:

a. a written notice before any action is taken or recommended that may change the child's school program
b. a right to examine all records related to the identification, evaluation, or placement of the child
c. a chance to voice any complaints regarding any matters related to the educational services the child is receiving
d. an impartial hearing before a hearing officer or a judge in the event that the school and the parents cannot agree on the type of school program for the child
e. adequate appeals procedure if parents are not satisfied with the due process procedure. The case may be taken to the state department of education, or finally to a court of law.

Each state has its own guidelines relating to due process and a copy of these may be obtained either from the state's special education department or from a concerned citizens group within the state. A copy of Public Law 94-142 may be obtained by contacting your senator or congressman, or by writing to the Superintendent of Documents, U.S. Government Printing Office, Washington, D.C. 20402.

THE EDUCATIONAL AUDIOLOGIST

The specialty of educational audiology is a comparatively new development in the field of communication disorders. Born out of a need for improved services to the hearing-impaired child in the school, and a shortage of qualified personnel to carry out a hearing conservation program, an educational audiology program was pioneered at Utah State University in 1966. (Alpiner, 1978.) Since that time, other states have followed suit in providing training programs for educational audiologists. According to Alpiner such training programs should be of help in providing more qualified individuals who are interested in working in the public school systems, since many clinical audiologists do not enter or seek employment in the schools. The problem as to who should provide therapy for mildly impaired children who are not candidates for special educational classrooms could also be alleviated. According to Alpiner:

> A more serious problem exists in smaller urban and rural communities where the number of children needing hearing therapy is comparatively small. It is not practical for these school districts to employ audiologists. Smaller geographical areas may be adequately covered by traveling audiologists from state health departments, but there is no provision for continuing therapy after the audiological and medical evaluations have been completed. It may then be the speech clinician's responsibility to provide rehabilitative audiology. This problem could be resolved by modifying university training programs so that the student preparing for speech pathology would be given additional training and practicum in audiology. This future clinician could then be more qualified to engage in speech-reading, auditory training, and hearing therapy. Whether or not such a course of action is feasible cannot be determined at this time, but this problem must be resolved. The public school clinician meeting the appropriate determined requirements would be able to work with both speech- and hearing-impaired children in any size school system. In any event, there is a need to provide qualified personnel for hearing-impaired children in all school hearing conservation programs. Evaluation alone does not constitute hearing conservation, and without the means for providing rehabilitative audiology, the program cannot achieve any degree of success. (1978, pp. 182.)

Growing out of the need for increased and improved services to the hearing-impaired student, educational audiology seeks to develop educational programs related to the unique characteristics of these individuals. Educational audiologists are in the process of developing model curriculums for the hearing-impaired child, as well as improved definitions of hearing disabilities.

The organization and management of school programs as well as the professional preparation leading to certification and licensing requirements, are also currently being developed.

Because this area of specialization is a recent one, there will be many geographical areas throughout the United States where the habilitative needs of the hearing-impaired child in the school system will continue to be met by the school speech-language and hearing clinician, the classroom teacher, and the principal until such a time as an educational audiologist is employed.

What are the functions of the educational audiologist? The Wood County, Ohio, Office of Education formulated a list of guidelines to assist teachers, principals, administrators, and clinicians in planning services for the hearing impaired. The guidelines list the services to be extended by the educational audiologist to the public school system in the county. (Miner, 1977) They are as follows:

FOR THE CHILD

Hearing evaluations
Hearing aid evaluations
Acoustic response of the hearing aid
Assessment of lip-reading skills
Auditory perceptual testing
Counseling
Speech and language assessment
Referrals
Follow-up

FOR THE PARENTS

Conferences
Home visits
Workshops
Referrals to other agencies and specialists
Child management recommendations
Information source

FOR THE TEACHER

In-service training
Classroom observation
Classroom management techniques
Consultation regarding specific children
Talks to class groups
Suggestions for materials, methods, resources
Conferences with parent-teacher-clinician

FOR THE CLINICIAN

Act as a referral source for difficult to test or severe cases

Serve as a liaison between parent-teacher-clinician

Assist in the planning and implementation of the hearing conservation program

Workshops

Demonstration therapy

Suggestions for methods, materials, resources

Assess audiological equipment status and needs

Calibration of audiometers

Measurement of noise levels and recommendations for sound treatment

FOR THE ADMINISTRATORS

Assistance in the preparation and design of educational programs for the hearing impaired

In-service training and workshops for teachers and staff

Liaison between community resources, parents, and educational staff

During the continuing phases of the program the following programs and projects constituted an attempt to extend the educational audiologist's function as a consultant:

1. Child Development Screening Program—a county-wide comprehensive screening program for pre-school and school-aged children.
2. Coordination and supervision of undergraduate clinicians—in-training to provide assistance in public school hearing screening programs.
3. Coordination and supervision of undergraduate and graduate level students in providing tutorial services for specific deaf and hearing-impaired children.
4. Workshops dealing with auditory perceptual diagnosis and remediation —designed for the public school clinician.
5. Establishment of the Wood County Hearing Aid Fund—to provide loaner instruments for specific children upon request.
6. Assistance in the coordination of Health Department Pediatric-Otologic-Diagnostic Clinics by acting as a liaison for school districts involved.
7. Formal and informal presentations to professional organizations, student associations, university classes, and Wood County Staff members to impart information (general and specific) about various aspects of program development.
8. Design and implementation of a statewide survey to assess the current status and needs of deaf education programs data presented to interested personnel in the Northwest Ohio Region as a workshop on deafness (in conjunction with the Bowling Green State University Psychology Department).
9. Act as hearing consultant for pre-school screening programs in Wood County.

10. Coordination of efforts in order to facilitate the development of a summer school speech and hearing program.

CONCLUSION

Before implementing organizational procedures, the school clinician must have a working knowledge of Public Law 94-142, an understanding of professional terminology, and an understanding of other professions involved in the education of the handicapped.

The continuum-of-services model, with its component, the delivery-of-services model, are helpful in the planning and implementation stages of a program.

A comparatively recent development in the habilitative management of the hearing-impaired child is *educational audiology*. A discussion of this professional specialization is included in this chapter.

4

the first steps in establishing programs

INTRODUCTION

In this chapter we will consider what is involved in the first steps toward organizing and carrying out a successful speech-language and hearing program in the schools.

Because change is an ever-present part of our profession, some school pathologists may be considering reorganizing their programs to meet current needs and improve services to communicatively handicapped children. Some of the questions and issues discussed in this chapter may apply to this situation also.

The person reading this text should keep in mind that the information contained in this chapter is a guideline for appraising the local situation in preparation for actually establishing the program. Many of the issues discussed will be further elaborated upon in subsequent chapters. One of the dilemmas facing the pathologist organizing a program (or in some cases, reorganizing a program) is that everything should come first! For that reason, detailed information regarding certain topics is provided in this chapter, and other topics which will be dealt with in depth later in the book have been briefly outlined.

APPRAISING THE LOCAL SITUATION

the number of children involved

Obtaining an estimate of the number of children and youth to be involved in the speech-language and hearing program in a school district is the first step in analyzing the needs of the program. It may be impossible to get an exact number, but it is important to utilize every source of information to obtain as close a number as possible.

In order to get an estimate of the number of children involved it is necessary to know the total school population. This is usually referred to as the *Average Daily Membership* or ADM figure, or the *Average Daily Attendance* (ADA) figure. Because school attendance is compulsory, all schools must report the attendance each day. At some point in the school year, usually in October, the ADM is determined. In many states, reimbursement from the state is determined by the ADM figure.

incidence

Chapter 1 dealt with the difficulties the profession has encountered over the years in attempting to assess the incidence of speech, language, and hearing problems in the school-age population. While numerous studies have taken place in the United States regarding incidence and prevalence, a reliable data base has not yet been established. Fisher (1977) reported in "An Open Letter to ASHA Members Employed in the Schools," that among the ten highest priorities determined at the 1975 Colorado Evaluation Conference was the need to collect reliable incidence/prevalence data.

Phillips (1975) stated, "Based on the majority of recent studies, it is probably safe to judge that between 8 and 10 percent of the children now enrolled in school exhibit some kind of oral communication disorder." This author would tend to agree with Phillips. There are even indications that the figure of 10 percent is a conservative one. There are possible reasons for this. In reporting it is often common practice to report the presence of only one handicapping condition. For example, a learning-disabled child may also have accompanying speech, language, or hearing problems, but in a survey that child is reported as being learning-disabled with no notice taken of the communication handicaps.

Another reason is that definitions and terminology regarding handicapping conditions may vary from state to state and from person to person so that the reporting of various conditions is not consistent.

Let us use the figure of 10 percent in estimating oral communication problems, and apply this to the total school-age population of Anytown School District. If there is a total school-age population of 5000, approximately 500 of these children can be expected to have communication problems serious enough to warrant intervention. Applying the figure of 10 percent to a building or an educational center containing 500 children, 50 of them can be expected to have communication problems.

As was mentioned earlier, the incidence and prevalence of language disorders are not known, but the numbers are believed by many to be high. Despite the fact that the data on incidence and prevalence is incomplete, it is useful for the school pathologist to have some estimates of the numbers of children with the various kinds of speech and language and hearing problems. The figures in Table 4-1 were ascertained from an incidence study by the National Institute of Neurological Diseases and Stroke (NINDS) in 1967.

TABLE 4-1   INCIDENCE OF COMMUNICATIVE DISORDERS
            IN CHILDREN

Communicative Disorders	Number per 10,000
Defects of speech affecting articulation	500
Severe hearing impairment	150-300
Voice problems	60
Stuttering (dysfluency)	60
Retarded speech development unrelated to deafness	50
Organic disorders affecting speech (cleft palate, facial malformations)	20
Organic speech disorders resulting from cerebral palsy	13
Total deafness	12

The incidence and prevalence figures which have been discussed so far have to do with the child in school. The mandatory education law (Public Law 94-142) refers to all children, some of whom may be in schools and some of whom may not be. The school pathologist must also include in the planning stages of an overall program those children who are of preschool age, in private programs, in residential programs, in detention homes, in sheltered workshops, or at home. The list would also include children who have dropped out of school voluntarily, who are employed in the community, or who are in continuing education programs such as vocational high schools and technical institutes.

child find program

Since 1974, states have been conducting a *Child Find Program* through their regional resource centers. Their purpose is to identify and evaluate all handicapped children in order to receive federal funding for special education programs within the state. Through the regional resource centers in the states it would be possible to identify the unserved handicapped children in an area.

In some areas of the United States where there is forced bussing of children, many youngsters will be found in private schools. Under the Child Find Program, all handicapped children in both public and private schools are the responsibility of the school district in which the parents reside.

In addition to the total school population, it is important to know the population of each building and the enrollments by grade level. The total number of schools in a district and what type of schools they are, is also necessary information. How many are elementary, how many intermediate, and how many high school? Are there any special schools? Are there any special classes, and in which schools are they located? How many children are enrolled in the special classes?

What are the socioeconomic levels of the various school neighborhoods? Do any of the schools have culturally disadvantaged children? If the school pathologist is concerned with human communication and its disorders, there must be a concerted effort to assume responsibilities for the "neglected" populations. This would include the disadvantaged inner city child, the disadvantaged rural child, and the child who comes from a bilingual background. The communication difficulties experienced by these children encompass not only language and speech, but listening, hearing, thinking, reading, and writing.

In summary, the school pathologist would first need to know the population figures including children both in and out of school. By applying incidence and prevalence percentages to the out-of-school population and to the populations in the various educational centers, it would be possible to obtain an estimate of the number of children needing speech, language, and hearing help. The speech pathologist would then have an idea of the magnitude of the task.

PHYSICAL FACILITIES

The next thing the school pathologist would have to assess would be the rooms used for therapy within each of the buildings being serviced. In setting up criteria for evaluating physical facilities, the factors of "realism" and "idealism" must be taken into account. While it might be ideal for the speech clinician to have a room in a school used exclusively for the purposes of the speech, language, and hearing program, it may not be realistic to plan such a room because the speech pathologist may be on an itinerant schedule and the space could be utilized by the reading teacher on the alternate days.

Another factor to take into consideration would be the existing facilities (things as they are today), and the potential facilities (things as they might be with some modifications). This is particularly true in setting up a new program. Because of this, it is important that there is a set of criteria, or a "yardstick", which would indicate that while the existing facilities may not be satisfactory, they could and should be modified in the future. In assessing this aspect of the program the policies of the school must be known. For example, is the supervisor of the speech, language, and hearing program involved in the planning of new facilities or the modification of existing facilities? Are staff members included in the planning? Are alternative plans considered, such as the use of mobile units, remodeling of areas of buildings, or the rental of additional space? What are the budgetary allowances and constraints?

According to Scarvel (1977) in considering criteria for physical facilities, the following questions should be asked:

1. Are the facilities of adequate size or space to permit total program flexibility? (The Key Term is Total Program Flexibility.) Can this be used by both Speech and Language Clinicians and Itinerant Hearing Clinicians?
2. Is the facility relatively free from extraneous noise? The Key Word is Relatively in being realistic in terms of the existing physical plant. (For example, one set of criteria required acoustically treated walls, and acoustic tile on ceilings.) This is fine; however, we may find ourselves in a room not having this, but still free from extraneous noise because of its location.
3. Are there adequate furnishings for the type of services offered? (The Key Word is Adequate.) Ideally, maybe there should be more than those appearing on this list; but, we're looking for *adequate* furnishings.
4. Are sufficient electrical outlets provided? (Key Word - Sufficient) This depends upon the type(s) of services to be delivered and/or equipment utilization necessary (rather than specifying an exact number).
5. Is the lighting adequate and the facility properly heated/cooled? (The Key Word is again Adequate.) For example, one source mentions the use of artificial light in addition to natural light; specifically, at least one window is needed.
6. Are facilities accessible to physically handicapped students? This criterion would apply only in those instances where physically handicapped students need to be serviced in a particular facility. As in the case with the other criteria, those criteria which are not applicable to a program, or to the specific services provided, would not be used.

The ASHA Committee on Speech and Hearing Services in the Schools, under the chairpersonship of Gloria Engnoth (1969), published a list of recommendations for the housing of speech services in the schools. This list may serve as a good checklist during both the planning stages of a program and the evaluation of an on-going program.

ROOM

Location: In a relatively quiet area near administrative unit with accessibility to classrooms, waiting area, secretarial services, and other special service personnel.

Size: 150-250 square feet to be used primarily (or ideally exclusively) for the speech and hearing services.

Number: One room, ideally with an adjoining office.

Lighting, artificial: 60-75 foot candles.

Lighting, natural:	At least one window with shade, ideally with drapes.
Heating:	Adequate heating, ideally with thermostatic control.
Ventilation:	One window which can be opened, or air conditioning.
Acoustical treatment:	Acoustical treatment of ceiling, doors, and walls, ideally draperies and carpeted floors.
Electrical power supply:	One 110V double plug on each wall. Ideally a rheostatic mechanism to facilitate use of audio-visual equipment.
Intercom:	Ideally, one intercom unit, connected to administrative offices.
Chalkboard:	One 3' x 5' (approximate) mounted on wall.
Mirror(s):	One 3' x 5' (approximate) mounted on wall at appropriate height for pupils. Should be able to be covered.

FURNITURE

Desk:	One office desk.
Chairs, Adult:	At least two chairs.
Chairs, Child:	Sufficient number of student school chairs to accommodate pupils at various grade levels.
Table:	One table adjustable in height to accommodate pupils at various grade levels.
Equipment stand:	One stand on casters suitable for tape recorder, record player, etc.

STORAGE FACILITIES

Storage space:	Locked storage space.
File case:	Locked file cabinet.
Bookcase:	Bookcase with 4'-8' (approximate) linear space.

EQUIPMENT

Audiometer:	Properly calibrated portable audiometer available.
Auditory training equipment:	Individual amplification units available according to need.
Tape recorder:	One assigned for exclusive use of clinician.
Phonograph:	One 3-speed phonograph available in building.
Telephone:	One telephone, ideally a direct outside line.
Typewriter:	Available.

Electric
clock: One.
Wastebasket: One.

(Electronic equipment is not included in this list and that information, along with other considerations, will be dealt with in chapter 6.)

other considerations regarding
physical facilities

In addition to evaluating the room itself, some other considerations should be dealt with in the planning stages. First of all, the room must be accessible to physically handicapped pupils and located in an area of the building convenient to all who use it. It should not be too far from the kindergarten and first-grade classrooms because these youngsters sometimes have difficulty finding their way to and from the room.

Space is often at a premium in school buildings and many buildings being currently used are old and not well planned for present-day needs. With a little imagination and resourcefulness, some simple remodeling and rejuvenation can transform unused space into completely adequate facilities for the school pathologist. For example, a portion of a large entry foyer may be partitioned and utilized for the speech-language and hearing program.

If a new building is being contemplated, the speech-language and hearing clinician will need to be in on the planning stages in order to insure adequate space allotment for that program. School architects are not always well informed as to the space and facility needs of the program, and the school pathologist can be of invaluable assistance in providing needed information.

The policies of the school in regard to space must also be known when planning physical facilities. For example, the school pathologist should know how space is assigned in a building and whether or not staff members are consulted when the assignments are made. The school pathologist should also know whether or not there are provisions for modifying the room. If space is to be shared, the speech-language and hearing staff members should know the procedures used for obtaining input from all the persons sharing the room.

(Alternatives to utilizing existing space will be discussed in chapter 7.)

ADMINISTRATIVE AND
FINANCIAL STRUCTURE

In organizing a speech-language and hearing program, it is also important for the school pathologist to have an understanding of the school system's overall administrative structure and to know where the program fits into the total structure. The same applies to the overall budgetary procedures for the school system, and specifically, the application of that information to the speech-language and hearing program.

School organization and budgetary costs for the speech-language and hearing program will be dealt with in a later chapter. The following questions apply to the planning stages of a program, and the school pathologist will want to seek answers to them.

What is the overall administrative structure of the school system? What are the lines of authority? Where does the speech-language and hearing program fit into the total structure? Is there a supervisor for the program? If there is more than one speech-language pathologist, what are the policies in regard to schedules, caseloads, recording and reporting practices, and referral policies? What are the staff responsibilities? What support services are available?

What are the school policies in regard to employment and dismissal practices, sick leave, salary schedules, and retirement? What are the policies on continuing education and staff development? What are the certification regulations and the tenure laws?

Is there a budget for equipment, materials, supplies, and travel? How are budget costs determined for the speech-language and hearing program?

reimbursement: state and local

How is the speech-language and hearing program reimbursed? A part of each program is paid for by the local board of education and the remainder is supported by the state. Each state is different, and more than one reimbursement formula may be used within a state. There are three general categories of state support. They are (1) unit, (2) per pupil, and (3) special.

According to *Project UPGRADE: Guidelines for Evaluating State Education Laws and Regulations:*

Under a unit financing procedure, school districts are reimbursed either a straight sum or a percentage of the costs for each designated unit of classroom instruction, administration, or support service. Michigan, for example, reimburses intermediate school districts for special education programs and services on the basis of five professional personnel per 1000 pupils enrolled in all public and nonpublic schools in the district, excluding programs for the severely and trainable mentally retarded. Recommended staffing patterns are outlined, but the local districts may designate professional staffing patterns at their own discretion. Texas, in contrast, allocates some teacher units on the basis of the formula in Table 4-2.

TABLE 4-2   TEXAS FORMULA FOR ALLOCATING
TEACHER UNITS

Teachers	One for each eight pupils or major fraction.
	One for each seven pupils or major fraction.
Principals	One for each 15+ teachers.
	One for each school.
Supervisors	One for each 10 teachers not to exceed three; however, a minimum of one for each school.
	Same as for countywide.

In both states, other allotments are given for transportation, other personnel, and services. Minnesota pays, in addition to these amounts, 60 percent of the salary of "essential personnel" involved in the educational program for the handicapped, not to exceed $5600 per year for each full-time person employed.

Per pupil funding is used in several states. Idaho uses a weighted per-pupil formula for pupils in special classes, but when speech, language, and hearing services are provided through itinerant personnel, districts are reimbursed 80 percent of their salary costs. Maryland has been using a straight-sum per-pupil formula. The sum of $100 is allotted for each pupil receiving language, speech, or hearing services on an itinerant basis, while $1,000 is allowed for each child in self-contained classes for the hearing impaired or language disabled. Maximum case-load and class size limits are set by regulations.

Excess cost formulas are also applied in various ways. In Massachusetts, excess costs of educating handicapped children are limited to 110 percent of the applicable state average expenditure for each special education pupil minus that state average expenditure.

The costs of instructional materials, administration, transportation, and pupil assessment may be included in excess cost formulas or may be reimbursed separately. (Jones and Healey, 1975, p. 21.)

school and community resources

Another item to consider in assessing the human resource potential of the program is what other services are available in the school. This would include psychological services, social workers, nurses, counselors, remedial and special education teachers, and others. It is also a good idea to get an appraisal of the resource services outside the school and within the community. Many communities maintain an active list of social service agencies in the area, as well as information on how to arrange for referrals, fee schedules, and who to contact for information. This information can often be obtained through the mayor's office, the local chamber of commerce, or a social agency clearinghouse.

THE STAFF: NUMBER, TRAINING, AND QUALITY

The staff needs should be based on the total needs of the program. After determining the approximate number of children in a school district who need speech, language, and hearing habilitation, the ratio of clinical staff to the communicatively handicapped population can be established.

It should be kept in mind in establishing a ratio that the staff members will play various roles. Depending on the size of the staff, a particular staff member may function in several capacities. For example, a supervisor may function for half his time as a supervisor and the other half as a clinical staff person.

In the event that the school system is a large one, a full-time supervisor or administrator may be needed, and, in fact, this individual's services may be augmented by several part-time supervisors who function the remainder of the time as clinical staff members. With the expansion of services to be rendered, it can be safely assumed that most school pathologists will spend at least part of their time supervising communication aides.

The various roles and responsibilities of the staff members should be taken into consideration in the overall planning of the program, particularly in establishing a ratio of staff to children.

In most states the ratio of staff-to-pupil is defined by state standards. With the mandate implicit in Public Law 94-142 of providing free, appropriate public education to all handicapped pupils, many staff-to-pupil ratios are no longer realistic. In a review of state plans submitted to the American Speech and Hearing Association, Healey and Dublinske (1977) found that some states reported a ratio of one speech-language pathologist to 150 pupils. According to Healey and Dublinske, "Ratios such as this will not allow communicatively handicapped pupils to receive an 'appropriate' education."

In the absence of any conclusive data on the best possible ratio of staff-to-pupil, it might be well to utilize the 10 percent figure of incidence of speech, language, and hearing problems (Phillips, 1975) to determine how many staff members will be required to service a given population in a school district. For example, a school system with a total population of 1000 pupils could be expected to have 100 children with serious communication handicaps. Taking into account the various duties and responsibilities of the school pathologist, the ratio could then be established.

ACCOUNTABILITY

A study was initiated in 1977 by the School Services Program of the American Speech and Hearing Association entitled, "A Normative Service Cost Analysis Model for Language, Speech, and Hearing Programs in the Schools" (Healey and Dublinske, 1977). Within this project are listed the services necessary to conduct a comprehensive language, speech, and hearing program in the schools. Included is information on the percentage of the population that receives the service, the personnel who provide the service, the number of times the service is provided, and the time needed to provide the service. The information will be computerized and interfaced with budget information from the twenty school districts participating in the project. This would provide a basis for determining the cost of providing each service included in the comprehensive program. A self-instructional manual on completing a cost analysis is being developed. Information regarding the manual can be obtained from the American Speech-Language-Hearing Association, 10801 Rockville Pike, Rockville, Maryland 20852.

Because states as well as local school districts are financially accountable to the public, the cost-accounting system would provide sound information in regard to the cost of the program, both state-wide and locally. By looking at the needs of the program and the cost to the school district, the school will then be better able to determine the number of personnel needed.

In further analyzing the information in regard to staff, the experience and education of the individual staff members will need to be taken into account— the number of years of experience of staff members, the average annual turnover rate, the degree of certification status of each staff member, and the number of staff members seeking advanced degrees and certification. It is also important in planning to note which staff members have particular areas of expertise that may enhance the program. Staff members may also express a need for in-service training and continuing education, and this needs to be noted.

CONCLUSION

Collecting the information in an effort to appraise the existing situation is the first logical step toward setting program goals. If the school pathologist is preparing to organize a program where none has existed previously, additional information may be needed. If the program is an on-going one, questions regarding current practices should be included. Whether the speech-language pathologist is organizing a new program or reorganizing an already established program, an appraisal is an appropriate place to begin. The information in this chapter may serve as a guideline in collecting information and utilizing it appropriately in the initial stages of planning.

5 | *applying management techniques to speech-language programs*

INTRODUCTION

When school speech-language clinicians are asked about their programs, services, and job performances, they are quite likely to make the following responses: "We need more time to plan," "There are too many children on my case roster," "We need more staff members," "I have trouble scheduling students because of all the other school activities," "My room is too small and not well ventilated," and so on. Interestingly enough the school clinician is generally pleased with the progress of the children in the program, and the school administration is pleased with the program. Why then the complaints? Very possibly the reason is that each school pathologist is constantly faced with the challenge of providing the highest caliber of services with the most efficient expenditure of time, money, and resources, including physical, technical, and human resources.

The emphasis on accountability and finances in schools has a direct relationship to both the planning and the carrying out of a school speech-language and hearing program. A close look at the services rendered, how effective these services are, how the services are viewed by parents, community, other professionals, and the children receiving the services, must be taken by the profession of speech, language, and hearing pathology. How then must the school pathologist proceed in order to insure accountability and to provide a flexible, viable program in the schools?

MANAGEMENT: BASIC PRINCIPLES

Perhaps the best place to start is to admit to ourselves that in the field of management we need to acquire new skills, new techniques, and new instruments, as well as an understanding of the principles of the management process; planning, organizing, staffing, directing, and controlling. The goal of comprehensive services for all handicapped children by 1980 points out the need for appropriate managerial skills at the local level as well as at the state and national levels.

The need for information on managerial skills and techniques has been recognized for some time. For example, a conference on "Supervision of Speech and Hearing Programs in the Schools" held in 1970 at Indiana University, Bloomington, Indiana, addressed itself to such topics as the role of leadership and group effectiveness, and program planning and evaluation. The conference, under the direction of Jean Anderson, utilized the services of personnel from the educational administration field and the business management field.

The American Speech-Language-Hearing Association's manual, *Essentials of Program Planning, Development, Management and Evaluation, A Manual for School Speech, Hearing and Language Programs* (Jones and Healey, 1973), utilized the management-by-objectives system. In the foreword to the publication it is stated:

> The present trend toward implementation of formal systems for program planning, development, management, and evaluation appears to be gaining acceptance at national, state, and local levels. Although the principles on which most systems operate have some commonality, their application in special programs requires interpretation and definition of specific procedures.

Many colleges and universities through their continuing education programs offer courses in supervision and management. Sometimes they are general courses in supervision, management-by-objectives, leadership, and communication and may be geared to specific professions or businesses, or particular groups of individuals. Seminars in management techniques are being offered at many places throughout the country, usually in addition to the regularly scheduled university courses in management. The proliferation of these courses and seminars in recent years points out the fact that state and local government agencies and departments are enlisting the aid of local universities and businessmen in developing and improving management techniques in the public sector.

It might behoove state and local speech-language and hearing associations to include programs on management in their meetings. Also, individuals in the profession, as well as students, might consider taking courses or attending seminars on management with the thought of applying the principles to organizing and implementing school, clinic, hospital, and agency programs. In the area of self-help there are some good basic books on management which would be of assistance to the speech-language pathologist. (These books and articles are listed at the end of this chapter.)

applying management principles

While it is beyond the scope of this book to provide a crash course in management principles and practices, let us take a bird's-eye look at what the field has to offer the struggling speech-language and hearing clinician about to organize a program in the schools.

According to Coventry and Burstiner (1977) in *Management: A Basic Handbook*, a common core of problems exists for any organization to be dealt with by its management. First, there is a need to establish major objectives and major policies. What is the purpose of the organization, and how can that purpose be attained? Does everyone involved understand clearly the objectives and policies?

Second, a structure must be set up to determine the responsibilities for the various tasks that must be accomplished in order to achieve the objectives. The relationships between these jobs must be established.

Third, there must be resources such as space, equipment, furniture, staff, supporting services, and supervisors, to mention but a few.

Finally, there must be long-term and short-term programs of work that conform effectively to the objectives and policies that have been laid down.

These basic principles seem fairly obvious, but sometimes the obvious is overlooked. For example, how many organizations know *exactly* their real objectives, as opposed to assumed objectives?

Management is the process of getting things done by people in the most efficient and effective way. It involves setting goals and objectives that are both understood and accepted, and then coordinating the activities of people toward the attainment of these goals.

In 1954, a system known as *management-by-objectives* was developed by Peter F. Drucker. This system has been utilized, in its various forms, by business, industry, governmental agencies, and educational systems concerned with efficient and effective organization and management. Table 5-1 illustrates the MBO process (Raia, 1974).

ESTABLISHING GOALS
FOR THE PROGRAM

Let us examine Table 5-1 with the idea of applying it to the organization and management of a school program. The first essential element is goal-setting and the major steps are: formulating long-range goals and strategic

TABLE 5-1   THE MBO PROCESS

The Essential Elements	The Major Steps

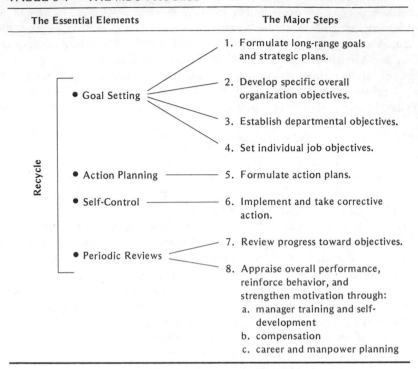

	1. Formulate long-range goals and strategic plans.
● Goal Setting	2. Develop specific overall organization objectives.
	3. Establish departmental objectives.
	4. Set individual job objectives.
● Action Planning	5. Formulate action plans.
● Self-Control	6. Implement and take corrective action.
● Periodic Reviews	7. Review progress toward objectives.
	8. Appraise overall performance, reinforce behavior, and strengthen motivation through: a. manager training and self-development b. compensation c. career and manpower planning

Recycle

plans; developing specific overall organization objectives; establishing departmental objectives; and setting individual job objectives.

Goals are long-term or short-term, tangible, measurable, and verifiable. They are not nebulous statements, but are specific statements of a desired future condition or accomplishment. Ideally, goals should be set by all persons involved in the structure so there is a commitment on the part of those persons. Once the goals have been determined it is crucial to get them down in writing. The language must be clear and concise, and must communicate the intent to all relevant parties.

Once specific overall goals have been established, the step-by-step process of translating them into required action begins. This brings us to the second essential element which is *action planning*. Action planning involves determining *when, who, what, to whom,* and *how much* is needed to reach the given objective. It also includes the criterion and the evaluation. It is a way of providing a connecting link between the statement of a goal and the more complete program of implementation. Another way of stating action planning is *setting program objectives*.

The third element is *self-control* and is based on the idea that the individual and not the superior will control his or her own behavior. According to Raia,

Self control requires meaningful participation in the goal-setting and action-planning process, resulting in a better understanding and a higher level of commitment to the objectives. The individual must also, however, be given the feedback and information he needs to assess progress and to take corrective action on his own. (1974, p. 18.)

The fourth element is *periodic reviews*. The purpose of the reviews is to evaluate progress and performance in the light of the established objectives. The problem areas can be identified and the obstacles removed so that new objectives can be established. It is a method of systematic stock-taking on the way to reaching the goal.

In setting up goals and objectives for speech-language and hearing programs, we would also include a statement of the criterion and the evaluation. The criterion indicates how successful you want to be in accomplishing the *what*. The evaluation indicates a method that will be used to find out whether or not the *what* was accomplished.

Also, keep in mind that in this chapter we are talking about *program* goals and objectives. The same general principles could be applied to *instructional* goals and objectives.

WRITING GOALS
FOR THE PROGRAM

Let us look at some examples of writing goals and objectives. We will first consider writing long-range program goals, assuming that you have already evaluated the existing situation and have determined the overall needs of the program. Keep in mind that although these are long-range and broad in focus, they still need to be stated specifically and concretely.

Example: One year from (date) the clinician will have developed and written a language curriculum guide for teachers of the adjusted curriculum classes in Ottawa County.

Example: By (date) the clinician will have completed a research project related to case selection at the kindergarten level.

Example: By (date) 90 percent of the pupils in Martin Luther King, Jr. School identified as having communication problems and needing therapeutic intervention will be receiving services.

Some goals and objectives may be narrower in focus and have a shorter time-frame.

Example: By (date) the clinician will have administered audiometric screenings to 95 percent of the second grade pupils in the Port Clinton School district.

Example: By (date) the clinician will have conducted group parent meetings for parents of all children enrolled at Lakeside School.

Some objectives are very short-term and have a very narrow focus. Sometimes they may be considered sub-goals and may be contained within a goal or objective and contribute toward its attainment.

Example: During the second week of school in September, 19___, the clinician will acquaint teachers at Jefferson School with referral procedures through an in-service meeting.

Example: By April 15, 19___, the clinician will write an article for the local newspaper and prepare items for the local radio and television stations regarding the prekindergarten communication evaluation program to be held during the first week in May at Catawba and Danbury schools.

A *criterion*, or a *standard of performance*, is the description of the results of a job well done. It should always be a number or an indication of quantity, that is, *how much* and *by when*. It should be realistic, control-oriented, and high enough so that when the task is completed it will have been of value to the program.

Example: Dismiss 30 percent of the pupils enrolled as functionally corrected and 50 percent as greatly improved by the end of the school year.

Example: By December 1, 19___, the clinician will provide three demonstration language development sessions in 50 percent of the kindergarten classrooms of Bataan School, and receive positive feedback, in written form, from 90 percent of the teachers involved.

The *evaluation* is an indication of the method to be used to determine if the goal or objective has been accomplished. An indication of the evaluation may be a report sent to the coordinator of speech-language and hearing services. Or it may be a list of post-test scores, a list of referrals made, or a chart indicating that change has occurred.

Example: By (date) the clinician will have administered speech-language screening tests to 95 percent of the third grade pupils in Marblehead School and a report will be submitted to the school principal and the director of speech-language and hearing services.

Occasionally, objectives are difficult to measure or confirm, even though they are activities or events which, when accomplished, lead to the overall improvement of a situation or a condition.

Example: The speech, language, and hearing pathologist will attempt to improve communication with the classroom teachers by:

    (a)   eating lunch with the teachers at least two times per week or more often if possible
    (b)   inviting teachers to observe therapy sessions
    (c)   attending as many school meetings and social functions as time permits.

importance of planning

Planning ahead is the key to a successful program. Setting goals and objectives is one of the most critical elements of the planning process. Once the goals and objectives have been determined, the next step is writing them down in such a form that they clearly communicate their intent to all the persons concerned and involved in the program.

The utilization of written goals and objectives has many potential advantages in the school speech-language and hearing program. First of all, it allows for change, because through the system of periodic review, objectives will need to be revised and rewritten. Also, it creates a positive pressure to get things done. Communication among professionals will be improved. There will be more precise definitions of the roles and responsibilities of the school speech-language and hearing clinician. A system for evaluating and assessing the overall program is inherent in the written goals and objectives. Better utilization of each staff member's time and capabilities will be encouraged. And finally, there will be a better basis for understanding the program both within the school system and in the community.

CONCLUSION

This chapter is an attempt to examine briefly some of the elements of management utilized by business and industry throughout the world, with the idea of applying these principles to school speech-language and hearing programs. The need to closely examine the school programs, what they are attempting to do, how they are doing it, and how effective they are, is vital. The school speech, language, and hearing clinician today and in the future will need to be acquainted with sophisticated tools and systems for evaluation and measurement of programs and personnel. A "cookbook" approach is not the answer because there is no single "recipe" for a good program.

At the end of this chapter is a list of references on management. School pathologists may want to examine the readings. There are also seminars, short courses, and continuing education programs available on the topic.

A helpful publication for school pathologists is *PDME, The Essentials of Program Planning, Development, Management, Evaluation, A Manual for School Speech, Hearing, and Language Programs*, published by the American Speech-Language-Hearing Association. This is also available as a telecourse and may be purchased or leased by writing to: Business Office, Continuing Education, 116 Stewart Center, Purdue University, West Lafayette, Indiana 47907.

SUGGESTED FURTHER READING

Albers, H. H., *Principles of Management: A Modern Approach* (4th ed.), New York: John Wiley, 1974.

Allen, L. A., *Professional Management: New Concepts and Proven Practices*, New York: McGraw-Hill, 1973.

Cleland, D. I. and W. R. King, *Management: A Systems Approach*, New York: McGraw-Hill, 1972.

Dale, E., *Management: Theory and Practice* (3rd ed.), New York: McGraw-Hill, 1973.

Drucker, P. F., *Management: Tasks, Responsibilities, Practices*, New York: Harper & Row, Pub., 1974.

Luthans, F., *Introduction to Management: A Contingency Approach*, New York: McGraw-Hill, 1976.

McFarland, E., *Management Principles and Practices* (4th ed.), New York: Macmillan, 1974.

Webber, R. A., *Management: Basic Elements of Managing Organizations*, Homewood, Ill.: Irwin, 1975.

Wortman, M. S., and F. Luthans, Richard D., *Emerging Concepts in Management* (2nd ed.), New York: Macmillan, 1975.

6 | essentials of the program

INTRODUCTION

An understanding of the structure of the public school system is of utmost importance to speech-language and hearing specialists in order for them to function effectively in that setting. In this chapter we are going to take a look at the structure and function of the school system. Obviously, in different parts of the United States there will be differences in various aspects of the school system's structure so it follows that in addition to having a general knowledge of the school system, you will need to make a close study of the educational facility in which you have been hired.

THE PROGRAM
ON THE STATE LEVEL

Because of our democratic philosophy of education we are committed to the idea of education for all. The major responsibility for education rests with each state rather than with the federal government. Through a state board of education, policies, regulations, rules, and guidelines are set. The laws for education in each state are enacted through the state legislatures, and money is appropriated through this body. A state superintendent of instruction is the chief education officer in each state. A state department of education is responsible for carrying out and developing policies, regulations, and standards related to schools.

State departments of education provide state consultants in various areas of education, and almost all states have consultants in speech-language and hearing. According to Garbee (1964), the consultants have the following responsibilities:

1. Providing statewide consultative services to all counties and school districts needing assistance.

2. Cooperating and participating in district, county, regional, and state conferences and in projects pertaining to meeting the needs of children with speech and hearing handicaps.

3. Promoting an understanding of sound professional criteria and the procedures used in establishing and maintaining public school programs for the speech handicapped and hard of hearing.

4. Identifying needs and areas for development and improvement in the state's programs for the speech and hearing handicapped as an outgrowth of objective study, research, and observation.

5. Promoting and assisting in establishing and organizing programs in locales where programs are nonexistent or in need of expansion.

6. Explaining state department of education policies, standards, and regulations.

7. Evaluating objectively speech and hearing services throughout the state.

8. Working closely with college and university personnel responsible for the preparation of speech clinicians and placing primary importance on keeping the colleges informed of public school needs, objectives, and unique characteristics.

9. Encouraging sound professional standards and practices for all speech clinicians.

10. Working closely with professional organizations promoting the enhancement of research and services to children with speech and hearing handicaps.

11. Representing within the department of education the interests of speech and hearing handicapped children.

12. Preparing information for dissemination which will assist those responsible for helping children with speech and hearing disorders.

13. Coordinating information on professional needs, with supporting evidence for meeting these needs, and channeling this information to the state department of education for consideration and possible action.

THE PROGRAM
ON THE LOCAL LEVEL

On the local level, school systems are organized into school districts. In some states these are known as *intermediate units*. The district, or intermediate unit, is a geographical area and may cross county lines. It is governed by a superintendent who is the chief administrative officer, and a district board of education which is elected by the people of the district and is responsible for developing and establishing policies.

The superintendent is the chief personnel officer for the school system in that he or she makes recommendations to the board concerning the hiring, promotion, and dismissal of school staff members. The superintendent is responsible for the total operation and maintenance of the school system, leadership of the school professional staff, and administration of the clerical, secretarial, transportation, and custodial staffs.

The basic responsibility for each school system rests with the citizens of that community inasmuch as they elect the school board. The school board selects the superintendent, who recommends the needed staff to operate the schools.

Depending upon the size of the school system, there may be assistant superintendents who have specific areas of responsibility, such as finance or buildings and grounds.

The structure of individual school systems may vary from state to state and from community to community. Usually there are directors of elementary education and of secondary education. There may be directors of pupil personnel services, instructional program services, special education services, child accounting and attendance, guidance and health services, and others.

A key person on the local level is the building principal. This individual is in charge of the administration and the instructional program in that building, and is also the chief intermediary between the school and the local community. The speech, language, and hearing pathologist is directly responsible to the principal in matters pertaining to that building's program. The working relationship between the principal and the school pathologist must be one of mutual understanding and cooperation if the program is to be successful.

The classroom teachers are responsible to the principal. They are the individuals who know the children best and who exert the most profound and lasting changes on the children's growth, development, and awareness. To say that the speech-language and hearing pathologist should work closely with the classroom teachers is a gross understatement. There is a more explicit discussion of the working relationship between the school pathologist and the classroom teacher, as well as between the principal and other members of the school staff, in chapter 9.

ADEQUATE ROOM
FOR THE CLINICIAN

If the school pathologist is to function efficiently and effectively, space must be provided by the school system. Too often in the past (and unfortunately in the present in some school districts) the school pathologist has been placed in the nurse's station where there are constant interruptions and exposure to illnesses, in a room next-door to where the band practices, creating an impossible situation for the child with a hearing loss or an auditory disability, or in a storage room which may have been inadequately lighted, ventilated, heated, and cooled.

Why do situations such as this exist? Surely the child with a speech, language, or hearing disability serious enough to interfere with his progress in school should receive therapeutic intervention in optimum surroundings. Sometimes the fault lies with the school system and the community, and as a result of carelessness, neglect, or thoughtlessness, adequate surroundings are not provided for their children. Another reason given is that there is overcrowding in the school and no space is available for the school pathologist. Occasionally the fault lies with the school pathologist who meekly accepts whatever space is assigned, however inadequate, without registering any complaint and without informing the school administration of what would be considered adequate space.

What can be done to remedy the situation? Perhaps the key word in answer to this dilemma is *flexibility*. Because of the needs of some children, a quiet, isolated area, such as a therapy room or a resource room, may provide the optimum environment. An *open education* environment where there are no walls and the clinician moves from area to area has certain advantages. A mobile unit that moves from school to school may eliminate some of the housing problems. Or perhaps a combination of the above may prove to be the best solution.

The ASHA Committee on Speech and Hearing Services in the Schools, under the chairpersonship of Gloria Engnoth (1969), published a list of recommendations for housing of speech services in the schools. This list may serve as a good checklist during both the planning stages of a program and the evaluation of an ongoing program. The committee's recommendations are included in chapter 4.

PLANNING FOR SPACE
ON THE SECONDARY LEVEL

Planning therapy rooms for grade schools will present different problems than planning for the intermediate or high-school-age student. The size of the furniture, for example, will have to be different as well as the use of space. For high-school students the use of individual practice booths might be advisable. A more complete description of rooms and facilities for high-school students is presented in chapter 10.

observation of therapy

The school clinician may want to have parents and teachers observe the therapy sessions. One way would be to have them in the room with the pupil. This may be especially desirable with young children in a situation where the clinician may wish to involve the parents in the therapy. Or in some cases it may be more desirable to have the parents or teachers observe from behind a one-way vision mirror. The addition of the one-way vision mirror, and possibly an intercom system, allows the school pathologist an opportunity to work more closely with parents and teachers by involving them in the therapy while it is taking place. Often school clinicians hear the comment from teachers, "But what do you actually *do* in a therapy session?" Having them observe would take some of the mystery out of therapy and would make vividly clear to them ways in which they could interface with the therapy process in the classroom and thereby help the child to generalize what he or she has learned.

rooms should be pleasant, comfortable, and functional

Most people feel better and do better in surroundings that are attractive, comfortable, and pleasant. Children are no exception. The additions of color, adequate lighting, and comfortable furniture are conducive to good results in therapy. A child who is seated on a chair that is too big for him or her is going to be very uncomfortable. In a short time the child will begin to squirm and wriggle and will be unable to focus on whatever the therapist is presenting. The child may seem like a discipline problem to the unseeing clinician, but in reality the little boy or girl may simply be attempting to find a comfortable position.

One of the most attractive therapy rooms this author has seen was in an old school building in a rural area. The whole building sparkled with cleanliness— wooden floors were polished and shone, walls were painted in soft colors, and furniture was in good repair and arranged harmoniously. The therapy room was pleasant, with a carpeted floor and colorful draperies. A bulletin board served both a useful and decorative purpose. The obvious pride in the surroundings was reflected by the way the children treated the therapy room and its furnishings. The clinician reported that everyone in the school, including the custodian, the principal, the teachers, and the children were proud of their attractive building and worked to keep it that way.

In furnishing and equipping the therapy room the clinician should keep in mind that garish colors and busy patterns are disturbing and distracting to some of the children. Children with sensory problems, children with problems related to brain dysfunction, and children who are mentally retarded, may have difficulty functioning in a room that is too stimulating and distracting. The clinician may wish to arrange one corner of the therapy room in such a way that all potentially distracting things are out of the child's range of vision.

The therapy room plans in Figures 6-1 and 6-2 suggest ways of utilizing space in a school for the speech, language, and hearing program.

mobile units

Overcrowded schools and substandard space within school buildings have prompted some school speech-language and hearing pathologists to look elsewhere for the solution to the problem. Howerton (1973), in an

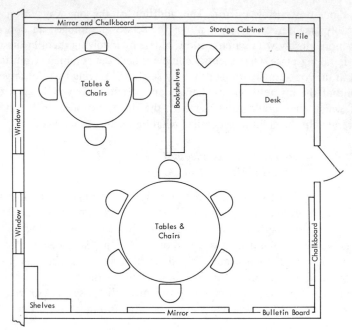

Figure 6-1.　Room Plan

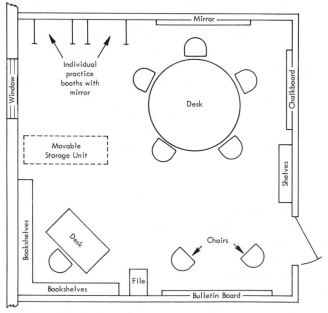

Figure 6-2.　Room Plan

article, "What Can Be Done About Substandard Space for Speech Correction Programs," described how he built a mobile unit to serve the speech and hearing program. He cited a number of advantages in using mobile units: they contain everything necessary for the program, thus eliminating gathering up and storing items every day; equipment is better cared for when it remains stationary and doesn't have to be transported in the trunk of a car; they provide quiet facilities for hearing, testing, and screening; and, they represent a saving in tax dollars in comparison to the cost of building permanent facilities.

The Gerstenslager Company of Wooster, Ohio, is one of the companies which designs and builds to specification self-contained speech and hearing vehicles. Figures 6-3 and 6-4 show some of the unit designs.

The Carteret, New Jersey, school district developed a mobile diagnostic speech, language, and hearing vehicle. The mobile unit provides for the evaluation of public and parochial (or private) school children with speech, language, and hearing problems. The program was developed through Project I.D.E.A.S.

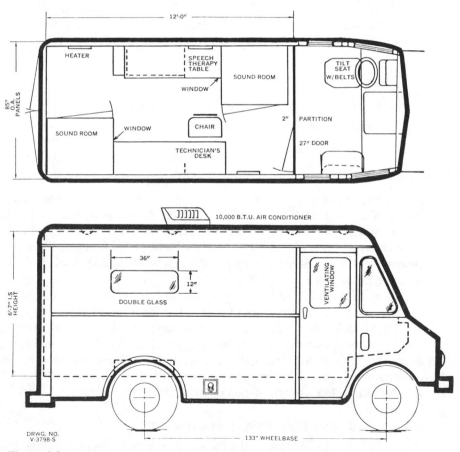

Figure 6-3

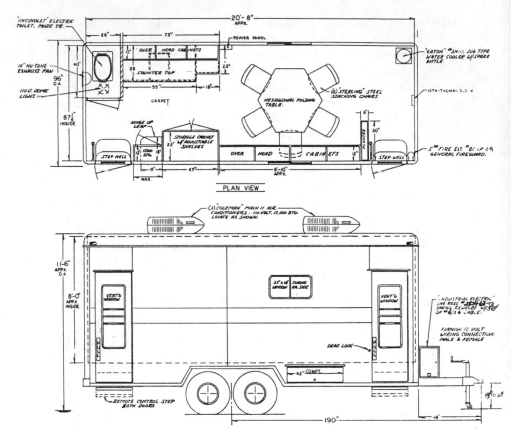

Figure 6-4

(Innovative, Developmental, Educational, Audio Speech) and was funded through a Title III E.S.E.A. Grant. The program allows communities to provide services which had been previously unavailable in a school setting. (Further information may be obtained by writing to: Mr. Louis J. Nigro, Director of Speech and Hearing Services, Project I.D.E.A.S., Columbus School, Roosevelt Avenue, Carteret, New Jersey 07008.)

Adequate space in which the school speech-language and hearing clinician must carry out a program is an essential item. It is the responsibility of the school clinician to make the needs of the program known to the superintendent, the director of special services, and the building principal. The clinician who fails to do this has no one to blame when inadequate facilities are designated for the speech program year after year. The greatest disservice, however, is to the child with the hearing loss, the articulation problem, or the voice problem.

MATERIALS AND EQUIPMENT

In addition to the therapy room, its furnishings, and the basic equipment described earlier in this chapter, there are other materials and supplies the school clinician needs in order to operate a successful program. In a new program the clinician should be prepared to submit a list of needed items along with the cost and the companies that manufacture or publish them. It might be well to consider the items on this list under the headings of *equipment* and *materials/supplies*.

Equipment may be considered an item which is nonexpendable, retains its original shape, appearance, and use, usually costs a substantial amount of money, and is more feasible to repair than to replace when damaged or worn out.

Materials and supplies, on the other hand, are expendable, used up, usually inexpensive, and are more feasible to replace than to repair when damaged or worn out.

sources of therapy materials

During recent years there has been an increase in commercial materials. Some of them are excellent and some of them are not useful for the purposes they claim to accomplish. On the other hand, there are many excellent homemade materials. These have the advantage of being inexpensive, and because many of them are designed for a specific purpose, they are useful.

Without decrying the use of materials, homemade or commercial, the clinician would do well to evaluate them from another point of view. Do they accomplish a goal in therapy for the child, or do they serve as a prop or a "security blanket" for the clinician? This letter from a staff member at a summer camp for speech, language, and hearing handicapped children, illustrates the point:

Before I went to camp they sent me a list of things to bring along. I didn't notice any mention of therapy materials. Should I take some along? I had been working as a school clinician and had therapy materials of my own. What should I do? Well, if they didn't tell me to bring any, perhaps they furnished staff members with them after you got there. When I got to camp no materials in sight! What was I expected to do for therapy! I panicked.

Within a very short time we were plunged into the camp program and things moved along at a fast clip. Suddenly, in the middle of the summer, I realized I had been doing therapy for several weeks and hadn't even missed any therapy materials. How could this be! In analyzing the situation I realized we had been using the life experience situations at camp, the activities, the surroundings, the educational programs and the other people in the camp as our "materials." The therapy grew naturally out of the environment.

Perhaps we often overlook the most obvious source of materials—the school situation itself. If therapy in the schools is to be meaningful to the child it must be a part of the school program. The school clinician needs to know what is going on at various grade levels in the way of instruction and should then tie the therapy to the classroom activities. Looking at the books children read, talking with the teacher about the instructional program, becoming familiar with the school curriculum, and looking about the classroom itself, will help the school clinician become more familiar with classroom instruction and will suggest ideas for therapy techniques and motivational devices.

In most of the states there are regional resource centers which provide local school districts with resources designed to improve the quality of instruction for handicapped children. Instructional and diagnostic materials are available on a loan basis to school clinicians. The instructional resource centers provide other services with which the school clinician will want to become familiar. Visiting the resource center gives the clinician an opportunity to examine a large number of tests, materials, and books before making a decision on which ones to purchase for the school. Personnel at the resource centers are also helpful in discussing the use of various items of material and equipment.

Regional, state, and national meetings of speech-language and hearing pathologists usually include displays by commercial companies of equipment, materials, and books. Demonstrations of equipment are carried on by company representatives. This is also a good opportunity to get on the mailing lists of commercial companies. The school clinician may want to maintain a file of company brochures and current prices.

Shared Purchasing of Equipment. Another way to become familiar with materials and equipment is to discuss them with other clinicians in the area or with university staff members, if there is a university training program nearby. School clinicians in a geographical area may want to consider joint purchase of expensive pieces of equipment that could be shared. Or one school district may purchase one item which could be loaned to a neighboring district, while that district may purchase another item with the idea of setting up a reciprocal loan system. Time-sharing policies and insurance considerations would have to be worked out in advance.

Portability. The portability of materials should also be taken into consideration. The clinician on an itinerant schedule should keep in mind the bulk and the weight of the materials. Lugging materials and equipment in and out of buildings, not to mention up and down long flights of stairs, several times a day requires the stamina of a pack horse, and has caused more than one school clinician to trim down the amount of materials used.

List of Commercial Materials. A partial list of commercial materials, equipment, and prices as of 1976, along with names and addresses of the publishers, is included in the appendix. The prices listed should be considered only as a guide and the school clinician should write to the company in order to obtain current prices.

A list of names and addresses of companies that publish catalogues containing materials, equipment, and tests is also included.

an activity file

Usually students enrolled in clinical practice classes start to collect their own materials and ideas. Many students have found it useful to start a file box of various therapeutic and motivational ideas. If the file is well organized it can be expanded and ideas can be added during student teaching and beyond.

The file should be organized in such a way that material can be easily retrieved and replaced. It is suggested that information be put on 5-inch by 8-inch cards so that an 8½-inch by 11-inch standard sheet of paper can be cut in half and will then fit the card.

Some students have found it convenient to color code the file while others have preferred to alphabetize the information under headings such as *consonants, vowels, expressive language, receptive language, stuttering, voice, hearing,* and others.

Here are some suggestions for the ingredients of a file for therapy ideas and motivational ideas:

1. Various ways to teach a child to produce a consonant or a vowel.
2. Lists of words containing sounds in initial, medial and final positions. (If the student already owns a book such as Fairbank's (1960) *Voice and Articulation Drillbook* or Schoolfield's (1937) *Better Speech and Better Reading,* it would not be necessary to make lists of words but rather, list the source of the lists.)
3. Sentences loaded with specific sounds.
4. Ideas for auditory discrimination.
5. Ideas for tactile and kinesthetic production of sounds.
6. Poems, riddles, and finger plays.
7. Flannel board ideas.
8. Worksheets for home practice.
9. Exercises for tongue and lip mobility.
10. Ideas for teaching-unit topics. (For example: astronauts, early American Indians, baseball, good nutrition, etc.)
11. Role-playing ideas.
12. Relaxation techniques.
13. Ideas for language stimulation and speech stimulation techniques that could be done at home by parents.
14. Progress sheets or charting methods.
15. Bulletin board ideas. (These could be related to seasons, holidays, or of general interest.)
16. Word lists and pictures related to holidays.
17. Utilizing puppets in therapy.
18. Laminated picture cards illustrating nouns or verbs.
19. List of records and books for children.
20. Lists of dos and don'ts for parents.
21. Ideas of movement activities that could be tied to therapy.
22. Ideas for speech development and speech improvement lessons in the classroom.

The card file can serve a number of useful purposes. It can be an inventory of available materials and publications; it can aid in lesson planning, and the cards can be easily removed from the file and used during the sessions. In addition, it can serve as an aid when consulting with classroom teachers in speech and language development and improvement, and serve as a source of ideas when working with parents. Plus, it is concise, easy to construct, convenient to use, and inexpensive.

budgeting for materials

Materials, supplies, and equipment are purchased by the schools. In some schools the clinician is given a fixed sum of money per year to spend for these items. In considering the purchase of equipment, it should be kept in mind that while the initial expenditure may be great, it may not have to be replaced for many years. There is, however, the matter of repair, maintenance, and general upkeep to be considered. For example, an audiometer needs yearly calibration. This should be taken into account prior to the purchase of the audiometer and discussed with the company representative.

Commercial therapy materials are subject to wear and tear if they are used frequently, and may have to be budgeted for periodically. Considerations in the purchase of therapy materials might be whether or not they can be adapted for a variety of uses and occasions, and whether or not they serve the purpose for which they are being purchased. They must be appropriate to age, maturity level, and interest of children.

evaluate before purchasing

At the present time there are numerous language programs on the market, but unfortunately many of them are untested. The clinician who purchases them may have no information as to their effectiveness, their validity, or their reliability. Connell, Spradlin, and McReynolds (1977) have suggested that clinicians should not obtain language programs unless the information necessary to evaluate their usefulness is available from the company publishing them. They recommend that the information should minimally include: (1) experimental analysis of mean or median trials to criterion and variance for each program step, (2) the percentage of clients who complete each program step, (3) a precise description of all the clients who were used in obtaining data, and (4) experimental analysis of the generalization of trained language behaviors.

The same cautions should be applied to the anticipated purchase of testing materials. New tests in particular should be evaluated carefully before they are purchased. Advertising brochures should not be the only criterion for selection, and the clinician should seek the pertinent information by querying the publishing company directly.

expendable materials

Supplies, such as paper, crayons, chalk, and some materials that can be used only one time, are usually supplied by the school, however it does not necessarily follow that the school clinician has access to an unlimited supply. These items may be rationed or budgeted to the clinician on a yearly or a semester basis. The clinician should be aware of the school's policy in regard to supplies. It should also be pointed out that because clinicians may function in several different schools within the same system, each school may have its own policy in regard to the availability of supplies.

Sometimes budget allowances are made on the basis of per pupil enrollment. Both money and supplies may be determined in accordance with the total number of children enrolled or the number enrolled at any given time. Because budgets must be made out in advance, the figures may be dependent on last year's enrollment, or on the estimated enrollment for the next year.

Budgeting for Professional Materials and Activities. Professional books may also be considered part of the school clinician's equipment and therefore would be justifiable budget items. The clinician may want to add to his or her own library of professional books, and these, of course, would not be a part of the school budget. The same is true of dues for professional organizations.

Budgeting for Travel. Some school systems allow travel money and expenses for personnel who attend professional meetings. It is wise for the new clinician to check the policy in regard to this.

If a clinician must travel between schools as part of the job, a travel allowance is available. Some school clinicians are paid a flat amount for a specified period of time, while others are paid by the mile. Some school systems make up for this difference by paying the clinician a higher salary than the person whose job does not entail travel between schools during the working day; for example, the classroom teacher.

THE MANAGEMENT OF TIME

The school clinician must take into consideration two factors in overall time management. The first is the need to plan time on a yearly, semester, weekly, and daily basis, while the second is the need for the clinician to manage his or her own time within the larger framework. In respect to both factors, planning is an essential first step. The next important step is setting priorities and sticking with them.

The school clinician going into a situation where he or she is the sole speech-language and hearing specialist will have much greater responsibility than will a person who is stepping into a job where there is an ongoing program with other school clinicians already involved. In the latter situation, the new clinician fits into a program that has already been set up. In the former, the clinician may be the key planner and organizer.

No matter how one looks at it, we are dealing with that precious and fleeting commodity—time. It is scarce, inelastic, does not have a two-way stretch, cannot be stored or frozen for future use, and cannot be retrieved. It can, however, be managed with effectiveness.

In planning time let us look first at what the school clinician's job entails:

1. *Screening.* In this activity the clinician identifies children with speech, language, and hearing problems. The bulk of it may take place at the beginning of the school year, however, many clinicians carry out preschool screenings in the summer or the end of the school year. Sometimes kindergarten and first-grade children are screened throughout the school year.
2. *Diagnosis and assessment.* This task includes formal and informal testing and is carried on throughout the school year.
3. *Staffing and placement.* This procedure is often carried out by a placement team and involves reviewing the data on individual students with the purpose of developing individualized educational programs for each student.
4. *Intervention.* This is the actual therapy and instructional activities provided by staff members to develop, improve, or maintain communicative abilities.
5. *Record keeping.* This includes all activities involved in maintaining information on the delivery of services to each student.
6. *Consultation.* These activities include the exchange of information with parents, teachers, psychologists, nurses, and others in regard to individual students.

Other services, not directly related to the communicatively handicapped students, are activities that maintain, promote, and enhance the speech-language, and hearing program. These activities are of an indirect nature, but at the same time are essential to the program. They include in-service training programs provided by the speech-language and hearing staff, as well as in-service training received by them for the purpose of upgrading their skills. Travel for the purpose of providing services is a necessary part of many school clinicians' programs. Many school speech-language and hearing specialists are engaged in research related to the school programs. Time is also spent organizing, planning, implementing, analyzing, and evaluating programs. Some school specialists spend time supervising student teachers in speech pathology and audiology, as well as paraprofessionals assigned to the program. Conservation and prevention programs may be carried out by the school clinicians, as well as public information activities such as talks to various groups, radio and television programs, and writing newspaper articles.

planning for the year

After the school clinician has taken a good look at what the job entails, he or she determines long-range goals based on a priority list. Inexperienced clinicians in a new situation sometimes try to do everything the first year. This is not only impossible, it is unwise even to attempt. The result may be spreading oneself too thin and not accomplishing anything satisfactorily. For example, the clinician may have to decide whether a teacher in-service program or a parent in-service program is more important during the first year. The clinician may then rationalize that the teachers are more readily available and need to understand the program more immediately than do the parents, so the in-service program for teachers would take precedence the first year. During the following year, however, the clinician may decide to devote more time and energy to the parent in-service program and that program would be given top priority the second year.

After priorities for the year are established, the long-range program goals are written. In chapter 5, information on writing goals is given. It should be pointed out that long-range goals need to be examined periodically and modified if necessary. The goals for the year should indicate the time (or times) of the year that the goals would be implemented and accomplished, as well as the amount of time involved.

Goals may be written for an entire school year, or some school clinicians may prefer to write them for a semester. A combination of the two time slots may also be utilized.

Program goals should not be confused with goals that individual clinicians establish for themselves. These clinician's goals and the program goals may not necessarily be at odds, but it should be kept in mind that while clinicians may come and go, programs, hopefully, go on forever. Setting goals for the program, with the clinicians as the implementers, will allow smooth, continuous functioning of a program despite changes in personnel. There is probably nothing more frustrating for a school clinician who is stepping into a job as a newcomer than to learn that the previous clinician left no records as to what was planned, what was accomplished, when it was accomplished, how long it took, and what has yet to be done.

In addition to establishing yearly or semester program goals based on a priority list of the tasks involved in the clinician's job, other information would have to be available, including:

1. Number of speech, language, and hearing clinicians on the staff
2. Number of schools to be served
3. Amount of travel time between schools
4. Enrollment figures for each school building. This would have to be further broken down into the following figures:
   a) Enrollment by grade level
   b) Enrollment of special education classes, including hearing impaired, physically impaired, mentally retarded, emotionally disturbed, learning disabled, and trainable mentally retarded.
5. Number of preschool children in the school districts based on Child Find figures.

The school clinician uses this information to decide on the appropriate methods of delivery-of-service and scheduling systems.

planning time for the week

In planning time for the week the key word is *flexibility*. The school clinician will have to decide how much time during the week will be spent in actual therapy and in travel if more than one school is involved during any one day. Specific blocks of time can be devoted to these activities. An activity such as screening must also be carried out in a block of time and the school clinician may want to reserve blocks of time at certain times of the year or the semester for this part of the program.

Such activities as diagnosis and assessment, staffing and placement, and consultation are necessary parts of the program, and time for these activities may be set aside in daily or weekly blocks. For example, the staffing and placement team may not meet every week, so the block of time set aside weekly could be used on alternate weeks for staffing and placement and diagnosis and consultation.

Record keeping and time spent in organizing, planning, implementing, analyzing, and evaluating the program could be scheduled at times of the day when school staff members are in the school but children are not present. For example, mornings before children arrive at school and afternoons after they are dismissed could be utilized for these activities. Many school systems set aside a time usually referred to as *coordination time* for tasks of this nature.

In-service training programs for classroom teachers may be part of the school's regular routine, and the speech-language and hearing pathologist may be asked to take part in them. Certainly they are an important part of a successful program and time should be set aside for them. Some school clinicians provide in-service programs for teachers, administrators, other school personnel, and parents.

If paraprofessionals and aides are assigned to the program, time must be planned for their in-service training programs, and time must be allowed for the supervision of such personnel.

For many of the activities mentioned, time is not planned on a regularly scheduled basis, but certainly must be set aside to include these important facets of the program.

planning time for the day

In planning time for the day the school clinician will have to know how many hours per day the children are in school. What is their arrival time and what is their dismissal time? How much time is allowed for lunch and recess?

The time that the teachers are required to be in school and the time they may leave in the afternoon is set by school policy, and school clinicians should follow the same rules that teachers are required to follow. This sometimes poses a problem for the school clinician who is scheduled in School A in the morning and School B in the afternoon, but who must return to School A for a parent conference in the afternoon after school is dismissed. The problem arises when the teachers in School B think the clinician is leaving school early. The problem can usually be alleviated by following the rule of always informing the principals of School A and School B of any deviation in the regular schedule.

The greatest percentage of actual therapy time will take place in the morning because the morning sessions are longer and children are available for a longer period of time. This is true in most school systems, but there will be exceptions.

The school clinician will have to decide the length of the therapy sessions.

There does not have to be a uniform length and sessions may range from fifteen minutes to an hour. The length depends on a number of factors, and before determining the pattern of the sessions the clinician may want to look at the school's schedule of classes, recess, dismissal time, etc.

Among the considerations are the number of children to be seen in total, the number in groups, and the number in individual therapy. Also, some children will be in the carry-over phase of therapy and do not require as much time as children who are just beginning therapy. It may be wise to schedule the sessions a few minutes apart to allow for children to arrive on time, or to allow time for the clinician to locate a child whose teacher has forgotten to send him or her to therapy. Children often assume the responsibility of remembering when to come to therapy, and for younger children who have not yet mastered the art of telling time, a clock face drawn on a sheet of paper with the hands pointing to the time of the session will allow the child to match the clock face with the clock on the wall.

In planning the daily schedule the school clinician will need to retain as much flexibility as possible. Children change and their needs change. The child who once required thirty minutes of individual therapy per day may later need only fifteen minutes twice a week. Or the youngster who once needed individual therapy may need the experience of a group situation in order to progress. This flexibility must also be understood by the principal and the teachers, and it is the responsibility of the clinician to interpret the rationale involved in making changes in schedules.

As a result of mainstreaming and the influx of more seriously disabled children into the public schools, the school clinician will need to allow time for working with classroom teachers of the mentally retarded, the emotionally disturbed, the hearing impaired, the learning disabled, and the multiply handicapped. In fact, any communicatively handicapped child may require direct or indirect intervention by the speech-language and hearing pathologist in the school, and, depending on the needs of the children in a specific school, the clinician will need to make allowances for the intervention both in the daily schedule and the overall scheduling of services.

Effective Use of the Clinician's Time.   Most school speech clinicians would like to add an extra hour to a day now and then or think in terms of an occasional eight-day week. Because time is scarce it must be managed with maximum effectiveness. Experts in time management tell us that selecting the best task to do from all the possibilities available and then doing it in the best way is more important than doing efficiently whatever job happens to be around.

How well do you manage *your* time?

CONCLUSION

This chapter stresses the importance of planning. One of the first steps in planning is an understanding of the structure of the school system. Other considerations are adequate room for the school clinician as well as equipment, materials, and furnishings.

Mobile units are discussed as an alternative to space within the school building.

The effective use of time is also discussed on the yearly level, the weekly level, and the daily level.

7 | *case finding, case selection, and the individualized educational program*

INTRODUCTION

In this chapter we will look at ways of identifying children with speech, language, and hearing problems. After the children have been identified we will consider ways of selecting those who are in need of intervention.

Placement decisions regarding each child are usually made by utilizing a team approach. The long-range and the short-range plans for remediation of each communicatively handicapped child are known as Individualized Educational Programs (IEPs). These topics will be discussed.

The information in this chapter is presented with the idea that it will provide a basis for assisting the school clinician in the many decisions that must be made in regard to case finding and case selection. The information should help school clinicians think their way through these various steps in a school speech, language, and hearing program.

CASE FINDING

One of the first major tasks confronting the school clinician is the identification of school-age and preschool children with speech, language, and hearing problems. This is usually done by utilizing two processes, either singly or in combination, *referral* and *screening.*

REFERRAL

Let us look first at the process of referral. The purpose of both referral and screening is simply the identification of the child with a communication problem. The school clinician needs to be alerted that a particular child might have a communication problem. The clinician, in the final analysis, is the one who is responsible for determining if such a problem exists, however, referrals can be made by anyone who has the child's welfare in mind and suspects the child has a problem. This would include the child's parents, teachers, family doctor, the school nurse, the school counselor, the principal, or the child.

Referrals should not be discouraged even though the clinician may sometimes feel that the classroom teachers overrefer or refer children who have problems other than speech, language, and hearing. The door should always be kept open for referrals. Teachers should be encouraged to refer any child they feel might have a problem, and the procedures and opportunities for referral should be presented to the teachers periodically. The school clinician will soon learn which teachers in a school are able to identify the communicatively handicapped child with a high degree of accuracy.

teacher referrals for speech problems

Diehl and Stinnett (1959), in a study regarding the efficiency of teacher referrals in a school testing program, found that elementary teachers with no orientation in speech disorders were able to locate speech defective children with less than 60 percent accuracy. They could be expected to fail to identify two of every five children who would be located in a regular school screening program. They were able, however, to locate with 80 percent accuracy children with severe articulation problems. According to Diehl and Stinnett, teachers have the least skill in identifying second graders with voice disorders.

Prahl and Cooper (1964) reported on a study in which thirty teachers in schools which had never had speech therapy programs were given a statement describing and defining speech problems. The teachers then referred children in their rooms whom they judged as having a speech problem. Each child in the classroom was later tested by an experienced speech therapist. The classroom teachers were able to identify approximately two out of five children with speech problems. The percentage of accurate referrals tended to rise as the severity of the disorder increased. Teachers were able to detect stuttering problems more readily than articulatory disorders and were least efficient in referring children with voice disorders.

Roe et al. (1961) have indicated that school clinicians frequently use teacher referrals as a method of case finding. Almost as frequent was the use of surveys by the clinician.

These and other studies indicate that the school clinician cannot rely solely on teacher referrals and other referrals if all the communicatively handicapped children in a school system are to be located. Teacher referrals are, however, an important adjunct in locating the speech and language handicapped children.

teacher referrals for hearing problems

In regard to identifying children with hearing loss in an elementary school, limited research has been done. Curry (1950) reported that teachers were able to correctly identify one out of four children with hearing loss. Kodman (1950), by comparing audiometric findings and teacher identifications, found that teachers were able to correctly identify one out of six children with hearing loss.

Nodar (1978) conducted a study in which teachers of 2231 elementary school children were asked to identify those with suspected or known hearing losses. An audiometric screening was then carried out and it was found that the teachers identified 5 percent of the children as being hearing-impaired while the screening identified only 3 percent. Following the teacher interviews rescreening and tympanometry were conducted and the results showed that the teacher screening and tympanometry were in agreement on 50 percent of the hearing-loss group. Nodar concluded that the observations and suspicions of classroom teachers can play an important part in identifying children with hearing loss in the elementary school. He recommended that teachers be included as part of the screening team and that their observations be given serious consideration.

referrals on the high-school level

In the elementary school, teacher referrals can be utilized along with a screening program. Because of the difficulties encountered in arranging a screening in the middle school or the high school, it may be necessary for the school clinician to rely more heavily on the referral from specific teachers who have the greatest opportunity to hear the child speak. For example, the high-school English teacher might be a good referral source. The same might be said of the physical education teacher or the school counselor, both of whom have an opportunity to hear the child talk in a more informal situation.

On the high-school level, self-referrals or parental referrals are often good sources of identifying individuals with communication problems. The high school student who has a speech, language, or hearing problem will have to know about the services offered if he is to refer himself. This means that the clinician will have to find ways of letting students know the services are available, as well as make it easy for them to refer themselves.

If teachers are to be used effectively as referral sources, they will need to know several things, including what is meant by an articulation problem, a stuttering problem, a voice problem, a language problem, and a hearing problem. The clinician will have to be able to define and describe the various types of communication problems as well as demonstrate them. As a prospective clinician, are you able to imitate or simulate various kinds of problems? A library of tapes of various types of problems would be helpful for demonstration.

Teachers will also need to have information on how children are referred and the criteria which the clinician uses in selecting children for therapeutic intervention. For example, why are some children included and why are some not considered candidates for therapy? Also, why would it be better not to include a particular child with a stuttering problem in the therapy sessions until after some parental counseling has taken place?

Many colleges and universities have a course in speech, language, and hearing problems that is required of all education majors. It would be helpful to the school clinician if all teachers were to have such a course, but this is not always the case. The school clinician may want to consider teaching an in-service course to teachers. For many years the Youngstown, Ohio, school system had the requirement that the speech, language, and hearing clinicians would not service a building until the teachers in that building completed an in-service course in speech, language, and hearing problems.

While teachers and parents are probably the most prolific referral sources, there are others that are also important. Other school personnel, such as the principal, the school psychologist, and the school nurse, are excellent referral sources. Outside the school, the welfare agencies within the community, physicians, health care specialists, and voluntary agencies such as United Cerebral Palsy, the Society for Crippled Children and Adults, and others, may all be considered valuable referral agencies.

Referrals can be initiated in person, by telephone, or in writing. The school clinician will also need to know and comply with the school system's policy regarding referrals. Usually there is a written referral form that must be filled out by the referring agent.

Following the initial referral, and depending on the information about the child gathered from the referring agent, the speech-language and hearing clinician will have to make a decision as to whether the student is to receive a battery of screening tests or a more complete assessment. In addition, parental permission must be obtained.

SCREENING

Public Law 94-142 and the various state laws regarding the education of handicapped children require that a process be implemented for the identification of children needing diagnostic assessment. One of the most widely used procedures is screening.

The purpose of screening is: (1) to determine whether or not a problem exists, (2) to determine whether or not further evaluation is needed, and (3) to determine if referral to other professionals is needed.

The first step would be a rapid screening process that would serve to identify children with communication handicaps. A second screening would be made of those children identified by the rapid screening or by referral as having possible communication problems. The second screening would be somewhat more extensive and would help the clinician pick out those children who are candidates for therapy. The third step would be a complete diagnostic evaluation for children who need therapeutic intervention and/or referral to other professionals.

The clinician must decide when and where the screening will take place, and which children will be screened. There are some general factors to be considered prior to making these decisions. According to Conlon et al. (1973) the following questions will have to be resolved if the school clinician is to make the best possible use of the screening time: What are the goals of the total speech, language, and hearing program in the school system? Is the speech, language, and hearing program new to the school? Is the school clinician new to the community? Is the school's population a mobile one, is there significant turnover in the population each year, and is the population increasing or decreasing each year? How long has 60 percent of the staff been on the school's staff?

When the answers to the above questions have been obtained, the goals of the screening program can be established. It is important that these goals are not only established, but that they are in writing and made available to the school administration. When the goals are established, the procedures for carrying out the screening program can be made. The procedures should also be in writing and should be available to the superintendent, the director of special education, the elementary and secondary supervisors, the principals of each school, and the teachers in each of the schools to be screened.

rapid screening

Let us look first at the rapid screening procedure. There are several models that can be utilized and there are some general principles that can be applied for the rapid screening for speech, language, and hearing problems. The major purpose is to determine whether or not a problem exists. Ideally, all children enrolled in the school are screened. The screening must be done quickly and accurately; that is, it must be done with a maximum degree of professional expertise and with a minimum expenditure of time, money, and professional energy. Planning is absolutely essential. In addition to a general plan, there must also be a plan to encompass all the details of the screening.

Much of the screening is carried on during the first few weeks of school, but it may be done at any time of the year. Many clinicians prefer to screen the upper elementary classes early in the school year and the kindergarten and primary grades later in the year. This allows the classroom teachers to become better acquainted with the children, and the very young child to become more accustomed to school. In some schools preacademic children are screened during a preschool roundup in May or August, just prior to enrolling in school.

Federal regulations do not require written permission of the parents prior to a group screening program; however, some states and some school districts do require that parents be notified of the screening.

Screening programs can be carried out by one clinician, by a team of clinicians, or by a team composed of clinicians plus trained aides and/or volunteers. If the school system is small and employs few clinicians on its staff, those individuals may want to team up with clinicians in adjacent towns or counties to accomplish the screening in both school districts by sharing the work and thereby cutting down on the time needed to screen. If more than one person is involved in a screening program, the procedures should be clearly understood by all in order to insure uniform administration and greater reliability.

class survey method of screening for speech and language

The *class survey method* of screening can be used with any grade level and can be carried out by one clinician or by a team of clinicians. It is done within the classroom or just outside, preferably as close as possible to the classroom. The clinician makes arrangements through the principal of the building and arranges a time schedule so that teachers know when to expect the screening to take place during the day. The clinician explains the procedure to the teacher and also prepares the children by giving them an explanation at their level of understanding. Young children are sometimes fearful of what to expect, and may not be as cooperative as the clinician would hope unless they are prepared.

The class survey screening can be carried out so there is little interruption of the classroom routine. The teacher supplies the clinician with a roster of the children, and indicates which ones are absent that day so the clinician can screen them later. If the roster is in the form of a seating chart, the clinician can take the children in order of their seating. In this way the clinician will not take up too much time trying to figure out the identity of very small children who have difficulty saying (or remembering!) their last names.

A procedure used successfully by many clinicians is to take three children at a time. While one is being tested the other two can observe and will know what to do when their turn comes without the clinician having to explain. As each child is finished he or she goes back to the room and gets the next child in the row. There is no interruption of the teacher's schedule, and the classroom activities go on as usual. A class of twenty-five children can be screened in approximately thirty or forty minutes.

General Considerations. Because the purpose of the rapid screening is detection, not diagnosis, the clinician will have to resist the temptation to spend more time than is needed with a child who obviously has a problem. Also, the clinician will have to tactfully discourage little Michael Motormouth from telling the lengthy, complicated, story of how his dog chased the neighbor's cat up the tree and how the firemen had to get it down.

The results of the screening task should be recorded immediately after each individual is seen. All absentees should be noted and arrangements should be made to screen them later.

The same general screening procedures may be applied to small groups of children. The clinician takes a group of six to eight children to the therapy room where the screening is carried out, returns the group, and gets the next group. If aides are available, they may take the children to and from the classroom.

In many school systems a team approach is used in the preschool screening program. The team members often include the school nurse, psychologist, speech pathologist, audiologist, and other specialists who test vision, hearing, speech and language, motor coordination, dentition, general health, and physical well-being. Paraprofessionals or volunteer aides also assist in this type of screening program.

screening tests

Instruments for assessing communicative abilities during a screening program differ according to the ages of the children. The instruments should be easily administered and should identify quickly those children needing further testing. In a school screening, whether one clinician or several are involved, the screening devices should be the same, and the standard for judging the results should be consistent from one tester to another. The screening procedures should also take into account differences in ethnic and socioeconomic backgrounds of the children being tested. The examiners need to keep in mind that they are attempting to detect differences in speech, language, voice quality, fluency, or any other problems in communication that might be potentially handicapping to the child's ability to learn in school or function as a useful member of society.

A comprehensive screening battery carried out by the speech-language specialist or as a part of a comprehensive screening program, could include the following:

A. Hearing evaluation
B. Articulation appraisal
C. Intelligibility appraisal
D. Voice appraisal
E. Fluency appraisal
F. Language appraisal (receptive and expressive) on the
   1. semantic level
   2. syntactic level
   3. phonological level

Screening procedures on any age or grade level are subject to the same degree of error. Some children will slip by undetected while others may not be identified correctly. School clinicians and classroom teachers must work together to recognize any children in which either of these situations has occurred.

screening for articulation disorders
in primary grades

According to studies, children in kindergarten, first grade, and second grade exhibit many phonetic errors. Some of these children will overcome their errors through the process of getting a little older and being exposed to the school environment; however, there are children in this group who will not improve without a therapy program. Differentiating between these two groups creates a dilemma for the school clinician. Obviously, because of the large numbers, all of these children cannot be included in the therapy program. Through prognostic testing at the screening level school clinicians will be able to sort these youngsters into two general groups: those who need therapeutic intervention, and those who would benefit from a general speech-language improvement program.

The Predictive Screening Test of Articulation (PSTA) was developed by Van Riper and Erickson (1968) for the purpose of identifying among primary school children who have functional misarticulations at the first-grade level, those who will, and those who will not, have acquired normal mature articulation by the time they reach the third-grade level. The PSTA consists of forty-seven items, requires no special testing equipment, and is available at cost from the Continuing Education Office, Western Michigan University, Kalamazoo, Michigan, 49001. The PSTA assesses the child's degree of stimulability—the ability to repeat sounds, nonsense syllables, words, and a sentence, after the examiner; the ability to move the tongue independently of the lower jaw; the ability to detect errors in the examiner's speech; and ability to follow the examiner in a handclapping rhythm.

In a study by Barrett and Welsh (1975), the PSTA was found to be a valuable speech-adequacy screening device for a first-grade population. The test was able to objectively substantiate with approximately 90 percent accuracy the opinion of the speech clinician that a child's speech is normal.

Other prognostic factors related to articulatory errors have been explored. One is the rate of change toward correction of kindergarten children. Steer and Drexler (1960) reported that the results of their study indicated that the most effective and reliable predictive variables appear to be the total number of errors in all positions within words, errors in the final position, errors of omission in the final position, and errors on the f and l consonant groups.

Another factor related to the predictability of the correction of functional articulation problems is the inconsistency of errors. It has been generally accepted that the more inconsistent the child's articulatory errors, the more possibility there is that he or she will outgrow them. The rationale is that the child may be able to produce the sound correctly sometimes but has not learned the appropriate times to produce it. Children exhibiting this type of error should be further tested with an instrument which provides more comprehensive and systematic testing on the way sounds are presented in all possible phonetic contexts. For example, the McDonald Deep Test (1964) would yield helpful information.

screening for articulatory disorders
in older elementary children

In older elementary children, speech and language screening can be accomplished by having them give their name, address, and telephone number, by counting to twenty-five, by naming days of the week or months of the year, or by responding to pictures of objects designed to test sounds. The best screening test is spontaneous speech because it is most likely to yield a sample of the child's habitual speech and language. If the child is asked to read words, sentences, or paragraphs, the clinician must be sure that the material is within his or her reading ability.

There are a number of picture articulation tests on the market which can be used for screening. For example, the Templin Darley Screening Test (1969) contains fifty of the most common consonants and blends in the English language. The Photo Articulation Test (Pendergast, 1966) can be used in a developmental articulation test.

The Picture Articulation and Language Screening Test (PALST) (Rodgers, 1976) is designed to be used in the classroom. It is easy to administer and score and the clinician may also make note of any anomalies such as dental deviations, tongue thrust, or characteristics of hearing.

The Goldman-Fristoe Test of Articulation (1969) tests phonemic proficiency in words and sentences.

Spontaneous speech samples will yield information on overall intelligibility of the child.

screening for language disorders

Screening for language disorders, deviations, or developmental problems is an important aspect of the total identification process.

Because this is not a book on diagnosis, it is not possible to include the theoretical concepts of language and language problems nor even a very complete discussion of diagnostic instruments and remedial procedures. Most of this information has developed recently and many school clinicians may feel somewhat at a loss in this area. On the other hand, many school clinicians have been dealing with language problems in the schools for many years and probably have much more information than they realize. Because this book is written for them as well as for new entrants into the field of speech and language, it should be pointed out that information on language is available in books, in periodical literature, in workshops, in continuing education courses, and in language courses on college campuses. Programs of national, state, and local professional organizations frequently contain presentations on language. The school clinician will need to keep up-to-date by partaking of these offerings.

What should a language screening include?

Keeping in mind the fact that screening is an identification process, we therefore need to *identify* the child with the language problem.

The facets of language include receptive (decoding) and expressive (encoding). The components of the language include phonology, semantics, syntax, and pragmatics. A complete language evaluation should include all of these aspects. On the screening level it is important to ascertain whether or not the language behavior of a child is adequate. The in-depth diagnosis could follow after the child has been identified.

Language screening may include the following tests but need not be limited to them:

1. Zimmerman, Steiner, Evatt *Preschool Language Scale*. Assesses skills in auditory comprehension, verbal ability, and articulation. (45 min.)
2. Stephens *Oral Language Screening Test*. Identifies children in need of more detailed evaluation. (10 min.)
3. Carrow *Screening Test for Auditory Comprehension of Language* (STACL). Identifies children in need of more detailed evaluation. (10 min.)
4. Rodgers *Picture Articulation and Language Screening Test* (PALST). Designed to be used in the classroom. (5 min.)
5. Bankson Test - Bankson Language Screening Test. Based on expressive modality but can be used to test receptive verification. (40 min.)

screening on the secondary school level

Case finding on the high-school level is carried out more often by teacher referral than by screening (Neal, 1976). School clinicians, while recognizing the need for improved case finding procedures at this level, point out the difficulties of a screening program because of the inflexibility of high-school class schedules and the greater mobility of high-school students within the school due to the changing of classes.

Another factor that would hinder both a screening program and a teacher referral program on the secondary level was pointed out by Phillips (1976). The study indicated that the higher the grade taught, the less aware the teachers were of speech disorders. She suggested that this might be a result of the fact that an increasing number of universities are requiring a basic remedial speech course of elementary education majors but not of secondary education majors.

One method of screening secondary students was described by Sommers (1969). In this program all of the testing was done on succeeding Mondays because this was the day during which there was a minimum of interruptions. It was done in the English classes because each student in the school was enrolled in those classes. The English teachers were made aware of the screening program in advance. The clinician was seated in the back of the classroom and each student was called individually to read a short screening passage. A brief phonetic analysis was completed for those students with speech problems.

If a sufficient number of clinicians were available, the task of screening the

English classes on the junior-high and high-school levels could be accomplished in a short period of time.

The screening devices on the junior-high and high-school levels usually include reading a short passage such as "My Grandfather" (Van Riper, 1954) in order to get an idea of the student's articulatory ability:

You wished to know all about my grandfather. Well, he is nearly ninety-three years old; he dresses himself in an ancient black frock coat, usually minus several buttons; yet he still thinks as swiftly as ever. A long, flowing beard clings to his chin, giving those who observe him a pronounced feeling of the utmost respect. When he speaks, his voice is just a bit cracked and quivers a trifle. Twice each day he plays skillfully and with zest upon our small organ. Except in the winter when the ooze or snow or ice prevents, he slowly takes a short walk in the open air each day. We have often urged him to walk more and smoke less, but he always answers, "Banana oil!" Grandfather likes to be modern in his language.

Voice quality can be noted at the same time. Spontaneous speech can be elicited by asking questions, and this will give the examiner some information as to expressive language. A short test of auditory discrimination might yield important information as well.

The examiner needs to be aware of the possibility of fluency disorders during the screening. Verification of this would have to be made by following the screening with consultation with the teachers who would be most likely to have heard the student in an informal speaking situation. These teachers might include the physical education teacher, the English teacher, and the guidance counselor.

IDENTIFICATION AUDIOMETRY

The role of the school clinician today in regard to the hearing-impaired child should be one of strong commitment. There are many tasks implied in this role. According to Northcott (1972), the school clinician should: (1) provide appropriate components of supplemental services directly to hearing-impaired children, (2) serve as a hearing consultant to teachers, administrators, and resource specialists, helping them make reasonable accommodations to meet the special needs of hearing-impaired children in the integrated class setting, and (3) serve as a member of an interdisciplinary team developing new components of comprehensive hearing services within the school district.

The early identification of children with even minimal hearing loss was one of the major recommendations of the National Conference of Identification Audiometry (1961). These children could then be referred for appropriate medical treatment in order to initiate remedial procedures and to prevent further problems from developing.

Educationally, children with even mild and intermittent losses can experience difficulties in the classroom. These children may seem only mildly inattentive and will be able to follow most face-to-face conversations, however, they may suffer from one to two years of educational retardation as a result of bilateral chronic otitis media (McCandless, 1975). Furthermore, these children may fail to develop their first words until over two years of age, and may maintain a delay throughout the early years if the condition persists.

According to McCandless, several factors may influence the degree of educational retardation caused by mild hearing loss. They are:

1. If the otitis media is sporadic and involves only one ear, the effects will be minimal or hardly noticed.
2. If it is bilateral and chronic, the effects are much greater depending on the child's intellectual ability.
   a. Superior intellects are usually able to compensate in the home and classroom and will appear only occasionally inattentive. They will progress at about the level of the average child, although they could be superior students and excel academically.
   b. Average or slower students are more seriously affected. Aside from appearing to be generally unresponsive and inattentive, they may be as much as one-third educationally delayed. They are difficult to motivate and tend to give up easily because they have to work so much harder to hear.
   c. The most devastating effects will be on the children who are educationally marginal.

One role we wish to examine is the clinician's role in identifying hearing-impaired children. The Model Regulations (Jones and Healey, 1973) make provision for identification audiometry as follows:

a. The hearing screening program shall be based on audiometric testing of individuals or groups of pupils. Individual tests shall be administered to pre-kindergarten through third-grade pupils, except in those cases where the (Department) approves computerized or other appropriate procedures. Individual or group tests may be used with pupils above the third-grade level.

b. Screening audiometers shall be calibrated to American National Standards Institute (ANSI) specifications initially, and recalibrated as needed, and at least (annually). Daily listening checks shall be performed to determine that audiometers are grossly in calibration and that no defects exist in major components.

c. The ambient noise level in any space used for audiometric screening shall not exceed 51 dB.

d. Identification audiometry programs shall be conducted or supervised by a qualified audiologist or speech pathologist with appropriate training in audiology. Support personnel may administer hearing screening tests under the supervision of a qualified speech pathologist or audiologist, after appropriate training. Control measures shall be included to validate and, where necessary, correct testing procedures.

e. Screening procedures shall be administered uniformly by all examiners, with specified test frequencies, screening level and criteria for failure. Minimum procedures shall include: screening at 20 dB HTL at 1000 Hz and 2000 Hz and at 25 dB HTL at 4000 Hz; failure to hear at the recommended screening level at any frequency is the criterion for failure.

f. Rescreening of failures shall be provided within a reasonable period after the initial testing, preferably within one week.

g. Comprehensive audiological evaluation shall be secured for failures on rescreening and be administered by qualified audiologists.

h. Pupils shown to have hearing loss as a result of comprehensive audiological assessment shall be referred for otologic examination to a licensed physician.

The typical hearing screening test utilized by school clinicians has been the pure tone audiometric test in which the frequencies 500 to 4000 Hz have been presented at 20 or 25 dB HL to each ear of the child being tested. Children failing to respond at any of these frequencies were then referred for further evaluation.

HEARING TESTING FACILITIES

School clinicians encounter a number of problems in respect to the hearing screening programs. One major problem is the lack of a room in the school sufficiently quiet to produce reliable test results. It would be extremely unusual to find a space in the school with an ambient noise level below 51 dB, as recommended by the Model Regulations (Jones and Healey, 1973). Testing in unsuitable rooms results in a large number of rescreenings, and eventually, in overreferrals. This can be translated into time wasted by the clinician and both time and money wasted by parents.

In order to overcome noisy testing conditions, the tester may compensate by raising the dB HL level above 20 or 25. As shown by Melnick, Eagles, and Levine (1964), this may result in serious limitations in identifying children with slight conductive hearing losses. Middle ear problems are often associated with slight conductive losses, so it is a possibility that many children with middle ear pathologies will not be detected if there is not strict compliance with recommended hearing screening procedures.

The school clinician should insist on good hearing testing facilities in the school. Sometimes this means demonstrating to the school principal and administration what is meant by a quiet room by actually measuring the ambient noise and comparing this to the recommended standards for testing.

mobile testing units

When good testing facilities are not available within the school buildings some schools and communities have attempted to solve the dilemma by taking the service to the client. Mobile testing units have been used with success in many parts of the United States and Canada. These vehicles are often custom designed to meet the purpose for which they will be used. They are self-contained units with their own water supply systems, heating and cooling systems, electrical power generators, and other necessities needed in such laboratories. The vehicles are fitted with sound-proof rooms, noise reduction barriers in the walls, clinic areas with desks, tables, and chairs, storage space for records, testing equipment, electronic calibrating equipment, as well as space for therapy equipment supplies, and other materials needed.

Mobile hearing and speech units are often joint cost-sharing projects of local school systems, local health departments, voluntary civic organizations, and universities. Many areas are served by mobile hearing and speech-language screening units which test preschool children and are also used in the hearing testing of adults and in industrial hearing conservation programs.

In Winnipeg, Manitoba, Canada, a mobile hearing unit is cosponsored by the Department of Health and Social Development, the Benevolent and Protective Order of Elks, and the Manitoba Health Services Commission, Department of Communication Disorders. The van provides on an itinerant basis a complete facility for screening, assessment, and rehabilitation of hearing disorders. The audiologist works closely with school officials, public health officials, and nurses, and services are available from the span of preschool children to adults. The van tours the northern Manitoba areas during the summer months and the southern part of the province during the winter.[1]

The Ithaca College Mobile Audiology Unit serves the area surrounding that part of New York State and provides hearing screening tests to both preschool children and the elderly. This mobile unit is particularly effective because it is in a rural area with a scattered population. Because of the costs of building and personnel a permanent clinic would not be feasible.[2]

IMPEDANCE AUDIOMETRY

Berg (1976) stated that a comprehensive program of identification audiometry should be conducted in each school system on a continuing basis. He recommends that the program include conventional and/or impedance audiometry to identify ear pathologies and hearing loss among children.

Navarro and Klodd (1978) feel that impedance audiometry is superior to pure-tone screening because it is capable of detecting middle-ear pathologies with greater reliability, due to the fact that middle-ear problems are often associated with less severe conductive hearing losses which may not be detected if the ambient noise level in the school testing facility is not adequate. In addition, Navarro and Klodd feel that impedance audiometry would be an advantage to the school clinician because it does not rely heavily on the cooperation of the child, enabling very young children to be tested with more reliability.

[1] Anderson, Gary D., and J. Brayton Person. "Mobile Audiologic Services Program (MASP)," Winnipeg, Manitoba, 1973. (Correspondence with Gerstenslager Company, Wooster, Ohio.)

[2] Woodford, Charles. "Mobile Audiology Clinic," Ithaca, New York, 1972. (Correspondence with Gerstenslager Company, Wooster, Ohio.)

Impedance audiometry is not influenced by the high levels of noise present in schools.

A possible disadvantage to impedance audiometry at the present time is the high initial cost of the equipment. This problem may be lessened as more units are sold and the cost hopefully becomes lower. The cost factor may also be somewhat alleviated if several school systems purchase the equipment cooperatively and share the use.

Cody (1976), in a paper presented at the West Virginia Speech and Hearing Association's annual meeting, stated that in his opinion impedance audiometry used in conjunction with pure-tone screening audiometry is the best possible means available of identifying children with ear problems. He further feels that the cost of the addition of this equipment to a school's budget is insignificant when compared to its ability to detect and thus allow early treatment and correction of ear problems which have proven to be educationally handicapping in young school-age children.

One disadvantage at the present time is the unfamiliarity with impedance audiometry by the school clinician. A helpful article on the fundamentals of impedance audiometry by Greenberg (1975) describes the terms and briefly explains the basic theory, procedures, and some of the results obtained in testing.

hearing screening procedures

The Task Force Report on School Speech, Hearing, and Language Screening Procedures (1973) suggested that the following procedures be utilized in the initial hearing screening in a school system. A clinician working alone with some supportive personnel could carry out this type of screening; however, it would lend itself well to two or more clinicians plus supportive personnel.

1. All forms for listing children's names, communicating with teachers, and follow-up procedures for further testing must be decided prior to hearing screening.
2. Fifth or sixth grade students can be assigned as "runners" for the hearing screening team.
3. Children are brought to the test area by the runners in groups of six children each.
4. While one tester uses the audiometer, the other tester keeps records.
5. Children are referred for further diagnosis upon failure of the predetermined levels in the hearing screening task.

PRESCHOOL SCREENING

According to Bergman (1964), with some individual exceptions, children from ages three to five years are ready for the application of monaural low-intensity screening tests.

A recent unpublished study of over 3,800 preschool children in New York City Day Care Centers demonstrated that the simple handraising responses to the test tones, as employed with older children, is a quick, efficient method for large-scale testing of children from three to five years. A key aspect of such screen testing of three-year-olds is the instruction and preparation of the children in groups. Ideally this is accomplished by the regular nursery teacher, who has been instructed by the test supervisor. In this way the test becomes a familiar game for all the children. The preparation involves group hand-raising responses to soft chirp sounds produced by the teacher, followed by individual children (first the more confident ones, then the more timid), each demonstrating to the rest of the children how well and how quickly he can raise his hand in response to the sound. On the day the tester arrives one, two, or three screening audiometers and testers are installed in one room of the nursery. The children come to the audiometers in groups of three for each instrument, are briefly reinstructed and two sit quietly by as one is rapidly screened. Each child, therefore, has had the benefit of previous instruction, reinstruction and observation while two of his peers performed the test task. With such preparation, from 85 to 95 percent of three-year-olds can be successfully tested on each ear with the simple pure tone screening audiometer. Approximately 96 percent of four-year-olds and 99 percent of five-year-olds can be thus screened in a nursery or similar group situation even with less preparation.

For children below three years of age the screening techniques described thus far do not apply. This is not to say that it is not important to detect and assess the hearing of very young children; it is extremely vital. There are today, however, guidelines and techniques which audiologists have found useful and effective in the testing of the newborn and infants.

IMPORTANCE OF SCREENING
SPECIAL POPULATIONS

Many children who have been labeled as learning-disabled, mentally retarded, cerebral palsied, and emotionally disturbed may also have hearing impairments which may go undetected because the other handicapping conditions are more obvious. In some instances these children may have been misdiagnosed. It is important for the school clinician to be aware of these children and apply the appropriate screening and diagnostic hearing evaluations.

It is also possible that many children who were thought to be retarded, schizophrenic, or brain damaged were hearing-impaired instead. A child who cannot hear speech or sounds in the environment will have great difficulty learning both in the schoolroom and in the preschool years.

The screening and assessment of special education children and children being considered for placement in special education classes should be included in the general testing program. When the facilities for further evaluation of these children are not available in the school (and this is most often the case), these children should be referred for audiological services to a university clinic, a hearing and speech center, a hospital clinic, or wherever they may receive the appropriate services.

The Pediatric-Otologic Diagnostic (P.O.D.) Clinic in Ohio serves as a referral facility for school clinicians. These clinics are a function of the Ohio Department of Health in cooperation with personnel from local health departments, university speech pathologists and audiologists, medical personnel, and school speech, language, and hearing pathologists. The P.O.D. clinics are held periodically, usually monthly, in forty-seven geographical areas of the state. Preschool and school-age children are referred to the clinic by nurses, doctors, and school clinicians, and are accompanied to the clinic by the parents and often the school clinicians. The clinic staff is composed of a pediatrician, an otolaryngologist, an audiologist, a speech-language pathologist, and the nurses in the local health department. There is no charge to the parents for the examination of the child by each of the specialists. The follow-up of the referrals is accomplished by the nurses.

APPRAISAL AND DIAGNOSIS

According to Public Law 94-142, all handicapped children must be assessed before placement in a special education program. This assessment cannot be racially or culturally discriminatory, must be administered in the child's native language, must be done by a valid testing instrument, and must be administered by qualified personnel. In addition, it must be administered so that a child with a sensory impairment, such as hearing loss, or a child who experiences difficulty using his hands, or a child who is unable to speak or whose speech cannot be understood, will be accurately assessed and the results will honestly reflect the child's true achievement and aptitude levels.

Native language as defined by Public Law 94-142 is meant to mean the language used by the child, not necessarily by the parents. For example, a child who uses English at school, but uses Spanish at home, could be evaluated in English. If it is obvious that the child is more competent in Spanish, then the testing must be done in Spanish.

Public Law 94-142 indicates that each handicapped child should be assessed in more than the suspected area of deficit. According to Dublinske and Healey (1978):

> The communicative status of all school children should be assessed. However, some state and local school agencies do not require the participation of speech-language pathologists or audiologists on child assessment teams. As a consequence, the ASHA School Services Program recommends that all pupils suspected of being handicapped be screened by a speech-language pathologist and audiologist to determine the presence or absence of communicative disorders. If the screening results suggest disorder, appropriate assessments should be completed and presented *at the child staffing by qualified personnel.*

The speech, language, and hearing specialist in the school system has the responsibility of providing diagnostic services for children referred by the assessment team (of which the speech-language and hearing specialist may be a member), as well as all the children picked up by the speech, language, and hearing screening program, and children referred by teachers, nurses, parents, and others.

A minimal diagnostic appraisal would include an assessment of the pupil's articulation abilities and language competencies, fluency, voice quality, and hearing acuity and perception. There should also be an examination of the peripheral speech mechanism. In many cases it may be important to have additional information, and this can be obtained through a case history. Such information would include developmental history, family status and social history, medical history, and educational history. A physical examination may be needed as well as a psychological evaluation and an educational evaluation.

Parental permission is required in most states for the diagnostic procedures. The permission should be in writing and usually a form is utilized for this purpose.

In some cases the school system may not be able to provide some of the diagnostic procedures because of lack of specialized personnel. In this event the school system may arrange to have these procedures carried out by a qualified agency with qualified personnel, in the immediate community or nearby. It is the responsibility of the school system to see that the required procedures are carried out. Such referrals are made only after written permission is obtained from parents.

It should be kept in mind that the purpose of the appraisal and diagnostic procedures is to select children who may be placed in the speech, language, and hearing programs in the school. The school clinician must be prepared to describe how the pupil's disability will interfere with his ability to profit from the instruction going on in the classroom.

steps in diagnosis

What are the steps in the process of obtaining a clear picture of the child's communication problems?

The first procedure is to gather as much pertinent information as possible. This is done through a case history and an interview with the parents, the teachers and, if possible, with the child. Each informant contributes information which is vital to the whole picture. The parents can give background information on the development of the child, the teachers may provide needed information on the present status of the child, and the child may be able to contribute information which may be of great value to the clinician.

After the background information is obtained, the clinician needs to add to that information by describing the problem. This is done by observation of the child and use of appropriate tests which measure the degree of the problem and suggest associated aspects. The clinician must be an astute observer and must be able to record information objectively and without bias. In other words, the clinician must be a good "reporter."

After all the information has been gathered, the clinician makes a diagnosis of the communication problem (or problems). A diagnosis, or an identification of the problem, is in reality a tentative diagnosis because as a human being grows and changes, the problem changes. A diagnosis is much more than putting a label on a person. It is convenient for professional persons to use diagnostic labels when communicating with one another if all parties concerned understand that the label is not the diagnosis. A diagnosis involves weighing all the evidence, discarding some of it as not being pertinent, and keeping that which merits further investigation.

On the basis of the information gathered, the testing done, and the tentative diagnosis made, the clinician then determines the prognosis and sets up a long-range plan for the remedial procedures. The long-range plan includes therapy appropriate to the communication problem as well as other strategies and treatment. The school clinician is involved in an interdisciplinary team approach with others who are interested in the child's welfare, and these individuals work as a team in establishing an Individualized Educational Program (IEP). The school clinician is responsible for the appraisal and diagnosis of the communication problem, but the clinician is a team member in the overall appraisal, diagnosis, and treatment of the child.

The clinician uses professional judgment as to whether or not to utilize a long case history form or a short one. The clinician should have available forms appropriate for specific problems including language and speech assessment, voice, fluency, articulation, and hearing. A form for the oral peripheral mechanism examination should also be available.

THE PLACEMENT TEAM

The appropriate placement of the handicapped child must always be made by a placement team involving, in addition to the child's parents (or surrogate parents), those individuals knowledgeable about the child. The federal law also specifies that the team should include a representative of the local educational agency, the teacher, and if appropriate, the child. While the law does not state that other individuals are required to be present, good educational practice would suggest that other team members also attend. This list would include those persons who by virtue of their professional backgrounds and the child's unique needs would reasonably be expected to be involved. It might include the school principal, the psychologist, the reading teacher, the occupational therapist, the physical therapist, the vision consultant, and the speech-language and hearing clinician.

The parent need not be the natural parent of the child so long as he or she meets the legal qualifications of the parent surrogate.

The child may be included *whenever appropriate*. Schools may develop their own criteria in regard to appropriateness.

The results of the evaluation and the possible placement options should be available when the placement team meets.

coordinator of the placement team

The representative of the local educational agency usually is the *team captain* and coordinator of this team, and as such arranges for the meeting, presides over the meeting, determines that all necessary persons are present, and acts as spokesperson for the school system. The chairperson presents the necessary information and data, or calls upon the person responsible for presenting it. The chairperson also has the responsibility of informing the parents of their rights. Setting the tone of the meeting and seeing to it that all the basic ingredients of the individualized education program are present, and that the procedures are carried out according to state and local guidelines, are also within the responsibilities of the chairperson (Sherr, 1977).

the teacher as a team member

The teacher is the person most responsible for implementing the child's program. The teacher in the case of the communicatively handicapped child may be the school speech-language and hearing clinician. The teacher may also be the classroom teacher. The teacher's responsibilities as a team member at the meeting include explaining to the parents various techniques used to meet the annual goals. The teacher will also explain to parents why one particular strategy was used instead of another. In addition, the teacher would answer questions parents might have in regard to events that occur within the classroom. In effect, the teacher is the main emissary between the school and the parents (Sherr, 1977).

speech, language, and hearing clinician's role on the team

The roles of the speech-language and hearing clinician on the placement team may vary according to the guidelines and practices of the local education agency. If the child in question has a communication problem, the person providing the language, speech, and hearing services in the school needs to participate in the placement process. While the placement team has the responsibility of developing an educational program for each pupil, the school clinician will need to provide input into the process of establishing goals, objectives, and intervention strategies for the child. The school clinician will also be responsible for sharing with the placement team the results of any diagnostic and assessment testing and may recommend further testing.

The school clinician will need to remember that he or she is one member of the team and that the team is composed of professionals from other disciplines and parents. Using professional jargon is out of place and does not contribute to helping the parents understand. Parents should not be talked down to or ordered to do something. They have a right to speak, ask questions, ask for clarification, and disagree. The school clinician should not become defensive either in responses to parents or to other professionals.

parents as team members

Public Law 94-142 clearly gives parents a much greater voice than they previously had in the decisions regarding the education of their children. Some may argue that parents are not really qualified to make judgments about educational or therapeutic matters, while others feel that parents have the total responsibility for the child and should be considered equal partners in making judgments concerning the individualized educational programs.

The rights and responsibilities of the parents are described under the *due process* section of the handicapped child law in the various states. Due process gives the parents the right to have full status at the meeting. They have a right to question why any one procedure is necessary, why one may be selected over another, how a procedure is carried out, and whether or not there are alternative procedures. If parents disagree with the recommended procedures they have the right of review with an impartial judge. The purpose of the due process is to guarantee the parents the right of having the school system explain to them and defend the recommended procedures. It does not necessarily make the parents adversaries to the system.

On the other side of the coin, the parents have the responsibility of dealing openly and honestly with the school system, accurately describing their child's behavior, and reasonably and realistically requesting services (Sherr, 1977).

the placement team's purpose

The ultimate result of the placement meeting is to develop an Individualized Educational Plan (IEP) for the child and to achieve agreement to that plan by the parents and the professionals. The plan must be a written document, filed and distributed according to the policies of the state and local educational agencies. Policies also regulate who shall have access to the report and how these copies shall be made available. A copy of the report is made available to the parents. All placement team members sign the report.

In most cases the speech, language, and hearing clinician is a member of the team if the child displays communication difficulties. If the clinician is not on the team (an unlikely, but not impossible situation), a copy of the document should be made available to the clinician.

THE IEP FORM

A sample IEP form is found in Table 7-1 (Dublinske, 1978).

TABLE 7-1 INDIVIDUALIZED EDUCATION PROGRAM (IEP)

1. Identification/Development Information

NAME: Bret I. Valip   D.O.B.   5/3/73

Case Coordinator: Mr. SLP   Approved by: Ms. S. E., Director

Service Year: 197X-7X   Date IEP Developed: 9/15/7X

IEP Entry Date: 10/1/7X   IEP Exit Date: 10/1/7X

Follow-up/Review Dates: 12/1/7X, 5/1/7X, 9/25/7X

Persons Developing IEP	Person(s) Implementing IEP
Mr. SLP	Mr. SLP
R. C. Teacher	
Mrs. I. Valip	

II. Assessment Information

Assessment Procedures	Date	Results	Examiner
LEA Spatial Relations test	8/28/7X	20% accuracy for spatial relations *in, on, under, behind, above.*	R. C. Teacher
Carrow Test of Auditory Comprehension of Language	8/30/7X	Obtained age equivalent score of 3.6. Analysis of preposition items found child identified 90% incorrectly	SLP
Spontaneous Language Sample	9/5/7X	Analysis of a 50-item sample found 10% correct use of prepositions	SLP

III. Special Education and Related Services Needed

Special Education and Related Services	Time	Participation in Regular Education Programs	Time
1. Enroll in the language teaching resource program one hour per day	33%	1. Enrolled in regular kindergarten class two hours per day	66%
2. Refer to the University Medical Center for otologic and neurologic assessments.			

TABLE 7-1 (continued)

IV.   Placement Justification

Analysis of the assessment information finds the child to have a communicative disorder with a severity rating of seven. The recommended frequency of service for this type and severity of communicative disorder is intensive continuous. The child initially will be enrolled in a special language teaching resource program for one hour per day of individual and small group instruction. With daily instruction, the child's prognosis for acquiring the language skills needed for academic success appears positive. For the remaining half day, the child will be enrolled in the regular kindergarten class.

V.   Present Levels of Performance

Language: Uses/identifies spatial relations (prepositions) *in, on, behind,* and *above* with only 10% accuracy

Speech:

Hearing:

VI.   Need Statements

---

1. There is a need to increase correct use of prepositions

VII.   Annual Goals

---

1. By June 12, 197X the child will use prepositions *in, on, behind,* and *above* with 80% accuracy.

_____

Signature (parent or guardian)

VIII.   Instructional Objectives
IX.   Recommendations
X.   Status Report

Status Code	*Partially Completed Code*

A - According to schedule	1 - 0-19%
B - Not Begun	2 - 20-39%
C - Completed	3 - 40-59%
D - Delayed	4 - 60-79%
E - Eliminated	5 - 80-99%
R - Revised	
PC - Partially Completed	

TABLE 7-1 (continued)

Performance Area	Goal Number	VII. Instructional Objectives	IX. Recommendations	X. Status Report							Revision or Comments
				A	B	C	D	E	PC	R	
Language	1	By December 1, 197X the child will be able to use the prepositions *in* and *on* with 80% accuracy in a conversational sample consisting of at least 10 *in* / *on* prepositions used in sentences. The speech-language pathologist will provide instruction and record correct/incorrect responses.	Use the LEA Preposition Teaching Program. Complete two lessons per day until program criterion is met for each preposition.								

The components included on the sample IEP form conform to the IEP requirements contained in Public Law 94-142. Many alternatives exist to develop the IEP and comply with the law. The suggested format is designed to provide speech-language pathologists and audiologists with decision-making information that can be used, if necessary, to improve program and case management procedures. The content included in the sample IEP shows how the information would appear on an IEP. Many IEPs will be more complex and detailed than the sample IEP.

I. Identification/Development Information

This section contains demographic information related to the child and information on IEP development and implementation activities. Components included in this section may vary depending on information required by the local education agency.

The "case coordinator" could be a staff person assigned to coordinate case assignments within the agency, or the person with primary responsibility for implementing the IEP.

If the IEP has to be approved by an immediate supervisor, this person can sign off in the "approved by" space.

The "IEP entry date" indicates the date services will be initiated. The "IEP exit date" indicates the date services included in the IEP will end. Since IEPs have to be reviewed on an annual basis, the duration of services indicated between the entry and exit date is typically one year.

The time between the entry and exit dates constitutes the "service year."

Space is provided to indicate the "follow-up/review dates." The IEP can be reviewed as often as necessary but must be reviewed at least annually. The review can take place anytime during the service year.

The "persons developing the IEP" must include as a minimum the parent, teacher, and person qualified to provide or supervise special education and related services.

II. Assessment Information

Informal and formal "assessment procedures" used to determine the child's eligibility for special education should be included. No child can be placed in special education based on a single assessment procedure. "Results" of the assessments should be described and interpreted in a manner that facilitates understanding by other persons viewing the IEP. Complete names of assessment instruments should be used. The "date" of assessment and the name and title of the "examiner" also should be included.

III. Special Education and Related Services Needed

This section must indicate all of the special education and related services the child needs to receive an appropriate education. Statements should include information on the specific placement alternative the child needs and the frequency service will be provided.

The percentage of time the child will spend in each special education and related service program and regular education program must be indicated. The percentage can be computed by determining the total number of educational hours available during the year and dividing the number into the number of hours spent in the various special and regular education programs.

IV. *Placement Justification*

If the IEP is used as a placement document, the parents' signatures must be secured to indicate they approve of the child's special education placement. As a placement document, the IEP should include a summary statement indicating the placement recommended and the rationale for the placement.

V. *Present Levels of Performance*

From the assessment information collected, data-based statements of performance must be developed. These statements indicate the performance level for specific tasks or behaviors. Preferably, each statement will include a numerical reference to the child's performance level. Performance levels can be indicated for such areas as language, speech, hearing, or any other breakdown appropriate for the child or the informational needs of the LEA.

VI. *Need Statements*

Need statements show the direction of change that is to occur as the present level of performance is modified. Need statements indicate that a behavior is going to increase or decrease.

VII. *Annual Goals*

Goals indicate the projected level of performance for the child as a result of receiving the special education and related services indicated in the IEP. Goals should include the components when, what, and criterion and should be numbered, 1, 2, 3 . . .

VIII. *Instructional Objectives*

"Area" refers to the specific performance area to which the instructional objective relates, for example, language or articulation.

"Goal number" refers to the number of the annual goal included in Section VII. By including the goal number, IEP viewers will know which objectives relate to which goals.

"Instructional Objectives" indicate the specific behaviors that will be acquired as the child moves toward accomplishment of the annual goal. Each annual goal may have a number of instructional objectives depending on the intermediate steps needed to accomplish the goal. Each objective should include the components when, who, to whom, what, criterion, and evaluation.

IX. *Recommendations*

Primary or unique methods and materials that are needed to complete the instructional objectives are included under "recommendations." Recommendations should include the following components: what, how many, and how often.

X. *Status Report*

The "status report" section provides a method for reporting progress made in accomplishing objectives. On the date the instructional objective is to be accomplished, or on any other regularly scheduled review date, the evaluation component in the instructional objective can be executed. Progress the child has made in completing the objective can be indicated by using the status code. The "partially completed" code allows staff to indicate the amount of progress made by the child in those instances when 100% of the indicated criterion has not been met. Under "PC" in the status column, the PC code number 1-5 can be listed. Under "C" in the status column the date the objective is completed can be indicated.

"Revision" made in any objective or "comments" on why the objective was not completed should be included to provide information that can be used in developing future IEPs. (Dublinske, 1978.)

CONCLUSION

The various methods of identifying children with communicative handicaps have been discussed in this chapter. After the children are identified, further evaluation is needed to select those students in need of therapeutic intervention, further testing, or referral to other sources. Or perhaps a combination of these strategies is appropriate.

A team approach is an integral part of the whole process. The school speech-language specialist is an important member of the educational team, and, as such, has the responsibility of providing information on language, speech, and hearing to other team members.

The Individualized Education Program (IEP) is the next step in the process of case finding and case selection. A sample IEP form is presented along with a discussion of the components of the form.

8 | *scheduling and implementing therapy*

INTRODUCTION

In this chapter we shall deal with the topic of scheduling services within a school system. Before the scheduling can take place, however, the school clinician will need to set up a priority system of case selection. The various methods of scheduling will be considered and the pros and cons of each will be discussed.

The therapy program itself will be discussed. In this area we will look at such things as planning for therapy, motivation, length and frequency of sessions, group and individual therapy, rationale for various therapy techniques, criteria for dismissal from therapy, achieving generalization through working with parents and teachers, coordination time, summer programs, and public relations in the schools.

The importance of writing good professional reports is also discussed along with some of the various records and reports the clinician may be utilizing.

PRIORITY SYSTEM FOR SCHEDULING

Before scheduling of children for therapy takes place, the school clinician will need to set up a priority system of case selection. One aspect of case selection has been discussed in the previous chapter. That aspect dealt with the identification and further diagnosis of individual children who were possible candidates for therapy. Let us now turn our attention to the priority system and the rationale for scheduling children on that priority list.

ASHA has provided guidelines for the establishment of a caseload selection priority system through its delivery-of-service model described in chapter 3. The guidelines are flexible and can be adapted to large, small, or medium-sized school systems. They can also be applied to pupils from preschool through high school.

The children falling in the first priority grouping will be those with severely handicapping communication problems in the areas of language, voice, fluency, articulation, and hearing disorders. This group would also include children with multiple problems as well as problems associated with irreversible conditions and unspecified etiologies. They would require direct and intensive remediation.

In the second priority group would be children with mild to moderate developmental or nonmaturational deviations. This group would include children with mild to moderate delays in language acquisition as well as mild to moderate problems in expression, reception, or integration of language. The articulatory category might include children whose speech is fairly intelligible, but contains some articulatory errors. These children would require direct or indirect clinical management. The category also includes children with moderate fluency problems, voice problems, and speech and language problems related to moderate hearing loss.

The children in the first and second priority levels would also require assessment and evaluation services from the school clinician. It is also possible that a child might "graduate" from the first priority level to the second priority level.

The third priority level would include children with developmental problems. These children need not be enrolled in direct therapy programs but would be served through speech and language development programs in the classroom. Reinforcement of the classroom teacher's services can take place through demonstration lessons by the school clinician. Parental guidance and in-service training of parents would also be appropriate for this group. The focus of service for these children would be the prevention of communication problems.

The children in special education classes and learning disability classrooms might also be served through third priority level strategies.

Also on the third level priority list are preschool children in need of speech and language stimulation approaches, children who had previously been enrolled in therapy but who need periodic evaluation, and children previously enrolled on the first and second priority levels who need to stabilize and generalize appropriate speech, language, fluency, and voice patterns.

It is important that in a situation where more than one clinician is employed in a school system, there is agreement on all the elements of the priority system. Periodic review of the system can be made by the entire staff of speech, language, and hearing clinicians, and if changes and modifications need to be made, this can be done.

Before a priority system can be put into use there would have to be the endorsement and support of the school administrator responsible for determining policy for the speech-language and hearing department. The understanding of the priority system and the cooperation of the school principals would have to be enlisted in order for the system to function satisfactorily. The school principal would be a key factor in the success of such a program. The classroom teachers would also have to be familiar with the priority system in order for it to work well.

One of the major advantages of the priority system is that it establishes a continuum of services for children based on their individual needs. It is far superior to a service program based on unrealistic and outmoded caseload numbers or enrollments of the schools. The priority system allows for flexibility both in terms of changes in school enrollments and in changing needs of the children.

A description of a program based on the continuum of services was reported by Zemmol (1977). It is located in the Ferndale, Michigan school district.

SCHEDULING

Scheduling children for therapeutic intervention and support services must be done with the best interest of each individual child in mind. The intervention can include services all along the continuum, from minimum services to intensive services, to meet the criteria of appropriateness and need-fulfillment for each child. The clinician who tries to work with too many children because of pressure from parents or from administrators does a disservice both to the children and to the program. Likewise, the clinician who arranges the schedule to satisfy personal needs, or on the basis of convenience, is not conducting the program in an efficient and effective manner.

Often the school clinician feels caught in a quandary when faced with outside pressures, and it is at this time that leadership and assertiveness must be exhibited. A good understanding of appropriate services for each child, plus a dash of diplomacy and a pinch of poise, can go far in winning the respect of others. Often adversaries can be converted to allies in this manner.

options available

There are a number of options open for the delivery-of-services in the schools, and it should be understood that it is not necessary to choose and utilize only one. A plan of possible alternatives was described in *Standards* and Guidelines for Comprehensive Language, Speech and Hearing Programs in Schools (Healey, 1973) and was discussed in chapter 3. The options can be used in combination and the combinations of options may be dependent upon a number of factors. One of the primary factors is the availability of staff. In a school system employing only one speech-language and hearing clinician the options may be considerably smaller than in a large school system employing a large number of clinicians.

Other factors include the following:

1. The geographic location of the schools, the clinician's "home" office, and the distance and travel time between these locations.
2. The availability of working space in each of the schools.
3. The type and severity of the communication problems within the schools.
4. The number and population of the schools. Would some schools warrant a full-time clinician?
5. Time allotted for coordination activities. This would include in-service training; supervision of paraprofessionals or aides; record keeping; parent conferences; placement team conferences; consulting with classroom teachers, special education personnel, and administrators; administration of diagnostic tests, etc.
6. School policies affecting the transporting of students from school to school in order to place them in locations where they may receive the appropriate services.
7. The level of the school. It is entirely possible that the junior high schools and the senior high schools may have smaller populations of communicatively handicapped students.

the itinerant model

Many of the children with severe communication disorders, as well as those with mild to moderate deviations will be in regular classrooms with speech, language, and hearing services provided by the school clinician on an itinerant basis. The itinerant model has been used from the time it was suggested in 1910 by Ella Flagg Young who felt that it protected the young teacher from "depression of spirit and low physical conditions resulting from confinement in one room for several successive hours while working with abnormal conditions." Not until recent years with the advent of mandatory legislation, more sophisticated tools of identification, evaluation and program management, larger numbers of children needing services, and the recognized need for an interdisciplinary approach, have other systems of scheduling been developed.

This is not to say that the itinerant model is not a good one, but it should not be considered the only one.

The itinerant model may be effective in situations where schools are within close driving range of each other or where school populations are low. It may also provide continuous therapy for children who need more frequent intervention over a longer period of time such as children with fluency problems, hearing problems, and problems resulting from such conditions as cleft palate or cerebral palsy.

the intensive cycle scheduling model

Another model of scheduling services is the intensive cycle or block system. In this model the child is seen four or five times a week for a concentrated block of time, usually four to six weeks. The block plan was used in Arlington County, Virginia, and it was reported by Ervin (1965) to be effective in terms of improvement for second and third graders with functional articulation problems. There are a number of variations of the block or intensive cycle model.

MacLearie and Gross (1966) reported on an experimental program in intensive cycle scheduling in the Ohio communities of Brecksville, Cleveland, Dayton, and East Cleveland city schools and the Crawford County schools. The research was carried on over a period of four years, and the results were reported both subjectively and objectively. The Ohio study indicated the following advantages to the intensive cycle scheduling plan:

1. A greater number of children could be enrolled during the school year.
2. A larger percentage of children were dismissed from therapy as having obtained maximum improvement.
3. The length of time children with articulatory problems were enrolled in speech therapy was reduced.
4. Although not statistically significant, the Brecksville study gave some indications that a greater carry-over of improvement occurred.
5. Closer relationships between the therapist and school personnel and parents was noted due to the greater acceptance of the therapist as a specific part of a particular school's staff.
6. Students appeared to sustain interest in therapy over a longer period of time.
7. Less time was needed in reviewing a lesson since daily therapy sessions occurred.

Participants in the study made the following suggestions as to the length and nature of intensive cycle scheduling:

1. The first block scheduled should be longer to account for screening and program organization.
2. Sessions should be a minimum of four weeks in duration.
3. A minimum of two cycles, and preferably three to four each year, are needed for best results.

Problems related to intensive cycle scheduling included:

1. Some problems of a psychogenic nature may need more frequent contacts on a regularly scheduled basis.

2. Administrative problems and reactions to students leaving a classroom on a daily basis may be a problem if the intensive cycle program is not carefully explained to the school staff.
3. Monopolization of a shared room for therapy services may cause scheduling problems.

One of the anticipated problems was the reaction of the classroom teachers to having children leave their classroom on a daily basis. In the Brecksville study, it was reported that of the thirty-five teachers responding, thirty felt that the intensive cycle method fitted better with other aspects of their daily program. Two stated they had no opinion and three preferred the itinerant method.

Results of the Cleveland study indicated that regardless of the scheduling method used, the group receiving the intensive program first had a greater average gain than the group using the intermittent method first. The implication seemed to be that an optimum program may be intensive therapy first and intermittent therapy second.

The Crawford County study concluded that the gains shown by the group scheduled four times per week were only slightly greater than the gains of the other two groups. Twice a week therapy was as effective as three times over a period of thirty weeks, however it was hypothesized that the lack of gain between eight and sixteen weeks was a result of a plateau of learning rather than a scheduling problem.

The Dayton study, involving nineteen public schools and five speech therapists, was conducted from 1961 through 1964. The purpose of the study was to compare the effectiveness of the intensive plan with the intermittent plan to determine the following: (a) the age at which children respond best to intensive scheduling, (b) the type of speech problem for which intensive scheduling seems most effective, (c) the optimum length of time for a "block" of speech therapy, and (d) the feasibility of scheduling both methods concurrently in one building. The results of the study were evaluated as follows:

OBJECTIVE EVALUATION:

a. A breakdown of the articulation caseload by grades indicated that best results were obtained in grades four, five, and six in terms of number and percent of pupils corrected.
b. The groups which responded least were made up of seventh and eighth graders
c. Intensive cycle scheduling seemed to be less effective with problems involving organic impairments such as cerebral palsy, cleft palate, and brain injury
d. Intensive scheduling provided the opportunity for a greater number to receive speech therapy, and for a greater percent of improvement
e. Experimentation with length of blocks revealed that the ten eight-week blocks enrolled more pupils than did the eighteen-week blocks. However, the ten eight-week block schools were first year schools. The previous

study showed that first year schools enrolled more pupils than did those using intensive therapy for the second time. The correction rate of total case loads was similar in each school

f. The limitation of four buildings per therapist was thought to:
    1) Provide an on-going program of once a week therapy for selected children between blocks on the intensive cycle plan
    2) Permit scheduling of selected children as needed.

SUBJECTIVE EVALUATION:

The project directors felt that intensive cycle scheduling tended to:

a. Provide better integration of speech therapy with the total school program
b. Result in more consistent oral practice at home and more sustained interest
c. Permit more frequent contacts between therapists and school personnel
d. Minimize the effect of pupil absence on speech progress
e. Shorten time allotted to speech screening
f. Result in fewer problems in scheduling therapy classes for upper elementary children as they could be seen at times which best suited their program
g. Stimulate more frequent conferences with parents and teachers
h. Permit the enrollment of a larger number of children with speech problems without detracting from the quality of the work accomplished
i. Provide a higher rate of correction.

Johnson[1] stated that approximately 47 percent of the public school programs in Ohio are currently using intensive cycle scheduling and 50 percent are utilizing intermittent scheduling. Three percent are using a combination of the two. Johnson further indicated that while many clinicians in Ohio are using the intensive cycle scheduling and the combination of intensive and itinerant systems, there seems to be a trend to more utilization of the itinerant system especially since the implementation of Public Law 94-142.

Another factor in the consideration of scheduling systems is the needs of individual children at different stages of their therapeutic intervention. A child may benefit initially from individual therapy on an intensive basis. After he has progressed to a point where the clinician feels that he would benefit from a group situation on a less intensive basis, he could then be shifted to an intermittent system.

In summary, regarding intensive cycle scheduling and intermittent scheduling, it might be said that the clinician should organize the program in such a way that both options would be available and could be utilized when needed. Obviously, this would be easier to arrange if there were more than one clinician on the staff, if communication aides were available, if the program were carefully coordinated and orchestrated, and if the clinicians and the school administrators were all in agreement on the program.

Scheduling in Junior and Senior High Schools. Some special considerations

---

[1] Jerry Johnson, Educational Consultant, Speech, Language and Hearing, Ohio Department of Education. (Personal correspondence, 1978.)

need to be taken into account in scheduling junior-high-school and senior-high-school students. Because of the inflexibility of the classes and the study programs on those levels the Task Force on Traditional Scheduling Procedures in Schools (1973) recommended these alternatives: (1) the clinician discuss scheduling periods with the school principal prior to the beginning of the school year, (2) consideration be given to regularly scheduled speech and language classes with credit as part of the academic curriculum for those pupils in need of such services, (3) a rotation system be developed so students do not miss the same class each time, (4) scheduling during the regular academic year be omitted completely and intensive services be provided during the six-week summer period, or (5) additional staff be employed to serve only these students.

THE THERAPY PROGRAM

The therapy program itself has many facets, many ramifications, and requires much from the clinician. Decisions must be made, and they will not always be the right decisions. It should be heartening to the neophyte clinician that while school clinicians are conscientious and bright people, they are not always infallible creatures. They usually learn by their mistakes and often by the mistakes of others. It might be wise for the beginning clinician to avoid getting locked into a course of action that might later be regretted. Allowing for some flexibility will enable the clinician to gracefully retreat from a position that seemed to be a good one initially, but later proved not to be.

The beginning clinician may feel somewhat like the young man who went out West to a ranch to learn how to ride horses. When the ranch manager said, "Have you ever ridden before?" and the young man said, "No," the manager said, "Fine. We'll give you a horse that's never been ridden and the two of you can start out together."

A PHILOSOPHY: THE BASIS
ON WHICH TO BUILD

Knowing who and what you are and where you fit in will provide the basis from which to make many decisions and plans for the program.

Traditionally, the concept of categorical labeling whereby handicapped children were diagnosed, tested, and labeled according to the functional area of the handicap, has been the approach to dealing with handicapped children in a classroom. This psychological-medical orientation approach has failed to provide information on the degree of educational handicapping for individual children. In order to provide better services for the communicatively handicapped child in the school setting it is necessary to describe the problem in terms of the educational deficits it is imposing on the child in school. Furthermore, it is important that the classroom teacher as well as the parents understand the connection between the communication handicap and the child's ability to profit from the instruction in the classroom. For example, it is not enough to label a child as *hearing-impaired* and let it go at that. In a school situation it is necessary to describe how the hearing loss affects the child's ability to hear the teacher's and other children's voices, to monitor his or her own speech, language, and voice, to discriminate among sounds of the language, and to receive information. The effect of the hearing loss on the child's self-image should also be explained.

Speech, language, and hearing clinicians work in many settings. The clinician who chooses to work in an educational setting has the responsibility of removing or alleviating communication barriers that may hinder the child from receiving the instruction that is offered in the school. The clinician who works in the schools also has the responsibility of evaluating the communication problem and assessing its impact on the learning process. Another responsibility of the school clinician is to serve as a resource person for classroom teachers and specialized teachers who have the communicatively handicapped children in their classrooms.

Perhaps it is the term *special education* that has led our thinking astray. It is in reality education for children with special problems. The education of handicapped children is not something distinct and set apart from education; it is a part of the total school program.

THERAPEUTIC INTERVENTION

The school clinician spends most of the working day involved in actually performing therapy. The type of intervention used will be the decision of the clinician and will be appropriate to the age of the child as well as the type of problem. It is not necessary at this time, nor would there be space in this chapter to discuss the various therapeutic approaches and philosophies. Suffice it to say that the school clinician should not only be well versed in the remediation approaches used in the past, but also should be aware of current developments in therapeutic approaches. There are a number of approaches available to the clinician, and the choice will depend on what best serves the child. Beginning school clinicians will reflect on what they learned in academic courses as well as in clinical practicum courses. They will gain additional information and practice during the student teaching experience.

myths

There are some myths to which beginning clinicians seem to be especially susceptible. One myth is, "Everything old is bad and everything new is good." Thinking in terms of intervention strategies, there are some therapy techniques which have been around for a long time and are still effective if used appropriately. Aye, there's the rub! They must be used *appropriately*, and this can be said for old approaches as well as newer approaches.

Another myth is, "If I learned it in my clinical practice class it must be the best approach." Students who go into student teaching with this attitude are often surprised to find that there are other approaches and techniques that are just as effective as the ones they learned in clinical practice. And, furthermore, there is often more than one "right" approach.

motivation

Much has been written about motivation and probably much more has been said about the topic. Everyone seems to be in agreement that motivation is necessary to produce good and lasting results in therapy. It is not uncommon to hear clinicians express the wish that they could motivate their client. This would imply that motivating is something one does to another person. Webster however, gives us this definition of the word:

> Some inner drive, impulse, intention, etc. that causes a person to do something or act in a certain way; incentive; goal .... Syn.-*motive* refers to any impulse, emotion, or desire that moves one to action (greed was his only motive for stealing); *incentive* applies to a stimulus, often a reward, that encourages or inspires one to action (he needs no *incentive* other than the desire to be useful); *inducement* always refers to an outer stimulus, rather than an inner urge, that tempts or entices one to do something (the money was an added *inducement*); a *spur* is an impulse or incentive that pricks one on to greatly increased activity or endurance (security for his family was the *spur* that drove him on)[2].

If motivation, then, is something that is within the person, driving him or her from inside, it is not realistic to think that clinicians are able to motivate clients. Rather, the recipient of our services will make a change in communication behavior only if personal values and attitudes impel him or her to do so.

The use of games, precision therapy, negative reinforcement, positive reinforcement, rewards, punishment, shaping behavior, etc. provide incentives, inducements, and spurs, which may bring about changes in behavior. If the inner drive, or the motivation is absent however, there may be regression or lack of what is commonly referred to as *carry-over* or *generalization*, or there may be no change in behavior.

While the clinician is highly anxious to change the child's speech behavior, it does not necessarily follow that the child will share that feeling. In some cases the child may be highly motivated to hang onto an immature speech and language pattern because it may be a way of coping with other members of the family. Or a child with a speech problem may enjoy the attention of the therapist so much that he does not wish to improve and end the therapy sessions.

What are the implications for the clinician in regard to motivation in students? Raph (1960) suggested that there must be a shift of focus from a teacher-centered orientation of motivation to an understanding of the attitudes and values present in the child's motivation for learning. She has suggested that it

[2]With permission. From Webster's New World Dictionary, Second College Edition. Copyright ©1978 by William Collins, World Publishing Co., Inc.

would be desirable for the clinician to have some background in developmental psychology, some sensitivity to the nuances of the therapeutic relationship, and a willingness to learn as much as possible about an individual child's emotional functioning. Raph has suggested that understanding the feelings of the child may be as important as any diagnostic information that is gathered.

COORDINATION TIME

In addition to the time spent in conducting therapy sessions and diagnostic activities, the clinician has many other duties to perform. Some time must be set aside during the week to carry out many activities necessary to the overall program. In some states this is referred to as *coordination time*. It may be a half day or a full day. Usually it is a block of time set aside on a regular basis in the week's schedule. Some school clinicians set aside a block of time during each day for this purpose.

Some of the activities carried on during coordination time are: parent conferences; staffing of cases; staff conferences; in-service training activities; correspondence; maintaining records and reports; classroom demonstration lessons for speech and language development and improvement programs; consulting with the school nurse, psychologist, guidance counselor, reading teacher, etc.; and other activities important to conducting an effective program. In some geographical areas school clinicians employed in different school systems "coordinate" their coordination days so that they can get together for professional meetings, and to assist each other in screening activities, in-service training programs, and other professional matters. This can be especially effective in geographical areas where there may be only one clinician in a school district, or in rural areas where the opportunity for getting together may be limited by distance and time.

Because of the myriad of activities carried on during coordination time, it is highly desirable for the school clinician to keep the school administrators informed of what is done during this time. Some clinicians use a monthly report form on which they record their activities during coordination day. Periodically, they send the reports to the school administrators. This serves the purpose of helping school administrators understand the program better.

LENGTH AND FREQUENCY
OF THERAPY SESSIONS

In considering the length and frequency of therapy sessions, the most basic consideration would be the best possible use of the time allotted. This is not much help to the beginning clinician, however, who must decide whether to schedule children for fifteen-minute sessions or thirty-minute sessions. Perhaps the best approach is to take a careful look at the schedule of classes in the school and then have the therapy schedule coincide with the class schedule. This does not necessarily mean that therapy sessions should be the same length as classes, but it would be helpful to both teachers and students if there were some coordination between the two.

Nor does it mean that all the sessions should be planned for the same amount of time. Some sessions may be ten minutes in length while some may be forty-five minutes. The decision as to the amount of time should be made by the clinician on the basis of the needs of the child. More time may be needed for group sessions. The child in the carry-over stages of therapy may require ten or fifteen minutes several times a week. In an intensive cycle scheduling system when children are seen more frequently during the week, less time per session may be sufficient. High school students who may be able to assume more responsibility for themselves may need only one one-hour session per week.

The amount of time needed for each child may change as the child progresses in therapy. Classroom teachers should be informed of the fact that this will occur during the year and that their input would be valuable in considering any changes in the time.

The key word in planning the amount of time per therapy session is *flexibility* and the criterion is *what is in the best interests of the child.* The responsibility for making good use of the time is up to the clinician.

LESSON PLANNING

For the same reason that a construction engineer needs blue-prints to build a building, the clinician needs a plan for therapy. The plan must contain several things. First to be considered are the goals for that particular lesson. What do you hope to have the student accomplish? Are your aims reasonable? Is the student aware of the goals for that lesson? Has he or she helped formulate them? Are the two of you agreed upon the goals? Will these goals bring you closer to the final goal?

All of these questions and more must be carefully considered in formulating the goals of therapy. It is true that clinicians may have many of these goals in their heads and rely on memory to keep them in mind, but only up to a point. As time goes on and as clinicians deal with more and more students, it becomes humanly impossible to keep in mind all the goals for all the students.

Furthermore, the setting down of goals for each therapy session helps the clinician and the student evaluate and reevaluate the progress and methods of therapy. It helps keep the clinician on the right track by focusing attention on where the student is going.

Along with the specific goals for each therapy session, the clinician and student must be in agreement on the general, or long-range goals. In other words, what is to be finally accomplished in the way of improvement of communication? In formulating the long-range goals, the physical, emotional, intellectual, and sociological limitations of the student must be taken into consideration. The vague goal or the unrealistic and unattainable goal must be avoided as these types of goals only produce frustration and disappointment both for the clinician and the student.

The next thing needed in the lesson plan is the list of materials. If the list contains stories or poems, the author, title of the book, and the publisher should be listed. The list should be so complete that a person unfamiliar with the session would be able to assemble the materials from the list. A complete listing of materials will provide a ready future source of reference not only for the beginning clinician but for the experienced therapist as well.

Following the list of materials, the lesson plan would then go on to the steps or the procedures in the lesson. These can be listed in order of use and the estimated time for each one could be noted. This would be particularly helpful to the beginning clinician who has not yet been able to accurately judge the amount of time needed for each step. It is a common occurrence for the novice clinician to complete all of the activities of the lesson in half the time allotted, or else to complete only the first few steps in the entire amount of time. It should be a comfort to the beginning clinician to know that with continued experience comes a more accurate judgment of the passage of time during a therapy session.

The steps in the lesson should be based upon the child's needs, the general and specific goals of therapy, and the evaluated results of the previous lesson. The clinician may wish to consult with the parents concerning home assignments, or with the classroom teacher on carry-over.

The clinician must have justification for listing the steps in a particular order, otherwise the therapy session becomes a hodge-podge of activities unrelated to the goals. On the other hand, the order of activities must not become so sacred that it cannot be changed. The author recalls one professor's lecture to a class in which she said, "I expect each student teacher to teach from a lesson plan, complete with goals, materials, estimated time for each activity, and the activities listed in order of presentation. But if I come into the room and find the student teacher teaching the right activity at the right time according to the clock and the lesson plan, I'll know there's something wrong with the lesson."

Her point, of course, is that any lesson plan, no matter how carefully thought out, should be abandoned or rearranged to suit the needs of the student. If Jimmy comes to speech class and proudly announces that he has a new baby sister, or if Susie wants to show off her new shoes, or if the first snow of the season has fallen during the night, all of these things are much too important for the clinician to ignore and not utilize in the therapy session.

By using meaningful activities and real-life situations, generalization becomes much less of a problem and the clinician doesn't fall into the trap of playing endless, meaningless games with the student.

Following the list of procedures there should be a place for evaluation of the lesson. What should the evaluation include? In order to decide this, let us look at the goals. Did this lesson accomplish the specific goals set forth in the lesson plan? Did the techniques employed bring about the desired results, or could the same results be accomplished by simpler, more direct methods? Did the student understand why he or she was doing certain things? In other words, did this lesson make sense to the student? Did it include an opportunity for carry-over? For practice? For review?

Did this lesson have any relationship to the student's specific needs? Were the techniques and materials adapted to the appropriate age level, sex, interests, level of understanding? Paradoxically, it is possible for a lesson to be well-taught and interesting to the student, yet still not have any bearing upon the communication problem and its eventual solution!

Was the clinician able to establish good rapport with the student? Was the clinician genuinely interested in both the student and the lesson? Did the clinician talk too much, or too little? Did both clinician and student seem to feel at ease? Was the clinician in charge of the lesson or did the student take over?

All of these questions and many more need to be answered concerning every lesson. Too often the criteria for a therapy session is based upon whether or not the student enjoyed it, and whether or not good rapport existed between the student and the clinician. While both of these things are important, there is much more to a successful lesson. Careful preparation and careful evaluation of therapy sessions, both group and individual, are essential ingredients of good therapy.

The most effective clinicians we have observed have kept a running log of therapy, usually written directly following each session. This is in addition to the lesson plan.

Lesson plans may serve still another purpose. When progress reports, case closure summaries, periodic evaluation reports, and letters are required, the lesson plan may serve as a source of referral and an evaluation of progress of therapy, and could facilitate the writing of letters and reports.

CRITERIA FOR DISMISSAL

Sometimes clinicians get so carried away with selecting students, diagnosing, providing intervention and maintaining students in therapy that a major factor is forgotten. This factor is dismissal. What we are doing as clinicians is trying to make each client his own clinician. In other words, we try to bring students to the point where they are able to monitor their own speech, language, or auditory problem to such an extent that they no longer need us. This is sometimes painful for clinicians to do, and at times the student is reluctant to be dismissed from therapy. Both of these factors must be objectively viewed by the clinician, and when the optimum levels of performance have been reached by the student, as stated in the long-range goals, the student is ready to be dismissed. The criteria for dismissal are unique to each child and must be carefully established, evaluated, and reevaluated during the course of therapy. If necessary, they must be adjusted or modified in the light of more knowledge about the student.

Dismissals need not be absolute. No clinician is wise enough to be able to dismiss a child from therapy with the absolute certainty that the child will never again need therapy. When a dismissal is made, the child should be scheduled for periodic rechecks to find out if the therapy has held. In a school situation it is important to have the classroom teacher check this also. It will be necessary to be very specific with the teacher on what to check. The same holds true for parents. A dismissal, then, could be called a *temporary* dismissal.

Sometimes a student may be put on *clinical vacation*. This may occur when the clinician feels that the student has reached a plateau, or has been in therapy for a very long time without a break. Before the point at which boredom and apathy set in, the clinician may put the child on a vacation from therapy for a designated amount of time. Clinicians have reported that gains in progress have been made during the time the student was on clinical vacation. Perhaps good therapy, like a salad, needs time to marinate.

The conditions of a clinical vacation should be explained to the student. The author recalls one little fellow who, when told he was going to be on clinical vacation, seemed elated. Several days later his mother called to report that he was disappointed when he found out that being on clinical vacation did *not* mean he was being sent to Disneyland!

GROUP THERAPY

In a sense all therapy is group therapy. A dyadic group (group of two) in the area of speech, language, and hearing consists of the clinician and the student. Therapy groups in the schools consist of the clinician and from two to five students, or in special instances, more students. The purpose of a therapy group is to help the client in such a way that in the future he or she becomes independent of the relationship. The clinician is in a leadership role whether he or she utilizes a nondirective approach or a direct approach. The clinician is a facilitator who is aware of the feelings, the values, and the tensions of the group participants. The clinician may play the role of an impartial judge in the event of friction. He or she keeps the group members moving toward the completion of the tasks at hand.

Initially, the clinician is faced with the task of deciding which children should be placed in a group. The answer would depend on the needs of the child at any given stage of therapy. Some children may need an intensive approach to master some skills and this may best be accomplished by working alone with the clinician. Later that same child may be ready to use these skills in a social situation, and a group experience would best fit this need.

The makeup of the group is an important factor in planning for optimal therapy results. Some clinicians find it more productive to work with a group of children who have similar problems, while for other clinicians the homogeneity of problems is not as important as grouping children of the same age level.

On the junior-high-school and senior-high-school levels it may be more productive to work with students with fluency problems in a group. On the other hand, some students with stuttering problems may not be ready for a group situation until after a series of individual therapy sessions.

Precision therapy lends itself readily to individual therapy because of the intensive nature of the tasks. Usually the precision therapy sessions are of shorter duration than other sessions.

Waters, Bill, and Lowell in an article entitled, "Precision Therapy—An Interpretation" (1977), described an approach to case management that combined the principles of programming, behavior modification, and traditional methods as applied to the school setting. At the conclusion of the program they raised several questions which they felt needed further study. The questions were: (1) would a group setting have facilitated conversational practice following the precision approach and prior to transfer to other settings? (2) would transfer have been more rapid if a group setting had been used? and (3) since individual training is not always possible in many school programs, could precision therapy methods be applied to groups of four or five children?

Beasley (1951) described the advantages of structuring a group therapy session around the development of social skills. Beasley maintained that practice and drill on speech patterns did not provide children a way of using them readily in social and interpersonal situations.

Backus (1952), in an article discussing the use of a group structure in speech therapy, viewed the role of the therapist as one who creates the kind of environment in which the client becomes able to change. She maintained that a group situation provides a greater possibility for this than does a two-person relationship. She also felt that the group situation has a wider availability of "tools" (social situations) than does the one-to-one encounter.

Backus and Coffman (1953) described a program of group therapy with preschool children with cerebral palsy. The children were enrolled for two hours each morning for a period of twelve weeks each semester at the University of Alabama. The program consisted of both individual and group instruction for the children, and a program of group therapy for the parents.

A knowledge of group dynamics is essential for the speech-language and hearing clinician. Some of this information can be obtained in university courses, some in reading, and some in supervised clinical practice situations. The book, *Group Dynamics: Research and Theory*, by Cartwright and Zander (1960) will furnish the clinician with basic information. Chapter 13, "Group Structure in Speech Therapy," by Backus, in the 1957 edition of the *Handbook of Speech Pathology* also has information pertinent to the topic.

Good group therapy means there must be interaction among the group members. The interaction may be active or passive. In other words, while one child is actively engaged in an assigned task, or is responding to the clinician, the other children could be encouraged to listen and in some cases they may be asked to evaluate a response. Enlist the aid of all the children by telling them they are expected to listen, watch, comment, use their "good" sounds, and be members of the group in every sense of the word by participating actively. This doesn't just happen; as the group leader, the clinician must encourage the students to do this.

There is no rule that says all therapy sessions must take place around a table. Working in front of a mirror, a flannel board, or a chalkboard, and using them, will help group members to become better participants. It has been said that learning is movement. If this is true, the clinician who sits on a chair without ever moving, and the children who remain in their places during the entire session day after day, may not be making the best possible use of the therapy time.

OTHER FACETS
OF A SUCCESSFUL PROGRAM

letter and report writing

The ability to express ideas on paper as well as verbally is essential for the speech-language and hearing clinician. Some persons seem to be born with this knack and others have to learn it. In any event the techniques of writing professional reports and letters can be learned.

Often, professional letter and report writing is highly stylized and follows a definite pattern. In addition to this, the basic essentials of good writing must be observed. First of all, the writing must be clear and concise. Simpler terms are much better than complex ones and the simplest and easiest way of saying something is usually the best. The professional vocabulary must be adequate and the terminology must be appropriate.

Emotionally charged words should be avoided. Such words provoke negative responses such as hostility, guilt, fear, and suspicion. Kindred (1957) has provided for teachers a list of negative expressions and has suggested a more positive way of saying the same thing.

NEGATIVE EXPRESSIONS	MORE POSITIVE EXPRESSIONS
Must	Should
Lazy	Can do more when he or she tries
Trouble maker	Disturbs class
Uncooperative	Should learn to work with others
Cheats	Depends on others to do his or her work
Stupid	Can do better work with help
Never does the right thing	Can learn to do the right thing
Below average	Working at his or her own level
Truant	Absent without permission
Impertinent	Discourteous
Steal	Without permission
Unclean	Poor habits
Dumbbell	Capable of doing better
Help	Cooperation
Poor	Handicapped
Calamity	Lost opportunity
Disinterested	Complacent

Expense	Investment
Contribute to	Invest in
Stubborn	Extremely self-confident
Insolent	Outspoken
Liar	Tendency to stretch the truth
Wastes time	Could make better use of time
Sloppy	Could do neater work
Incurred failure	Failed to meet requirements
Nasty	Difficulty in getting along with others
Time and again	Usually
Dubious	Uncertain
Poor grade of work	Below his usual standard
Clumsy	Awkward in movements
Profane	Uses unbecoming language
Selfish	Seldom shares with others
Rude	Inconsiderate of others
Bashful	Reserved
Show-off	Tries to get attention
Will fail him	Has a chance of passing, if

For the beginner who is learning the skill of professional writing it is best to keep in mind the person to whom the report is being written. This person may be another clinician, the teacher, the family doctor, or the parents. Appropriate word choices should be made in keeping with the understanding of the person who is the potential reader of the report. Avoid professional jargon when writing to parents and do not assume they know the meanings of technical words.

Here we will list and describe the different types of reports that may be written during the course of the school clinician's professional career.

The Daily Log. The daily log is written for the clinician's own information. It may be nothing more than a simple jotting down of notes following each therapy session. These notes may indicate the child's reaction to the therapy, any progress made on that particular day, and suggestions and ideas the clinician may want to include in the next therapy session.

The Progress Report. The progress report covers a span of time. For example, the reports may cover a period of one month, two months, six weeks, six months, or a year. They may be written for the clinician's own information or at the request of the person responsible for the management of the students in that particular setting. The progress report could include such information as the specific dates of the therapy time covered, the number of therapy sessions, the name of the clinician, an evaluation of the progress, a listing of the therapy goals and a statement as to whether or not they were accomplished, the methods of therapy, and the overall results of the treatment to date. In a school situation the progress report may be written for the teacher's use and should be specific as to what was done in therapy and what would be recommended for the teacher to follow up on. Progress reports are usually filed in the child's cumulative folder, and if the child moves from one school to another the reports may follow to the new school. Progress reports may also be sent to parents. The clinician must be sure the terminology is geared to the parents' understanding.

Final Reports. Final reports or closure reports may follow a checklist format or they may be narrative style, or they may be a combination of the two. The factual information included in the closure summary may include: name, date of birth, type of problem, date of the latest service, name of the clinician and the supervisor, date when student was first seen, starting date of the therapy, and the date of recheck and results of recheck. Information about the therapy and the number of sessions may also be included, as well as whether the therapy was in group or individual sessions. A rating of the progress during the time covered by the report could also be included. The rating may be on a continuum such as, "no progress, very slight, slight, moderate, good, excellent." Clarification of these categories should also be included.

If other services were utilized during this time it would be necessary to include a reference to them and, if available, a summary. Such services would include psychological, social service, remedial reading, medical, vocational, educational, psychiatric, etc. In some cases it might be necessary to attach a copy of the report. The report should indicate whether the service was obtained within the school system or in a community agency.

General Information. In writing professional reports the school clinician should keep in mind that opinions, rationalizations, hunches, and unsubstantiated ideas should not be included unless they are labeled as such. They may be included under *clinical impressions* or a similar category. As long as they are labeled it is permissable to include them.

Report writing, as the name implies, means a reporting of the facts without any editorializing by the writer. The reader of the report must be allowed to draw his or her own conclusions from the facts submitted. In keeping with this idea, personal pronouns are not acceptable in professional reports.

Clinicians must realize that reports are available to parents and, in some cases, to the client. The reports, therefore, should be as accurate as humanly possible and written so that they will not be misconstrued.

CONCLUSION

In this chapter many aspects of the therapy program itself were discussed. The importance of a priority system related to case selection and scheduling of students for therapy is a fundamental consideration. The various options of scheduling procedures, along with the rationale of each, were considered.

Elements of therapy such as motivation, group and individual therapy (note: we did not say "group *versus* individual"), lesson planning, criteria for dismissal, length and frequency of therapy sessions, coordination time, and letter and report writing were discussed.

As each of these topics was considered it undoubtedly became clear to the reader that the school clinician must make many professional judgments and that these judgments will be based on each clinician's philosophy. A philosophy does not spring fullblown at any given time. Rather, it evolves over a period of time. The basis for the philosophy comes from the student's training and early clinical experiences, books and articles by the student, discussion in academic classrooms, and the opinions and thoughts of professors and other students. The beginning speech-language and hearing clinician will probably hang onto these early learning experiences, and they will serve as a temporary life-raft. But as the clinician grows in experience and wisdom, his or her philosophy will grow, expand, change, and develop. Eventually, each clinician's unique philosophy will emerge, and professional judgments will be made on this basis.

9 | *working with others in the school*

INTRODUCTION

The functions of the school speech-language and hearing clinician are not carried on in isolation. Other persons are important to the program and the school clinician must learn to work with them. This involves becoming aware of their duties and obligations as well as helping them become aware of the school clinician's responsibilities. In previous chapters we have looked at the roles and responsibilities of the speech-language and hearing pathologist, and in this chapter we will look at the roles and responsibilities of others and consider how they interface.

The boundaries between speech and hearing will probably never be clear. The work of the educational audiologist is important in increasing services to the hearing handicapped in the school. The functions of the educational audiologist will be dealt with in this chapter.

Paraprofessionals are becoming an increasingly important part of the program, and information about them will also be presented.

Someone said that public relations is putting your best foot forward, then telling people about it. School clinicians are engaged in a many-faceted program and there are many ways of letting parents and the community know about the services offered. This topic will also be discussed in this chapter.

A team approach implies a productive working relationship in which the beneficiary (in the case of the speech, language, and hearing program) is the communicatively handicapped child. The team may include the school principal, the classroom teachers, the school nurse, the psychologist, the guidance counselor, the social worker, the reading teacher, the learning disabilities teacher, the educational audiologist, and the health and physical education teacher. Administratively there are school personnel who play an important part in the program. These persons are the director of special education, the curriculum coordinator, the elementary and secondary supervisors, assistant superintendents, and the superintendent of schools. Their roles have been discussed previously.

THE SCHOOL PRINCIPAL

A key person in the program is the building principal. This individual's attitude toward speech, language, and hearing can make or break a program. Without the understanding and cooperation of the principal it would be extremely difficult to carry out an effective program. The principal is the administrator of the building, and, in a sense, the school clinician is responsible to him while in that building. The school clinician is a member of staff of that particular building in the same way that other teachers are staff members.

The principal is often the representative of the local education agency in the development of individualized educational programs for children, and may serve as the coordinator of the placement team.

What can the school clinician expect from the principal? First of all, the principal is responsible for arranging for adequate working space and facilitating the procurement of equipment and supplies. The principal acquaints the clinician with the school policies, rules, regulations, and all procedures in that school.

The principal may assist the clinician in scheduling the screening programs and in setting up the schedule for children to be seen in therapy. The principal may help the therapist in integrating the speech, language, and hearing program into the total school program.

The interpretation of the program to other members of the school staff, the parents, and the community, is an ongoing thing, and much of this may be done by the principal. In addition, the principal may arrange opportunitites for the clinician to interpret the program to the staff, the parents, as well as professional and lay groups in the community. The principal is the liaison person between the school and the community, and between the school clinician and the school staff. When a parent, a classroom teacher, or a member of the community has a question regarding the speech-language and hearing program, that person will ask the principal who may answer the query or refer it to the school clinician. Clinicians may not always be immediately available for questions that come to the school because on that particular day they may be scheduled at another school. When this occurs, the principal will be the one to handle the questions.

The principal can be expected to visit the therapy sessions and observe. Indeed, a wise clinician will invite the principal to observe therapy sessions and will encourage questions by the principal.

The principal can smooth the way for school clinicians in many situations. Perhaps one of the most important is in helping the school clinician gain acceptance of the program by the school staff and the parents. The attitude of the principal may be reflected by the teachers, and the attitudes of the children may stem from the way teachers perceive the program. Because of a myriad of duties and heavy administrative responsibilities, principals cannot be expected to know everything about the school therapy program, but a willing and cooperative principal with a positive attitude toward the program is excellent insurance for a good speech, language, and hearing program.

On the other side of the coin the school clinician has some important responsibilities to the principal. If the clinician is itinerant, more than one building and more than one principal will be involved, therefore, the clinician needs to know the policies and procedures in each school served.

Providing information about the program to the principal is one of the most important factors in maintaining a good relationship. The principal needs to know the children on the active caseload, the children dismissed from therapy, the children on the waiting list, and have a brief statement on the progress of each child enrolled. The children on these lists should be identified by name, age, grade, room number, and teacher's name.

The clinician should also provide information to the principal on screening policies and procedures, the children screened, the criteria for case selection and those children selected, as well as scheduling policies and procedures. In many schools the clinician will want to confer with the principal regarding each of the steps of the program. Some of the information can be conveyed through a conference, however. It is advisable to furnish the principal with periodic written reports, such as a monthly report, on the various aspects of the program.

The clinician should discuss with the principal any plans for parent conferences and should furnish a schedule of the conferences. Any plans for in-service programs for teachers and group meetings with parents should be discussed with the principal prior to inception.

Any written reports or correspondence pertaining to a child in that school should be shared with and approved by the principal. This would include information to other professional personnel as well as letters and notices to parents.

If the school clinician keeps in mind that the principal is legally and educationally responsible for each child enrolled in the school, the answers to many of the clinician's questions will be self-evident. Generally speaking, the school clinician should keep the principal well informed on every aspect of the program.

Because clinicians work in several buildings and with several principals at one time, it is good practice to keep all the principals informed in a general way about the programs in the other schools. This practice serves to keep the principals well informed about the total program in the school system, may suggest ways of cooperation and coordination among schools, and helps keep the clinician's workload well balanced.

THE CLASSROOM TEACHER

A study was conducted by Phelps and Koenigsknecht (1977) on the attitudes of classroom teachers, learning disabilities specialists, and school principals toward speech, language, and hearing programs in the schools. The results of the study were that the overall disposition of these educators was moderately favorable; however, they perceived the size of the clinician's caseload as too large to effect desired behavioral change. They also found that the classroom teachers of grades 4-6 evidenced the least enthusiasm for and support of elementary-school speech and language programs.

While the results of this study are, and should be, disturbing to the entire profession, it is evident that there are many school clinicians who are doing a good job. The study should prompt us to take a good look at some aspects of the programs in the schools and take whatever steps are necessary to remedy potentially dangerous situations and conditions. In addition to remedying any unsatisfactory conditions such as caseloads which are too large, the clinician must also focus on cultivating good relationships with classroom teachers. The role of the classroom teacher in the success of the program cannot be over-emphasized.

The integration of the speech-language and hearing program into the school's curriculum is a basic factor. It is essential that the classroom teacher understand the speech and language program, but it is equally important that the speech clinician understand what is going on in the classroom. It is not enough to give lip service to the idea of integrating the program into the educational framework; it must be put into practice.

How can this be accomplished? The answer is not a simple one, but let us first consider some of the things the clinician can expect of the classroom teacher, then let us look at some of the expectations of the classroom teacher in regard to the clinician.

The clinician can expect the teacher to provide a classroom environment that will encourage communication and will not exclude the child with the stuttering problem or the articulation problem, or the child who is hearing-impaired. A teacher who shows kindness and understanding toward the handicapped child is not only assisting that child, but is showing other children in the classroom how to treat handicapped individuals. Sometimes it takes more time and patience to deal with handicapped children, but the rewards in terms of the child's performance are many. The teacher in the classroom takes the lead in establishing the emotional climate in that setting, and the children learn by example.

The classroom teacher is also a teacher of speech and language by example. If you doubt this, watch a group of children playing school sometime. Teachers provide the models for communication and children imitate the teachers. Teachers must have an awareness of their use of language, the quality of speech, the rate and volume of speech, and the use of slang or dialect.

The clinician can expect the teacher to help identify children in the classroom with speech, language, or hearing problems. Some children with communication problems are not spotted during a routine screening, and teachers who see children on a day-to-day basis will have more opportunity to identify the children and refer them to the clinician.

The clinician can expect the classroom teacher to send the children to therapy at the time scheduled. The clinician will need to supply the teacher with a schedule, and both teacher and clinician should stick to it. The clinician can also expect the teacher to inform the clinician of any changes in schedules which would necessitate a child being absent from therapy.

One of the most important areas of cooperation between the clinician and the classroom teacher is in the carry-over, or generalization stage—when speech and language behavior learned in the therapy setting is brought into the classroom setting. In order for this to be accomplished it will be necessary for the clinician to keep the teacher well informed as to the child's goals in therapy, progress in therapy, and steps in development of new patterns. This must be done, not in general terms, but in very specific terms. The teacher needs precise information on the child's problem and what is being done in therapy before there can be a carry-over into classroom activities. The teacher can provide the clinician with information as to how well the child is able to utilize the new speech or language patterns in the classroom.

When confronted with the idea of helping the communicatively handicapped child in the classroom, the teacher's reaction is apt to be, "I don't have time to work with Billy on his speech when I have twenty-five other children in the room." The clinician's role in this situation is to give the teacher specific suggestions as to how this can be accomplished as a part of the curriculum. This of course means that the clinician will have to be well-acquainted with classroom procedures, practices, and activities. It also means the clinician will have to know what can be expected of children of that age and on that grade level.

In order to fully integrate the speech, language, and hearing program into the school setting, there must be a continuous pattern of sharing of ideas and information between the clinician and the classroom teacher.

We have considered what the clinician can expect of the classroom teacher. Now let us look at the other side of the coin—what the teacher can expect of the clinician.

If you are the new clinician in the school, starting off on the right foot is important. Being friendly and open with teachers, showing an interest in what they are doing in their classrooms, and showing a willingness to share information with them, are all things that can be done to help build trust and understanding. There are many ways in which this can be accomplished. One way is to plan to eat lunch with the teachers in the teachers' lunchroom. Another way is to participate in some of their social activities. Because clinicians deal with many teachers in different schools it is not wise to become identified with little cliques and associate only with a very small group. Outside the school you will have your own circle of friends, but inside the school be friendly with all persons.

If you have a schedule, keep with it, and if you make changes in it, as you surely will, be sure to tell the classroom teachers who are affected. If you send a child back to his classroom late, you will have no basis for complaint if the teacher fails to send a child to you on time.

Share information with teachers. This can be done through informal conferences, arranged conferences held periodically, by inviting teachers to observe therapy sessions, and by observing in classrooms. Always make arrangements in advance for conferences and observations. The principal can often help make arrangements for any of these activities. In one school where the author worked the principal volunteered to take over each classroom for a half-hour so that each teacher in the school could observe in the therapy room.

Information can also be transmitted in written form. Short descriptions or definitions of the various speech, language, or hearing problems or any aspects of the program, will help teachers understand the program better. *Short* is emphasized because realistically teachers are not going to take the time to read long treatises.

Providing in-service programs or short courses for credit are excellent ways of providing teachers with information about communicatively handicapped children.

Dopheide and Dallinger (1975) described a pilot in-service program carried out in Maine in a district that had been providing language, speech, and hearing services to children for only one year. It was seen as a potential model for other schools in the state. Enrollment by the teachers was voluntary, and the course consisted of eight workshop sessions that spanned a four-month period and carried three credits toward state recertification.

The objectives of the workshop were: (1) to design the program so that teachers and the clinician would engage in free and open professional communication, (2) to deal with problems in developing teacher support of the clinician's work, (3) to help teachers understand definitions of speech problems, criteria for making referrals, procedures used by the speech pathologist to help children with communication problems, and how to assist in the change process, (4) to prepare a series of videotapes to effectively stimulate discussion of improved cooperation between clinicians and teachers.

Mainstreaming means that regular class teachers will be faced with the task of integrating exceptional children into regular classrooms. The school speech-language and hearing clinician can help teachers to understand children with communication disorders by providing in-service programs.

What are some of the things that classroom teachers will need to know about communication and communication disorders? Following is a list of topics that might be included in an in-service program:

1. The relationship of speech, language, and hearing to the educational process.

2. The speech, language, and hearing program in the school, including the preventive, diagnostic, and remediation aspects.
3. Normal speech and language development.
4. Articulation disorders—characteristics, possible causes and related factors, diagnosis and assessment, therapy, and the role of the classroom teacher.
5. Delayed language development and language disorders—characteristics, causes and related factors, therapy, the role of the classroom teacher.
6. Speech and language—characteristics of mentally retarded children, diagnosis, therapy, and the role of the classroom teacher.
7. Stuttering—characteristics, possible causes and related factors, the various stages of stuttering, the role of the classroom teacher, therapy.
8. Voice disorders—characteristics, causes and related factors, medical diagnosis, assessment and diagnosis by speech pathologist, the role of the classroom teacher, the prevention of voice problems.
9. Cerebral palsy—characteristics, diagnosis and assessment, roles of the physician, the physical therapist, the occupational therapist, the role of the speech-language and hearing pathologist, suggestions to teachers.
10. Cleft palate—characteristics, related factors, medical and dental intervention, importance of early diagnosis and treatment, possibility of concommitant hearing loss, therapy, the role of the teacher.
11. Hearing problems—anatomy of the ear, the nature of sound, types of hearing loss, causes of hearing loss, identification and measurement of hearing loss, role of the classroom teacher, rehabilitation and habilitation of hearing deficiencies.

In working with classroom teachers the school clinician is a partner in effecting the best possible services for the communicatively handicapped child. The more help the school clinician is to the teacher, the more opportunity there will be for integrating the speech, language, and hearing program into the schools.

The book, *Speech and Language Services and the Classroom Teacher* by Gerald G. Freeman (1977), was written specifically for teachers, and provides much useful information regarding classroom management of communicatively handicapped children and emphasizes the team approach.

Some universities require that students majoring in elementary education take a course in speech, language, and hearing problems.

SPECIAL TEACHERS

A diversity of options exist in the delivery of educational services. The services may include self-contained special classrooms, part-time resource rooms, or full-time integrated classes with monitoring or support services. The individual needs of the children determine the amount and type of supplemental services required. The speech-language clinician may be working with teachers of the mentally retarded, the emotionally disturbed, the hearing impaired, and the learning disabled. The children in these modules may also require the help of the reading teacher, the academic tutor, the psychologist, and others. This means that the school clinician will be working, not only with the child's classroom teacher, but with other specialists as well as with the parents of the child.

In working with personnel in the other specialized fields, it is important to keep in mind that the instruction should be child-oriented. The specialists involved work as a team and each team member has specific responsibilities which are known to themselves and other team members.

For example, in a program described by Parker (1972) in which the speech-language clinician was on a learning center team, the other full-time members included a teacher of the educable mentally retarded, a reading specialist, and a special learning disabilities teacher. Part-time members included a psychologist, a social worker, a hearing consultant, two tutors, a vocational rehabilitation counselor, and a school counselor. According to Parker, the team members did not teach content area subjects, but they did assist classroom teachers in developing and acquiring more diversified methods and materials. The team identified those students requiring team services, diagnosed the students' learning strengths and weaknesses, prescribed behavioral goals according to the students' needs, prescribed plans to carry out these goals, managed the prescribed plans, and evaluated the students' progress, the prescribed plans and the methods.

THE SCHOOL NURSE

Depending on the size of the system, there may be a number of school nurses, only one school nurse, or a part-time school nurse. In some localities the school nurse may be part of the staff of the city, county, or district health department, and work either part-time or full-time with the school. The new school clinician will want to know in which of these arrangements the school nurse functions.

The school nurse maintains the health and medical records of the children in the school. Children with hearing loss, cleft palate, cerebral palsy, and other physical problems are already known by the school nurse. She is the one who arranges for medical intervention when it is needed, makes home visits, and knows the families. The school nurse is a storehouse of medical and health information. It goes without saying that the school nurse and the speech-language and hearing pathologist work closely together and need to share information on a continuing basis.

In some states, Ohio for example, the school nurse is legally responsible for conducting hearing screenings. The nurse, the school clinician, and the educational audiologist may work together in organizing and administering the hearing conservation program of detection, referral, and follow-up. All medical referrals and follow-ups involving family doctors, otologists, and other medical specialists are carried out by the school nurse. This would include medical problems in addition to those connected with hearing loss.

The school nurse is one of the best sources of information for the school clinician and should be one of the clinician's closest working allies.

THE PSYCHOLOGIST

The school psychologist is a member of the team of professional persons helping the communicatively handicapped child. The school clinician may make referrals to the psychologist for the purpose of obtaining additional information about the child in regard to educational diagnosis, school adjustment, personality, learning ability, or achievement. The child's speech, language, or hearing problem may be closely related to any of the above factors, either as a result, a cause, or an accompanying factor.

The school clinician and the psychologist will find that a close working relationship is mutually beneficial. The school clinician will want to know the kinds of testing and diagnostic materials the psychologist uses. On the other hand, the clinician may be helpful to the psychologist in interpreting the child's communication problem so that the best possible tests may be used. In making a referral to the psychologist the clinician should ask specific questions in regard to the kind of information being sought. The school clinician can also furnish the psychologist with helpful information that would facilitate working with the child.

The school psychologist's role differs from one school system to another, so the clinician should make note of that role, and find out what additional kinds of psychological help are available in the community.

THE GUIDANCE COUNSELOR
AND VOCATIONAL
REHABILITATION COUNSELOR

Another professional person with whom the school clinician works closely is the guidance counselor. The guidance counselor works with students with adjustment or academic problems, helps students plan for future roles, and makes available to them information that is pertinent to their situation. This individual may also do individual counseling of students.

The guidance counselor is especially helpful in dealing with students on the junior-high and high-school levels. Students with communication problems are often known by the guidance counselor, so the school clinician may depend on this person for referrals, supplementary information, and cooperative intervention.

The vocational rehabilitation counselor is usually employed by a district or state agency. This individual assists students sixteen years of age and older in overcoming handicaps that would prevent them from being employable at their highest potential. The vocational rehabilitation counselor, while not a member of the school staff, may work in conjunction with the school system.

THE SOCIAL WORKER

A major role of the social worker is to facilitate referrals among tax-supported and voluntary agencies. This individual's thorough knowledge of social agencies in an area can be of considerable aid to the school clinician. The social worker not only knows about the various agencies, but is a key person in helping families find places where they may receive needed help. The social worker may do some counseling, both individually and in groups, may make home visits, and can be the liaison between the school and the family. When financial assistance is required for supplemental services, the social worker is the one who can be of assistance to the family in locating that aid.

Not all school systems are fortunate enough to have a social worker on the staff, but if there is one, the school clinician should explore ways in which they may work cooperatively.

THE READING TEACHER

The relationship between reading and speech has been recognized for some time by classroom teachers, reading teachers, and speech and language clinicians. Often they find that the child with a speech or language problem also has difficulty with reading. The precise relationship between the problems, however, has thus far eluded many researchers. There are studies that show that there is a relationship between speech and reading, and between language and reading, but whether the problems are in a causal relationship or whether they exist concomitantly has not been established. Nonetheless, there is much evidence to indicate that the speech and language clinician can contribute significantly to the treatment of reading problems. The reading teacher, likewise, will be able to offer much valuable information to the speech and language clinician in regard to the child with both a reading problem and a communication problem.

Research suggests that children with reading failure need to learn the rules of spoken language. Stark (1975) indicated that they need to develop strategies for processing morphophonomic and syntactic units and learn the logic of the language system. He suggested that teaching so-called *word attack* skills, teaching sound and letter correspondences, blends, and improving perceptual-motor skills must be questioned. He also felt that an overwhelming amount of attention is being given to visual motor testing and training despite the fact that in 21 of 25 studies from 1960 to 1975 it was found that concomitant improvement in reading cannot be expected as a result of systematic visual motor training. According to Stark (1975):

. . . we believe that there is a significant amount of evidence to indicate that speech and language pathologists can make a very important contribution to the prevention and treatment of reading problems. Assisting parents, teachers, and other specialists by providing information about the nature of language acquisition and training children in linguistic processing may produce highly desirable results. At the least, speech and hearing clinicians may be able to modify currently used teaching techniques and materials so that teachers can more effectively understand the role that language development plays in reading.

Rees (1974), in the article entitled "The Speech Pathologist and the Reading Process," stated:

The speech pathologist has an essential contribution to make to the process of reading acquisition, in normal and learning-disabled children. The speech pathologist can make this contribution when he functions as a language specialist rather than in the limited role of articulation therapist. As a language specialist, the speech pathologist makes use of research findings and theoretical accounts of the foundations of reading in language and speech. The speech pathologist has the responsibility to assess and develop the linguistic prerequisites for reading, as well as to assist the child in developing the specific linguistic awareness required for reading. Specific training in auditory perception is probably of limited value.

According to Sanders (1977):

The arguments concerning whether or not auditory perceptual problems arise from deficiencies in specific auditory skills has its corollary in the area of reading difficulties. There is little doubt that auditory perception plays an important role in learning to read. Certainly, the widely used phonic approach to reading depends heavily on the child's ability to process patterns of speech sounds and their linguistic values. Examination of existing theories about how a child learns to read reveals a surprising parallel to theories . . . concerning how the spoken word is perceived. Many of the same questions are asked and many similar hypotheses are made concerning how the process might operate. It seems quite logical to assume that a common basis exists for an understanding both of speech perception and reading.

Sander's book, *Auditory Perception of Speech*, provides reference information on neurophysiological, psychoacoustic, and psycholinguistic aspects of the auditory processing of speech. He also discusses auditory learning difficulties as a language processing dysfunction, and the correlation between auditory perceptual skills and the process of reading.

Discussions on auditory processing and the assessment of cognitive and linguistic skills, as well as suggestions for remediation, are included in Wiig and Semel's book *Language Disabilities in Children and Adolescents*. Muma's book, *Language Handbook: Concepts, Assessment, Intervention*, also contains information helpful to the clinician.

Gruenewald and Pollak (1973) described the clinician's role in helping primary classroom teachers develop strategies for teaching the auditory skills necessary in learning to read. They suggested that the clinician utilize knowledge of auditory processes in diagnosing and analyzing auditory skills such as listening attention, identification and localization, discrimination, auditory sequencing and memory, and auditory association and closure. According to Gruenewald and Pollak the appraisal of reading readiness is often weighted heavily toward visual discrimination tasks or the combination of visual and auditory tasks, to the exclusion of auditory learning tasks.

Gruenewald and Pollak stated that while speech clinicians are generally not trained to teach reading as a process, they are trained in the auditory aspects of speech and language development and must not isolate themselves from the total learning process. According to Gruenewald and Pollak:

We are suggesting that the clinician use knowledge of auditory processes to assist the primary teacher in diagnosing needs and implementing group and individual programs in the developmental aspects of reading. Our unique contribution to the educational team can be the analysis of speech, language, and auditory learning upon which further symbolic and academic skills are built.

Following is a diagnostic outline showing auditory activities involved in reading readiness (starred items). The outline was developed by Gruenewald and Pollak, along with the developmental reading specialist in the Madison, Wisconsin public schools to provide a framework for the classroom teacher in assessing reading readiness skills (starred items indicate auditory activities):

1. Some components of reading readiness assessment
   A. Following directions
      *(1) Attending behavior (visual and auditory contact)
      *(2) Language of instruction (comprehension of task)
      (3) Performance of task (at what level?—motor, perceptual, conceptual, verbal)
   *B. Language
      (1) Nonverbal
      (2) Social
      (3) Comprehension (nonverbal-verbal)
      (4) Verbal (structure and content)
      (5) Conceptual parameters (classification and relationship)
   *C. Auditory behavior
      (1) Listening behavior
      (2) Recognition, identification, and localization of sound
      (3) Discrimination
         a. Concept: same-different
         b. Nonverbal: sound, pitch, rhythm
         c. Verbal: letter sounds, words
      (4) Auditory memory and sequencing (nonverbal and verbal)
      (5) Auditory association
      (6) Auditory closure
   D. Visual behavior
      (1) Visual reception
      (2) Visual recognition and identification
      (3) Visual discrimination
      (4) Visual memory and sequencing
      (5) Visual association
      (6) Visual closure

E. Motor behavior
   (1) Gross motor performance
   (2) Fine (visual-motor)
       a. Hand-eye functioning
       b. Eye focus
       c. Tracking
       d. Midline structure

Reading is one of the most important skills taught in the school. Classroom teachers in the primary and early elementary grades are responsible for teaching reading and the reading specialist in the school system is responsible for helping the child with a reading problem. Sometimes this is done directly with the child and sometimes it is accomplished indirectly through the teacher.

Classroom teachers often use quick screening instruments to place students at appropriate reading levels. Children experiencing reading difficulties are referred for a thorough reading analysis which is done by the reading specialist.

The speech clinician and the reading specialist should strive to learn one another's professional terminology. Often they are talking about the same things but using different terms.

The reading specialist and the speech-language pathologist have much in common and much to offer one another. A close working relationship between them is an important aspect of the school speech, language, and hearing program.

OTHER MEDICAL PERSONNEL

There are other professional personnel, not members of the school staff, who the speech-language and hearing pathologist will undoubtedly encounter in the context of a team approach.

The occupational therapist works under the prescription of a physician and helps people obtain better coordination of the hands, improved posture, balance, and motor speed. The occupational therapist also works with swallowing, chewing, and sucking skills.

The physical therapist works under a physician's prescription and helps persons with ambulatory problems. Improved use of the lower extremities in sitting, standing, walking, and movement with and without aids, is the goal of physical therapy.

The speech, language, and hearing clinician often works in conjunction with these therapists. If a student is receiving speech or language therapy in addition to physical and/or occupational therapy, it is best for the student if there is coordination and cooperation among the various therapists.

PHYSICIANS

Nothing is more important than good health. The child who is ill, or the child who is in need of medical attention, cannot be expected to perform well in school. School clinicians should be alert to the child's physical condition, and if there are any suspicious conditions, referral should be made first to the school nurse who will then make the referral to the family doctor. In making a medical referral, specific questions should be asked, and any helpful information from the clinician should be considered. Observations, results of any diagnostic procedures, and general impressions should also be included.

A good relationship with the physicians in the community enhances the school speech-language and hearing program. School clinicians should take every opportunity to establish such relationships by conducting their programs in a professional manner. This includes following established protocol in referral procedures, writing letters and reports that are professional in content and style, and giving talks to local medical groups if invited to do so.

A competent school clinician never oversteps the bounds by giving medical advice, or advice that could be construed as medical in nature. The school clinician may feel that a child's enlarged tonsils are interfering with voice and speech production, but the clinician does not advise the parents to have the tonsils removed. Instead, the clinician refers the child to the physician through the school nurse, accompanies that referral with a letter stating the reasons for the referral, and asks the physician to assess the situation from a medical point of view.

In summary, the speech-language and hearing clinician who works in a school program is a member of the educational team which functions cooperatively to aid the student with a communication problem. The school clinician may be a member of the placement team or the diagnostic team, or may work with any of the other specialists in alleviating the problems of an individual child.

SUPPORTIVE PERSONNEL

Referred to variously as supportive personnel, paraprofessionals, communication aides, speech and hearing technicians, and therapist's assistants, there is no question that these individuals are present and that they are providing a service. In a study by Blanchard and Nober (1978) regarding the impact of federal and state laws affirming the right of handicapped children to free, public, individualized, and appropriate education, professional activity changes were rated by speech-language and hearing clinicians in Massachusetts approximately fourteen months after implementation of the laws. Among the most evident activity increases was the supervision of paraprofessional workers and students.

Interestingly enough, the ASHA Committee on Supportive Personnel (1970) developed some guidelines and, although much has happened since that time, these represent our only present policies on supportive personnel.

Moll (1974) pointed out some questions which must be resolved by the profession as a whole in regard to supportive personnel. The ASHA guidelines provide almost complete flexibility which means that the titles used, the training provided, and the duties performed are determined individually by the facility in which the person is to be employed.

Under this concept, according to Moll, horizontal mobility is not ensured. In other words, the persons would not be able to move from job to job because their training is specific to a given facility. Another question which Moll raises is, should it be only on-the-job training? Should there be academic work, and if so, how much and where?

Another dimension involved, according to Moll, is vertical mobility which can be provided through establishing various hierarchical categories of supportive personnel, according to the training and experience, types of responsibilities, and amount of supervision appropriate to each category. This approach has been taken by other professions such as occupational therapy.

Moll (1974) states:

> Personally, I believe that we must move toward the establishment of specifically defined categories of supportive personnel to achieve consistency and uniformity and to provide horizontal mobility; that specific training programs for supportive personnel should be established; and that vertical mobility, at least through various levels of supportive personnel categories, must be provided.

A number of pilot programs utilizing communication aides have been reported in the professional speech, language, and hearing journals. One of the earliest was a pilot program undertaken by the Colorado State Department of Education. It involved ten aides working in nine school districts of metropolitan Denver for one semester. The aides observed clinicians at work for four days and worked under their assigned clinicians for two days. Instruction also covered school organization and administration; the role of the speech clinician; professional responsibilities and ethics; child growth and speech and language development; the speech and hearing mechanisms; disorders of speech, language, and hearing; and the identification and remediation of these disorders (Alpiner, 1970).

The majority of the aides' time was spent working with children with articulation problems; the remainder of their time was divided between clerical duties and working with children with language disorders. The result was that these areas matched those in which the clinicians felt the aides were most helpful. In general, the communication aides were accepted by the classroom teachers, school administrators, and school nurses in the buildings in which the aides worked. Several of the clinicians had some reservations about the aides; they gave many reasons, but their major complaint was a problem in keeping the aides occupied. They also felt that the use of aides should not be mandated by the state. The majority, however, wished to continue working with the aides but expressed a desire to interview them before employment to increase the likelihood of compatibility.

A pilot project was reported in the Montgomery County Public Schools of Maryland (Braunstein, 1972). This program was designed to aid in the remediation of language problems. The aides' responsibilities were as follows:

> ... to meet groups of children on a daily basis and conduct activities, to record daily progress, to record comments on students' behavior and re-

sponses, to tape-record weekly group sessions for evaluation, to confer with the clinician regularly, to participate in in-service activities designated by the clinician and approved by the principal, and to assist in the preparation of materials.

Each aides' caseload was made up of children with mild to moderate language problems in kindergarten through the second grade. Each aide worked with three groups of eight children for at least twenty-five minutes daily. The remaining time was allotted for conferences. All the materials used in therapy were part of a prepared programmed language development series. The aides received thirty-five to forty hours of training and analyzed twenty-five to thirty hours of audio and video tapes. At the outset of teaching the clinician and aide alternated the duties three times a week.

Another paraprofessional program involved language remediation for culturally different children in Prince George County, Maryland under a program called "Operation: Moving Ahead" (Lynch, 1972). Begun in 1966, it involved children in kindergarten through the third grade. Its primary objectives included the acquisition of standard English vocabulary, increased standard English familiarity, and the use and refinement of standard English language.

The aides were divided into two groups: children's aides and parent helpers. The children's aides' function was to help small groups of children by reinforcing the instruction program planned and provided by the classroom teacher. These aides were supervised by the *helping teacher* who did the diagnoses, further planning, and evaluations. The parent helpers' functions were to help parents learn about the school program, to understand the importance of language in the child's future success in school, and to suggest ways of working with the children in the home. They primarily worked in the community by visiting homes and distributing materials. They also developed a language box for stimulating language in preschool children and a folder containing ideas for making materials and equipment from inexpensive objects found in the home.

During the 1972-73 school year, the Los Angeles Unified School District established a paraprofessional/volunteer program to supplement and expand the services of the language, speech, and hearing clinicians (Scalero and Eskenazi, 1976). These supportive personnel were intended to work with the remediation of articulation and language disorders. The aides received an intensive seventy hour preservice training course; they then worked six hours five days a week. The volunteers attended a condensed form of the training course—mainly in-group sessions which emphasized practice with the programmed materials; they then worked in two-hour blocks a minimum of two days each week.

At the outset, the speech clinicians tested all potential clients. The fifteen aides and fifteen volunteers then used programs designed specifically for their use. They each kept a log of pupil performance and the particular lessons completed. The clinicians then evaluated the clients' progress and determined when they were to move to the next stage; they also supervised and rated the aides through the use of checklists and rating scales. Throughout the year the supportive personnel worked with 125 articulation cases and 136 language problems. A postinstruction evaluation of the clients revealed 90 percent of the articulation problems had 80 percent or more carry-over in fifteen weeks or less of therapy. These successes were independent of the age, education, or previous training of the aides but were related to their rapport with their pupils and their ability and willingness to follow directions. The children who worked with the volunteers attained the same goals as the children who worked with the aides, but in longer periods of time.

A slight variation of the paraprofessional program was attempted in Maine to meet the requirements of Public Law 94-142 in the isolated rural districts without speech clinicians (Pickering and Dopheide, 1976). Instead of being trained to perform supervised therapy, these aides were to screen for communication disorders. In two separate workshops, fifty-one people from twenty different schools were trained; the majority of these trainees were school aides, but classroom teachers and "floating" teachers were also involved. Each workshop lasted two days and had performance-based success levels.

As a result of the screening by the paraprofessionals, 11 percent more children were identified in the first testing. Voice quality was the most difficult judgment for the trainees to evaluate and for the instructors to define. A total of 1700 children were screened with the aides referring 35 percent of the children tested and the teachers referring 28 percent; of these referrals one-third needed remediation. The program significantly reduced the amount of time the language, speech, and hearing clinicians had to spend in screening children.

Some school speech, language, and hearing programs utilize the services of volunteers or unpaid aides. These individuals have been used in assisting with hearing screening programs. The school clinician must train the volunteers in the specific tasks they are to perform. Often mothers of school children will serve as the volunteer aides in the screening programs.

Strong (1972) reported on a program in northern Minnesota designed to utilize supportive personnel in screening school populations for speech problems and managing direct therapy with children over eight years of age who exhibited frontal or lateral distortions of sibilant phonemes or distortion of the phoneme /r/. The program was carried on in a rural area and the results indicated that the use of supportive personnel allowed the school clinician to devote more time to the more severe cases.

Galloway and Blue (1975) described a program in Georgia which was carried out over a period of three years. The paraprofessionals were trained to administer programmed materials to first- through fifth-grade students who had articulatory errors. The errors exhibited were in the mild to moderate range of functional articulation problems. The findings suggested that paraprofessionals using a preplanned program and materials can enhance the program carried out by the school pathologist by allowing more time for problems that require greater expertise.

A pilot program for training and utilizing communication aides in Head Start programs in Wyoming was reported by Jelinek (1976). According to Jelinek benefits other than the statistical inferences were realized from the program. The aides became skilled in the delivery of language programs and more knowledgeable in child development and behavior management. "Project staff were able to develop a liaison with Head Start staffs, parents, and other professionals in the community which might not have been possible without the development of the pilot program. Because of the success of the pilot communication aide program, this model has been expanded to include all Head Start centers in Wyoming."

Costello and Schoen (1978) studied the effectiveness of paraprofessionals in an articulation intervention program in California using programmed instruction. The results indicated that paraprofessionals using a clearly written, previously tested programmed instruction format compared favorably with the results obtained using a fully qualified speech clinician. The use of audio- and video-tape aids insured a standard quality program presentation and reduced the responsibilities of the paraprofessionals. Costello and Schoen suggested that a possible future role of the speech clinician would be that of a program writer, program researcher, trainer, and supervisor of a paraprofessional staff. This would leave more time for clients with special and more complex needs, and would also enable the program to serve larger populations more effectively.

While many programs throughout the country are providing their own training agenda for aides and paraprofessionals, there is at least one college that is offering training programs leading to certification. This is Community College of Baltimore in Maryland (Brunson, 1978).

One of the programs offered by Community College of Baltimore is an associate degree program which has been designed to train a person in two years to be an assistant to a speech pathologist or an assistant to a special education teacher. In this program special emphasis is given to the problems of the hearing impaired.

The certificate program at Community College of Baltimore is directed mainly toward training a person in a year's time to be an assistant to a speech pathologist.

The programs provide preservice/in-service course work and practicum to prepare supportive personnel to assist special education teachers, speech pathologists, or other professionals in any setting where specification needs exist. Trainees receive experience with the severely and profoundly handicapped, trainable and educable mentally retarded, learning disabled, emotionally disturbed, and speech impaired on preschool to adult levels. The programs include identifying and screening exceptionalities, speech and language development, executing articulation and language programs, managing lessons, drafting behavioral objectives, and preparing reports of client progress for review by supervising teachers or clinicians.

COMMUNITY INFORMATION PROGRAM

Keeping the community informed about the speech, language, and hearing program in the schools has a number of advantages. First of all, it interprets the program of prevention, assessment, and remediation to the public at large and may remove any possible stigma attached to having a child enrolled in the program. It also builds a feeling of trust and confidence in the program, and toward the school system in the community.

A community information program should not be a haphazard affair; it should be well planned and executed. It should not be a "one-shot" deal but rather it should be continuous, consistent, and persistent. It should also be varied, informative and interesting.

The school clinician may want to survey the types of media available within the community. The most commonly utilized are newspapers, radio, television, service clubs, lectures and presentations, and displays.

The school clinician may wish to make arrangements with the local newspaper to run a series of articles on such topics as types of communication problems, how parents can help children learn to talk, the school therapy program, dos and don'ts for families of children with fluency problems or hearing-impaired children, the importance of early referral of children with problems, and the many other topics of interest to parents and community members.

In preparing articles for release in the local newspapers, it is best to inquire of the editor how long the article should be, and then stick to the length suggested. If an article submitted is too long the editor is likely to trim it and may inadvertently cut out an important part. Most editors like to have articles submitted, but the articles should be well-written and interesting. The school clinician can usually obtain from a member of the newspaper staff the pertinent facts on style, length, and other information. If pictures are used and they contain any children, it is an absolute *must* to first obtain written consent of the parents.

Some school systems have a person in charge of community information or public relations and this individual will often assist the clinician in preparing articles for publication.

Radio interviews or other types of radio programs are a good way of getting information across to the public. Local radio stations often welcome suggestions on programs of special interest. Clinicians can utilize such timely events as "National Hearing Week" in May to publicize information on the importance of hearing conservation programs.

The same can be said of television programs. Often local television stations have programs during which various community figures are interviewed. Or the television station may cooperate in preparing a program on various aspects of the speech, language, and hearing program.

Talks to community service clubs, professional organizations, and other groups can yield innumerable benefits. Many of these groups sponsor special projects or programs as part of their community service activities. Interest in the speech, hearing, and language program can be generated through talks to these organizations.

Another effective way of informing the community about the program is through displays at health fairs and similar events.

Public libraries are often willing to add to their shelves books of interest to parents of handicapped children. The school clinician can make suggestions for specific books which could then be made available to the public.

CONCLUSION

In this chapter information has been presented on the working relationships between the speech, language, and hearing clinician in the school and other professional specialists. These include the school principal, the classroom teacher, special teachers, the school nurse, the psychologist, the guidance counselor and vocational rehabilitation counselor, the reading teacher, the occupational therapist, the physical therapist, and the physician. The paraprofessional's function in the program is also presented.

The importance of maintaining a good community information program is emphasized and there are specific suggestions on how this may be accomplished.

10 | *special categories of programs*

INTRODUCTION

In this chapter we will look at special categories of programs such as speech-language improvement programs, high-school programs, vocational school programs, and summer programs.

A sampling of various programs in the United States is included. The information was gathered through a questionnaire sent to speech-language pathologists in Arizona, California, Delaware, and Ohio. As is true in many thousands of programs throughout the United States, these programs are in the process of complying with state and federal mandates, and at the same time are providing services to speech, language, and hearing handicapped children.

THE SPEECH-LANGUAGE IMPROVEMENT PROGRAM

Speech-language improvement programs are generally thought of as taking place on the kindergarten, first- and second-grade levels. They include children whose differences may be within the normal range, and children with minor deviations. A major focus would be on the prevention of communication problems. Another major goal of such a program would be to encourage better listening habits as well as to provide practice in more effective communication skills.

The benefits of such a program are substantiated in studies by Wilson (1954), Sommers (1961), and Byrne (1965). The results of these studies indicate that articulatory errors in kindergarten and first-grade children were reduced following speech improvement programs.

Speech-language improvement programs involve work done with an entire class or a large group of children. The speech-language clinician's role may be one of conducting the speech-language improvement program in the classroom, or one of serving as a consultant to the classroom teacher who conducts the speech-language improvement activities. In many cases it is a combination of the two roles. The clinician may carry out several demonstration lessons for the teacher and may, along with the teacher, plan the remainder of the speech-language improvement sessions which are then carried out by the classroom teacher. Both the school clinician and the classroom teacher should be involved in the speech-language improvement program, but the major task of carrying out the program rests with the classroom teacher.

Several hurdles must be cleared before embarking on the speech-language improvement program. One is the reluctance of the classroom teacher who may feel unprepared to conduct such a program. The speech-language clinician can help to alleviate this problem by conducting a program with the classroom teacher present and then furnishing the teacher with outlines, materials, and suggestions for subsequent lessons. It would also be helpful to the classroom teacher for the clinician to conduct in-service training sessions on speech and language development and improvement. The in-service meetings could include goals, guidelines, materials, and programs for speech and language improvement. It might also be necessary to convince the teacher of the merits of such a program.

It would also be important for the school clinician to make sure that the information presented to the children during the program would not conflict with the approach used in teaching reading in that particular classroom or school system.

The speech-language improvement program may enrich the child who has already demonstrated proficient language and listening abilities. Such children could be encouraged to further develop speaking skills through such activities as creative dramatics, speaking before a group, participating in group discussions, and improving social skills.

Some school clinicians may wish to initiate programs in speech improvement and language development for high-risk preschool children and children in Head Start programs. Such a program would include a parent guidance program as well. Another group of children who would profit from a speech-language improvement and development program would be the mentally retarded children in special classes.

In the evolving role of the school speech, language, and hearing specialist, more emphasis is being placed on the prevention of communication problems. The speech-language improvement program, carried out cooperatively by the school clinician and the classroom teacher works toward this end. In addition, minor deviations can also be handled in the speech-language improvement program. Parents can do much to help young children develop speech, language, and voice proficiency and must be considered part of the program.

On the high-school level speech-language improvement programs can be correlated with academic subjects, speech classes, debate and dramatics, as well as with activities such as student government, class organizations, assembly programs, and clubs.

While the school clinician's role in speech-language improvement is a consultative one, time must be allowed on the weekly schedule for all the activities necessary in implementing such a program. At the present time there is a paucity of literature available on the organization and management of speech-language improvement programs in the schools and little time is given to the subject in university training programs. While speech-language improvement programs are not new, they are not widespread and are often loosely defined. They have been beneficial where they have been utilized, by reducing the numbers of children in remediation programs, and it is time for the profession to consider them as a viable aspect of the school communication program.

commercially available programs
for speech-language development

There are a number of commercial programs available for speech language improvement geared to group or individual use. One such program is the *Goldman-Lynch Sounds and Symbols Development Kit* (1971), which is for preschool to primary children. It is a phonetically oriented program with one symbol for each sound. It includes a manual of lesson plans, stories, songs, workbooks, and puppets for teaching speech production.

The *Peabody Language Development Kits* (Dunn, 1968) were designed for use with educable retarded and culturally different children and can be used with large groups, small groups, and individuals. They are available on four mental age levels ranging from 3 to 9½ years. Materials include pictures, color chips, puppets, records, tapes, and a Teletalk set which can be used as a telephone or a two-way communication system.

Think, Listen, and Say (Sayre, 1967) is an audiovisual kit which utilizes records and filmstrips to improve listening abilities, auditory discrimination and comprehension, and is designed for preschool through primary grades.

Distar Language—An Instructional System (Engleman, 1969) is designed for preschool through primary grade levels. Originally it was planned for culturally disadvantaged children. The purpose of the program is to teach language concepts.

The book, *Correction of Defective Consonant Sounds* (Nemoy and Davis, 1945) contains stories, poems, and activities correlated with consonant sounds. The book also contains suggestions on how the clinician or teacher can teach the production of the sounds, as well as suggestions on helping the child attain proficiency in auditory discrimination. The material in the book is appropriate for the lower elementary grades.

The Child Speaks (Byrne, 1965) outlines a speech improvement program based on a three-year research study carried on in two public school systems in Kansas. The program is appropriate for kindergarten and first-grade levels. The book is a syllabus and is used with materials which the school clinician or the teacher would already have in the classroom or could find in the school's media center. The program is flexible in regard to time spent on each lesson, materials used, phonemes, and pictures.

HIGH SCHOOL PROGRAMS

One of the most neglected areas of intervention is the secondary school. In a survey conducted by Neal (1976), some interesting questions were raised as the result of a questionnaire sent to 250 school speech clinicians in the United States.

> Has the school clinician merely adapted elementary programs and techniques for use at the secondary level? Do we need innovative approaches to working with older children? Do we need more experimentation with different school scheduling patterns or is the clinician satisfied with traditional methods? Does the clinician continue to use methods for which validity has not been properly established? How can the clinician improve the delivery of services at the secondary level in view of the variety of problems inherent in that particular setting?

The survey also revealed that the factors judged most important by the school clinicians at the secondary level were as follows: (1) consistent attendance by clients, (2) the client's motivation for self-improvement, and (3) the client's opinions of other peoples' attitudes toward himself and his speech defect. The least important factor at the secondary level was the cooperation of the classroom teacher. Parental cooperation at the secondary level was given a relatively lower ranking than at the elementary level. Neal concluded that the comparisons may reflect a decreasing role of parents and classroom teachers in the therapy program as the age of the child increases. According to Neal:

> While decreasing importance is attached to these two adult roles, the student's opinions of other people's attitudes seemed critically important at the secondary level. Even though the active role of parents and teachers decreases as the child gets older, the attitudes they reflect concerning the child and his defect seem to become increasingly more important to the success of the therapy program.

DeKalb County program

The communication disorders program for adolescents and adults in the DeKalb County School System, Georgia, provides service to secondary students partly through a central clinic and partly through itinerant services to the high schools in the county. Also served are college students and the adult residents in the school system's district. The case finding is accomplished through a continuation of services from the elementary program, and through referrals from counselors, teachers, students, parents, physicians, and specialists. Because of difficulties associated with carrying out a screening program on the secondary level, a teacher education program is carried out by the staff[1].

The caseload is composed of individuals with problems in articulation, fluency, voice, language, as well as speech and language difficulties associated with hearing impairment, cleft palate, cerebral palsy, cerebral vascular accidents, and laryngectomy.

The models of delivery-of-services include: (1) diagnostic evaluations and individual and small group therapy at the clinic; (2) consultative services at the clinic or in the schools which aid students with mild communication differences who do not require direct therapy, and students who have been dismissed but may need occasional contact; (3) itinerant services which include diagnostic evaluations and therapy scheduled in the schools, therapy administered by a trained aide, and structured home programs provided and monitored by the speech therapist; (4) resources offered to teachers and students in special classes.

The system used in DeKalb County has significant features and advantages (Beall, 1977). These include:

1. Therapists who work four extended days providing services after school and work hours
2. Flexibility of delivery models; servicing model is dependent on individual student needs and circumstances
3. Staff was redirected and reassigned at no cost to the school system
4. Problems associated with workspace, scheduling conflicts, and interference with extra-curricular activities were minimized; absenteeism was reduced
5. With students seen in the high schools the referring counselor or teacher is responsible for securing workspace and arranging the schedule
6. Cooperation of counselors and their awareness of special needs and programs were significantly increased
7. Services were centralized allowing for a more efficient and prompt referral system and improved instruction and evaluation
8. Motivation and interest of students enrolled for therapy appeared significantly improved
9. Program procedures and development of new, effective delivery systems are the responsibility of the staff; the flexibility of the present administration has facilitated the establishment of this non-traditional approach

Two full-time clinicians, two part-time clinicians, and one teacher-assistant comprise the staff. The teacher-assistant provides secretarial help in addition to administering structured programs to high-school students and adults. Also,

[1] Kathy Hosea, "Exemplary Speech Pathology Programs in Secondary Schools." Presentation at American Speech and Hearing Association Convention, Chicago, 1977.

student aides, identified by counselors, are trained to work with their peers in the high schools.

The staff serves twenty-four secondary schools, grades eight through twelve, with approximately 34,000 students. They also serve a community college and a continuing education program having approximately 34,000 students.

Evanston Township High School program

The Evanston Township High School program in Illinois has been functioning continuously since the late 1930s. Started as an outgrowth of the Northwestern University Speech and Hearing Clinic, it is now a division of the Special Education Department of Evanston Township Schools and has been guided by Helen Sullivan Knight and Marjorie Burkland[2].

In addition to the continuity of the program, there are some unique features. The *Speech Modification Program* is part of the regular curriculum of the high school. Students receive grades and high-school credit for enrolling and attending. The credit is one-quarter as much as a regular school course and therapy may be repeated for credit. The grades are on a scale of A, B, C, D and N.C. (no credit).

According to Burkland, the students are graded on the following criteria:

(1) They must attend and they must be on time
(2) They must carry out semiweekly assignments
(3) There must be participation in the therapy process. In other words, all students in a therapy group must participate in the activities planned for that session. The participation may consist of critical listening or carrying out a specific task, but there is no just sitting back and being present
(4) There must be some personal improvement. A student may get an A even though he or she may not have perfect speech

Perhaps the single most significant feature in the delivery of remedial speech and language service at Evanston Township High School, according to Burkland, is that all scheduling is done by computer in the scheduling office along with academic scheduling during the spring quarter preceding enrollment. The clinician provides the scheduling office with appropriate times for such courses as articulation improvement, fluency, individual lessons, etc., and these appear as requested on the students' respective schedules. In this way ability grouping (as to overall academic functioning) as well as disability grouping (related to a given communication problem) can be provided for. An additional advantage is that students begin the year with the speech modification elective clearly *a part of* rather than added to their programs. Basically the clinician provides therapy four days a week (with most lessons being semiweekly) and surveys and diagnoses one day a week, thereby developing a prospective caseload for the ensuing year. A speech aide assists as a critical listener in carrying out lessons prescribed by the clinician and devises materials geared to accomplish listening, language formu-

[2] Marjorie Burkland, Speech-Language Pathologist, Evanston Township Schools, Illinois. (Personal correspondence with the author).

lation, articulation goals, etc., agreed upon in conference with the clinician.

Ideally, motivation for enrolling in a remedial course comes from a student's inherent interest in enhancing personal adequacy, but very real motivation is provided by Evanston Township High School because speech modification courses are listed in the *Program Planning Handbook* and carry elective credit. Also, grades are given and attendance kept, thereby making this elective like all others in the curriculum.

There are minimal scheduling conflicts, according to Mrs. Burkland, because the course appears on the school's regular schedule of courses. The course meets on a Monday-Wednesday or Tuesday-Thursday pattern, with Friday used for screening, testing, conferences with teachers, and seeing students for extra sessions. The screening is done through students' homerooms with all freshmen being screened. Screening takes place during September, October, and November. Reevaluations continue during December, January, and February. In March and April the students are scheduled for the speech modification course which appears on their programs the following September. Generally students are not enrolled after the course starts, but emergency enrollments do occur throughout the year. Students are scheduled for the course for a year but may be dismissed earlier if they meet the proficiency standards set by the clinician.

Burkland, plus a part-time therapist and an aide, serve a population of 4,300 students. In September, 1979, an additional clinician was added on a part-time basis.

A specially designed therapy room is located in the high school. The plan for the room is shown in Figure 10-1.

Figure 10-2 shows the card used to keep a speech record of every student in the school.

Figure 10-1   Speech Modification Suite, Evanston Township High School, Evanston, Illinois.

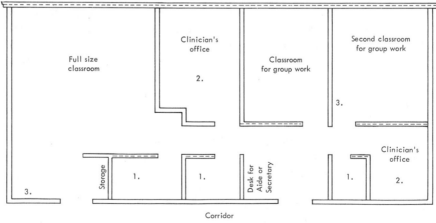

1. Practice room
2. Phone
3. Sink
– – – – – Windows and glass

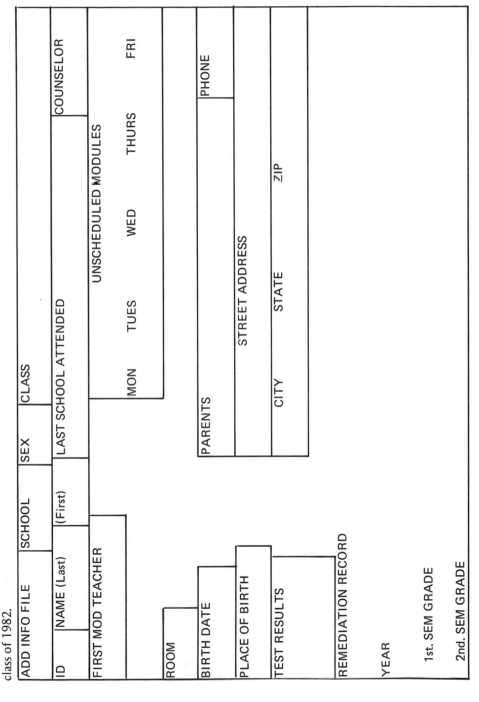

Figure 10-2 Information is IBM printed each September for the entire class. Color coding of card is used to indicate class level of student. For example: green is used for class of 1979; yellow for class of 1980; pink for class of 1981; and white for class of 1982.

ADD INFO FILE	SCHOOL	SEX	CLASS		
ID	NAME (Last)	(First)	LAST SCHOOL ATTENDED		COUNSELOR

FIRST MOD TEACHER

UNSCHEDULED MODULES

MON	TUES	WED	THURS	FRI

ROOM

BIRTH DATE

PLACE OF BIRTH

TEST RESULTS

REMEDIATION RECORD

PARENTS

STREET ADDRESS

CITY	STATE	ZIP

PHONE

YEAR

1st. SEM GRADE

2nd. SEM GRADE

Speech, language, and hearing programs on the junior-high and high-school levels cannot be duplications of the programs on the elementary level. The subject matter must be geared to the interest of the students and to the subjects they are studying in their regular classrooms. Materials and unit topics can be found in abundance within the classroom and by working with the classroom teacher. Scheduling must be flexible enough to accommodate the student's varied and busy school day. Counseling students on the secondary level appears to be one of the most important factors in the success of the treatment program. The initial interview with the student may well be crucial in convincing him or her of the value of therapy. If the student has had therapy during the elementary years and has been exposed to a "speech game" approach, it may be necessary to emphasize that this type of approach will not be used on the high school level. Because the student is now an adult, he or she deserves a clear explanation of each step of the procedures used and the progress made. Many clinicians working in high schools make enrollment voluntary and have found this approach successful.

VOCATIONAL SCHOOL PROGRAMS

The increase in vocational high school education in recent years offers the speech, language, and hearing therapist a unique challenge to provide services. It is not known exactly how many school clinicians serve vocational schools, but the number is probably quite small. However, this fact should not preclude the possibility of investigating the needs of students in vocational high school settings.

A vocational high school is usually jointly operated by a group of existing school districts. In some cases, if the school district is a large one both in numbers and in size, the vocational high school may serve only one school district. Students often retain membership in the "home" school district, but may attend classes at the vocational school for all or part of the school day.

The curriculum of the vocational high school may include basic academic classes such as English, American history, and government. It would also contain classes related to the students' vocational choices, and laboratory classes during which the theory and training are applied to actual job projects. The students upon graduation receive a diploma from the home school and a vocational certificate from the vocational school.

Because the purpose of a vocational school is to prepare a student for a specific vocation, the needs and the motivations of students in this kind of setting differ from those of students in the normal high school.

Awareness of the psychology of this age group is important to the school clinician. A strong desire to be accepted by peers and not to be different from them sometimes underlies a resistance to therapy on the part of the student. A good working relationship with the vocational instructor can do much to encourage students enrolled in therapy to maintain good attendance in therapy sessions.

Penta County program

Madaras and Wozniak[3] have indicated that regardless of how severe the communication deficit may be, it is of secondary importance to the student at this age level. They have recommended that the intervention program be based on the student's personal and vocational vocabulary. Remedial sessions may be developed around such topics as hairdressing, automobiles, getting a job, and other subjects of interest.

In addition to a remedial program in the vocational school, a speech improvement program may fulfill the needs of many of the students. In one such experimental program initiated with senior dental students at Penta-County Vocational High School, Ohio, the students preparing for their rotation assignments as assistants to area dentists were reintroduced to the following topics: (1) selecting correct word choices, (2) eliminating slang, (3) speaking clearly with the appropriate volume and rate, and (4) eliminating syntactical errors.

The vocational instructor worked closely with the clinician on noting common errors and providing the vocational vocabulary. A pre-test was designed to disclose other areas of weaknesses. The clinician instructed the entire class for one forty-five minute period per week for eight weeks. The results of the post-test showed that each student received a much higher score on the post-test than on the initial test. Furthermore, the students seemed to be more aware of their overall speaking habits.

The Penta-County Vocational High School program also includes in-service training programs for both students and staff members. Topics for vocational instructors included information on speech, language, and hearing problems and the recognition of them. In-service topics for students include speech, language, and hearing behavior in the young child for the students enrolled in the child care program, as well as the effects of prolonged and sudden loud noise on students working in shop areas such as auto mechanics, industrial, carpentry, and agricultural shop areas.

In the Penta-County program the clinician initiated a hearing conservation program. Staff members and students involved in noisy laboratory and shop classes were made aware of the various ramifications of noise pollution and the effects on the hearing of the persons involved. The clinician arranged for decibel readings to be conducted in the suspected loud noise areas. Measures were then taken to make ear protectors available in the school supply store for students and instructors.

SUMMER PROGRAMS

One way in which many school clinicians have extended their services is to offer a summer program. There may be several reasons for carrying out a summer program. One would be to provide more intensive therapy for

[3] Roberta Madaras and Jean Wozniak, "A Speech, Hearing, and Language Program in a Joint Vocational School." (Unpublished article, 1978, and correspondence with author.)

children who need it. Another reason would be to provide services of an intensive nature to children with such problems as stuttering or communication problems associated with cleft palate. Another reason would be to offer a preventive program of therapy along with a parent guidance program.

School clinicians have provided summer programs for a number of years. Some of the programs have been financed by the local education system while some have been underwritten by such organizations as Crippled Children's Society or a local service club. In some cases, the program has been a joint effort of both the school system and a voluntary organization. In this sort of program, usually the building, facilities, supplies, etc., have been furnished by the school while the clinician's salary has been paid by the community group.

The clinician in charge of the program will need to establish criteria for accepting children for the summer program and will need to carry out the necessary diagnostic procedures. Often only a limited number of children can be accepted into such a program depending on the number of staff members available.

Summer programs are usually well received in a community, and once started are often repeated during subsequent summers.

A SAMPLING OF PROGRAMS

Students-in-training have often expressed interest in how school speech-language pathologists are organizing and managing programs. In order to obtain information on the various aspects of the programs, a questionnaire was sent out in 1977 to school clinicians located in various geographical areas of the United States. The purpose of the questionnaire was to obtain a sample of the programs in different parts of the country. No attempt was made to query representative programs or to quantify the information received or even to draw any conclusions from the comments returned. Rather, it was felt that the information these individuals provided would be helpful to prospective school speech-language and hearing clinicians.

It might be added that all respondents at the time the questionnaire was returned were actively engaged in school programs, and all were holders of the Certificate of Clinical Competence in Speech Pathology from the American Speech-Language-Hearing Association. The school pathologists are: (1) Barbara DeWeese, (2) William Freitag, (3) Ruth Terry, and (4) Polly Young. The school systems represented are located in Arizona, Ohio, Delaware, and California.[4]

---

[4]Barbara De Weese, Speech-language pathologist, Pinal County Schools, Arizona. William Freitag, Speech-language pathologist, Sylvania City Schools, Ohio. Ruth Terry, Speech-language pathologist, New Castle County School District, Delaware. Polly Ann Young, Aphasia teacher specialist, Los Angeles County Schools, California.

The questionnaire contained the following questions to which the school pathologists responded in respect to their various programs:

A. Under which of the delivery-of-service models does your program fit?
B. How and by whom are children referred?
C. In regard to evaluation, what testing instruments are used? Who does the evaluating and what is the procedure?
D. Could you describe the class, the classroom, the equipment and furnishings, and the scheduling procedures?
E. What is the rationale of your program?
F. What about reevaluations?
G. If it is part of your program, how do you foster return to the regular class?
H. What are the advantages and disadvantages of your program?

The answers to these questions are not given in the order of the pathologists listed above. However, the order given here is consistent throughout the series of answers (e.g., number 1 is the same pathologist each time).

A. UNDER WHICH OF THE DELIVERY-OF-SERVICE MODELS DOES YOUR PROGRAM FIT?

1. A full-time special class for children with severe language disorders and aphasia.
2. Contractual and, or, cooperative services. I have been employed by the County Special Services Cooperative for the past two years and worked in 2-3 different school districts.
3. The itinerant model combined with the consultant model.
4. This program falls within the itinerant diagnostic-educational team concept for its delivery of services.

B. HOW AND BY WHOM ARE CHILDREN REFERRED?

1. Referrals may be initiated from numerous sources—preschool screening specialists, district psychologists, speech and language clinicians, pediatricians, private schools or nursery schools, parents, etc. Each student must be referred from the contracting school district of residence. That school district supplies referral letter, doctor's report, and a parent questionnaire to the county severe language disorders/aphasia program and the referral is then dealt with in the closest severe language disorders and aphasia office (SLD/A) to the contracting district.

Children from three to six years of age, as soon as can be managed, are placed in a preschool diagnostic class which involves diagnostic teaching to determine the child's learning style and an appropriate instructional plan. The child is in the class approximately six to eight weeks. School-age pupils are seen by the diagnostic team which consists of a consultant, psychologist, language program specialist, principal, language teacher specialist, and is assisted by consulting physician, school nurse, audiologist, and other specialists.

2. Children can be referred by anyone such as a classroom teacher, principal, coordinator, psychologist, nurse, aide, parent. The largest number of referrals come from classroom teachers. In one instance, a child referred himself.

Referrals have been received verbally or in writing and include information such as name, grade, teacher, and a brief description of the problem. Usually the children referred have been seen at least once by the speech-language pathologist because the entire school district population has been screened.

3. A brief referral form is usually used by teachers, nurses, psychologists, social workers, guidance counselors, principals or other administrators. Parents, other concerned adults, and the individual himself make verbal referrals. The completed form or referral message is sent to a SLH person.

4. Children with speech and language handicaps are identified through routine speech surveys conducted by the speech and language pathologists and supplemented by teacher and parent referrals. Referrals are also received from the county nurses who work within the system, and from the otolaryngologists in the area as well as from the orthodontists for myofunctional therapy when these children have concomitant speech problems in addition to the myofunctional problems.

We also utilize the "Strategies in Early Childhood Education" program which we implemented in 1976. Dr. Robert Wendt was one of the facilitators and original authors of the program which was developed in Wisconsin. This program is administered to kindergarten children in the fall and hopefully we will move it into first and second grade in the near future. This program assesses the visual and auditory perceptual language development and physical coordination of each child to compare his ability levels with his peer group so that we can descriptively provide educational programs at the kindergarten level for these children. Children who do not perform well in the language areas of the Strategies Program are referred to us for further testing.

C. IN REGARD TO EVALUATION, WHAT TESTING INSTRUMENTS ARE USED? WHO DOES THE EVALUATING AND WHAT IS THE PROCEDURE?

1. Children three to six years of age are placed in the preschool diagnostic class as previously mentioned. A language teacher specialist does informal assessment and takes a 50 to 100 utterance language sample. The language program specialist does formal testing which usually consists of the *Illinois Test of Psycholinguistic Abilities* (Kirk, 1968), *Assessment of Children's Language Comprehension* (Foster, 1969), *Peabody Picture Vocabulary Test* (Dunn, 1965), *Northwestern Syntax Screening Test* (Lee, 1969), or any other test that may prove informative. The school psychologist does intellectual testing utilizing a performance test such as the Leiter performance part of the *Wechsler Intelligence Scale for Children* (1949). The nurse does vision and hearing screening. If a child fails the hearing screening, an audiologist

will do further testing. For children of school age the same testing procedure is used, but there is no placement in a diagnostic class, and the psychologist does academic as well as intellectual testing. An admittance and dismissal committee meeting is held when all assessment has been completed and a decision is made whether to admit the child into the SLD/A program. Members of the committee are the diagnostic team as mentioned above in question B and the child's parents.

A child is admitted into the program according to the state's Administrative Code, Title V Regulations. The child has a severe language disorder which is not due to deafness, mental retardation, or autism.

2. Each evaluation includes receptive and expressive aspects of the language. Additional testing is done when warranted such as in cases of severe language development problems.

Articulation is tested with an informal picture test, a reading sample, or the *Goldman-Fristoe Articulation Test* (1969). Other commercial tests used include: *Auditory Test for Language Comprehension*, Carrow 1973; *Northwestern Syntax Screening Test*, Lee, 1969; *Illinois Test of Psycholinguistic Abilities*, Kirk, 1968; *Peabody Picture Vocabulary Test*, Dunn, 1965; *Goldman-Fristoe-Woodcock Test of Auditory Discrimination*, 1970; *Houston Test of Language Development*, Crabtree, 1963; *Wepman Auditory Discrimination Test*, 1958. Informal tests are used for verbal absurdities, syntax, auditory memory and blending, and expressive language usage.

I do the speech and language evaluations in entirety but frequently check the results of Title I Reading testing and those of psychologists when they are involved with a particular child.

The procedure used (after obtaining parental permission and conferring with parent when requested) is to "test" the child by himself. The evaluation includes: articulation; imitation of word series and sentences; auditory discrimination; oral examination; informal voice assessment; hearing test; receptive vocabulary; basic information such as name and address; descriptive speech noting parts of speech used; informal assessment of fluency; absurd sentences; sound blending; similarities and differences.

A summary of the evaluation is written in duplicate or triplicate. The results are submitted to the classroom teacher, the coordinator, and sometimes the psychologist. A conference is held with the parent unless the parent waives such a requirement. Those persons who must be consulted with and notified of such a conference are the principal, coordinator, teacher, parent, special education teacher, and other persons involved with the child.

Primary language (if other than English) has to be considered among much of our school population. The primary language of the home and the child has to be documented. Some testing, such as articulation, is done in English and the child's primary language to determine whether there are articulation errors in both languages.

3. SLH person does evaluating. Initially the following tests might be used: (1) C. Van Riper (1973), *Predictive Screening Test of Articulation*, (2) E. T. MacDonald (1974), *A Screening Deep Test of Articulation*, (3) Hejna (1955), *Developmental Articulation Test*. Further testing might include: (1) Wepman (1958), *Auditory Discrimination Test*, (2) Zimmerman, Steiner, Evatt (1969),

Preschool Language Scale, (3) *Peabody Picture Vocabulary Test* (Dunn, 1968), (4) for particular problems: certain sub-tests of *Illinois Test of Psycholinguistic Abilities* (Kirk, 1968), (5) audiometric testing.

4. Children who are not identified during a screening may be referred by the teacher, a parent, the nurse, or member of the Special Services Department. The speech pathologists do all the evaluations of the children referred for suspected communicative handicaps.

The testing instruments vary. We will begin with the pure tone audiometric evaluation and, or, impedance testing to determine whether or not the child has any kind of hearing acuity problems. Some of the more frequently used tests include: *Picture Articulation Test,* Pendergast, 1969; the *Fisher-Logeman Test of Articulation Competency,* 1971; or the *Goldman-Fristoe Test of Articulation,* 1969. The following tests may also be used: The *Wepman Discrimination Test,* 1958; the *Goldman-Fristoe-Woodcock Auditory Selective Attention Test,* 1970; the *Goldman-Woodcock-Fristoe Auditory Memory Test,* 1970; the *Goldman-Fristoe-Woodcock Sound/Symbol Test,* 1970; the *Token Test,* DeRenzi and Vignalo, 1962; the *Boehm Test of Basic Concepts,* 1971; the *Peabody Picture Vocabulary Test,* Dunn, 1965; the Auditory Sub-tests of the *Illinois Test of Psycholinguistic Abilities,* Kirk, 1968; the Carrow test for *Auditory Comprehension of Language,* 1973; and the *Northwestern Syntax Screening Test,* Lee, 1969. We also use the *Assessment of Children's Language Comprehension Test,* Foster, 1969; the *Utah Test of Language Development*, Mechan, 1967; and the *Wiig-Semel tests of Linguistic Concepts,* 1976.

D. COULD YOU DESCRIBE THE CLASS, THE CLASSROOM, THE EQUIPMENT AND FURNISHINGS, AND THE SCHEDULING PROCEDURES?

1. Classroom organization:

    Location—space is rented from school districts

Levels	No. of Students	Usual Age Range
Preschool	6	3 - 6
Primary	6	6 - 9
Middle	8	9 - 12
Junior High	8	12 - 14
High School	8	14 - 21

Each class of six pupils has assigned to it a language teacher specialist and a full-time communication teacher aide. Ancillary staff available to the teacher are language program specialist, psychologist, nurse, audiologist, and occasionally a remedial speech therapist.

Classroom furnishings, organization, and scheduling are largely left up to the teacher. The pupils are bused to their school site and attend class five and one-half hours. The special classes are located at regular schools and at minimum allow for integration during lunch and playground. Pupils who the teacher deems ready to integrate, attend regular class for part of the day.

Teachers are responsible for meeting the total needs of the student and teach academics as well as language and speech. Junior and senior-high classes are career education oriented and some students at the senior-high level spend part of their school time in a job situation.

A remedial physical education teacher serves preschool, primary, and middle grade students approximately one half-hour per day.

Instruction is largely individualized, and geared to reach each pupil's unique needs. Cross-age tutors from the regular classes are often used as well as the teacher and aide.

2. Since my services are itinerant, I have many classes usually one half-hour in length twice weekly. Many of the children are seen in groups of three to four, but some are seen individually because of their communication problems and ages. The "classroom" facilities vary from school to school. Usually these are classrooms or conference rooms with oversize tables and chairs. Filing facilities are in the school office. No storage areas can be located in the rooms used for therapy.

Almost all equipment for therapy is obtained from the cooperative office. Such equipment is kept in a school office or at my home when not in use. Quite an extensive amount is available including tests, therapy materials, audiometers. Much of what I use is my own, such as teaching materials and a tape recorder. We have been fortunate in that equipment we have requested has either been available or has been ordered for us through the cooperative office.

Scheduling is done by me and is a hassle! Since I innovated the practice here of conducting therapy twice weekly in each school building, I have found it necessary to compromise and change groupings of children a number of times. The times to be avoided in scheduling include Title I Reading and Resource Room sessions. It has been necessary to schedule some students during physical education, music, and crafts. Generally the teachers have been cooperative.

Each building has been serviced twice weekly except for some students in the kindergartens and junior high school. The buildings having the greater number of students in need receive the longer half of the school day (morning). Usually grouping is based upon the nature of the child's problem, particular grade, and age.

3. The class is made up of four or less students who are the same age or grade placement. Some individual work is done. Size of group is often determined by size of room. The room itself is usually a storage closet, empty regular classroom, library, or whatever isn't in daily use by other persons in the school. Chairs and tables of appropriate size are usually available. Each SLH person has a tape recorder.

In regard to scheduling, the children to receive therapy are listed in groups as the SLH person would like to see them. Then the SLH person talks with teachers and attempts to work out a mutually agreeable schedule. Usually this plan works.

4. We look at each child individually and try to provide as much therapy as is needed. We use a combination of the itinerant and the intensive cycle scheduling. For example, I am scheduled at Jones Elementary School on Monday

morning, Thursday morning, and Tuesday and Wednesday afternoons. This allows me to see a child on Monday, Tuesday, Wednesday, and Thursday if it is needed. As the child shows progress, I can drop him or her to three times a week, two times a week, and eventually visits can be phased out completely.

Furnishings meet state standards; we exceed any maximum standards for equipment. We have a Language Master, with both long and short cards; three pure tone, one pure tone bone and one impedance. We have an auditory trainer for working with children who have hearing problems and for children who need to work on discrimination. We also have tape recorders and a cassette library on some of our students. Through the Media Center we have access to video taping equipment which we may use with voice or stuttering cases and with the preschool language program. We also have a very extensive professional library and materials center to go along with our different tests.

We have tried to correlate most of the tests with available remedial materials for the classroom teacher's use.

The scheduling, whether individual or group, is determined by the needs of the children.

E. WHAT IS THE RATIONALE OF YOUR PROGRAM?

1. The County SLD/A program provides special day classes for students who exhibit severe language disorders as outlined in the state's Administrative Code, Title V Regulations.

2. This is governed largely by both a state mandate which went into operation for the 1976-77 school year, and now a Federal mandate. It requires special services for all school children identified as handicapped with emphasis upon individual rights, due process, primary language, and cultural background. Primary throughout is the requirement for staffing with school personnel and parents involved. The least restrictive environment for the child is stressed. A great deal depends upon parental permission and cooperation.

The rationale is to provide a program which meets the needs of those students identified as having communication problems. It also involves consultant and informative kinds of service, such as conferring with school personnel and parents and providing some in-service training for staff members.

3. The program exists to identify, evaluate, and provide therapy for children with SLH problems in district schools K-12 including children in a school for the TMR. The therapy is directed toward teaching children to attain a standard of speech-language skills that enables them to function satisfactorily in other areas of their school life.

4. Our philosophy is to accept each individual child as he or she is and to provide opportunities to learn effective communication skills so as to insure his or her rightful place in society. In keeping with this philosophy, our program is designed to give the most communicatively handicapped child the highest priority, scheduling him or her intensively, and reducing the caseload as needed to assure the most effective program of remediation.

F. WHAT ABOUT REEVALUATIONS?

1. Each student in the SLD/A program is brought before an admission and dismissal committee meeting at the close of every school year. The following guidelines apply to all students;

 1) Students must have performance intelligence measures within the past three years. Those who do not have a qualifying performance test within the normal range when admitted to the program will be recommended for a performance test. 2) Students must have formal language testing within the past two years. Previous language tests with scores falling below two standard deviations will be recommended for retesting. Reading and math test results below the normal range will be recommended for retesting. 3) Students must have reading, or math measures. 4) All students whom teachers consider at this time to be possible candidates for dismissal at the end of the year will be recommended for complete testing. 5) Teachers make any other recommendations that they may have and may suggest additional testing.

2. The mandate requires reevaluation every three years of children enrolled in special education programs. Reevaluation procedures are the same as those used for reevaluation.

Also required are reviews once each semester or whenever requested by the parents. The results are to be submitted to the parents. Such reviews amount to informal assessments of therapy—what has been accomplished and what remains to be done.

3. There is continuous evaluation in therapy. Reevaluation is done: a) when in the course of therapy it seems advisable, b) always at the end of the year, c) at the beginning of the next school term after the summer therapy break, d) periodically, for children not active in the program who are being watched.

4. We reevaluate the child the year following dismissal from therapy and usually one more evaluation is made six months later. Thus a child is followed after dismissal for about a year and a half before we deactivate the folder.

G. IF IT IS PART OF YOUR PROGRAM,
HOW DO YOU FOSTER RETURN
TO THE REGULAR CLASS?

1. Since the SLD/A classes are located at regular elementary schools, integration of SLD/A pupils is widely encouraged in any activity which the teacher feels they could succeed. When an SLD/A student is returned to the district into a regular class, that student is assigned to an itinerant aphasia teacher specialist who works with the pupil several hours each week at the student's neighborhood school upgrading language skills as well as aiding the pupil's academic achievement.

2. This is not an integral part of the therapy program. If a student has progressed to the point of dismissal from therapy, he or she is checked periodically during several school years following dismissal.

As a student has made progress, he or she may then be seen for therapy fewer times per week or perhaps once every two weeks.

3. Does not apply to this program.

4. This is not applicable.

H. WHAT ARE THE ADVANTAGES AND DISADVANTAGES OF YOUR PROGRAM?

1. *Advantages*

Our program is fairly well-funded and ample equipment and supplies are available for use by teachers. The county has written a special education curriculum to use as a guide in dealing with Special Education students. The communication aide is a full-time employee and works a six-hour day. The class size is especially advantageous and aids in individualizing instruction. The preschool diagnostic class serves well to ready youngsters for testing and test results are usually deemed reliable. Various ancillary staff are made available to assist teachers when the need arises.

Disadvantages

Classes are located at various sites—two to four classes to a site and twenty to twenty-five classes are under a principal. The sites and classes are spread apart geographically and sometimes communication channels are not clear and open. Teachers must deal not only with their own SLD/A principal but also with the principal of the building in which they are located. Since the program falls within a large county government and the state is now requiring so much accountability, there is a huge amount of paperwork required of the teachers and this seems to take time away from reaching the students.

2. *Advantages*

a) Working out a cooperative offers the opportunity to share and become informed about other special services programs within the county, such as physical therapy, the hearing-impaired, and psychological services. b) Without guidelines or an effective program previously, it has been possible to set up the program the way I want it except for the restrictions of the mandates and the limitations of number of days contracted by each school district for such services. One example is that of scheduling students twice a week instead of the previous schedule of once a week or once every two weeks. c) Among the Special Education staff, there is a sharing of information and concern about the children served. Each of the staff members is respected for the expertise he or she can provide. There is a strong team approach particularly in regard to children with multiple handicaps.

Disadvantages

a) The mandates generate a great amount of paperwork. A considerable portion of time is spent on that instead of on providing therapy. b) Because of the use of Spanish and Indian tongues by parents, it is difficult to explain the program to them and gain their cooperation. c) The mandates make the same requirements of Speech and Language Therapy as of every other area of Special Education without consideration for the nature of the program, the number of students involved, and the role of the speech-language pathologist in diagnosing, consulting, and providing treatment. d) There are no state guidelines for Speech and Language Therapy programs regarding caseload, frequency of therapy sessions, limits on populations served, and facilities. e) State funding is based upon the number enrolled in the therapy program; thus, administrators can use this to pressure the therapist into providing services for larger numbers of students than would otherwise be considered practical.

3. *Advantages*

a) We deliver service to a large number of children who need it. Many of them would not otherwise get the service. b) Language gains are great with use of conversational experiences/language stimulation with urban children who don't get it at home. c) Teachers often report that certain children are able to do better work in reading after having had speech therapy.

Disadvantages

a) Lack of adequate working space on a continuing basis. b) Lack of adequate furnishings such as locked storage cabinet. Often the room is piled with junk. c) SLH person is classified as a teacher, not a specialist (such as social worker, psychologist) yet is often expected to play role of specialist. d) It is often difficult for SLH person to communicate the nature of his or her responsibility to school personnel—particularly administrators. e) Lack of opportunity to take advantage of many continuing education programs that are offered during the school year.

4. *Advantages*

Probably the most important asset we have is the diversity of interest within the staff itself. By this, I mean each member has a particular area in which he or she excels, and we each recognize each other's strengths. When we are involved in the diagnostic evaluation, and we find that we have a child who is exhibiting a problem that falls within the expertise of a colleague, we do not hesitate to call that individual to our school, and ask that person to help in the evaluation. We can then consult and hold a staffing. When we have in-service meetings, members of the staff attend workshops and come back and report findings. I feel that we have a dynamic program because we have a dynamic staff. Members of our staff participate actively in national and local professional organizations. We have become involved in research and we have published our research findings. We have an early childhood strategies program in our kindergartens which is an adjunct to our identification program. A diagnostic-educational team concept is utilized and we consult with the classroom teacher, the school psychologist, the parents, and, in many cases, the children. We have received over $60,000 in the last seven or eight years for research and development. We have a language program for the communicatively handicapped preschool child which includes a parent guidance program.

Disadvantages

One of the difficulties we face is the amount of time required to comply with the federal mandates. In the long run I think this will be beneficial, but the short-term effect is very constraining. Another disadvantage that results from, perhaps, a lack of emphasis and training at the university level, is that we find ourselves being asked to play the role of a reading consultant. The lack of training and the lack of information about some of the new testing instruments places us at a disadvantage when we consult with the classroom teacher. I am just barely holding my own in this area. Fortunately, there is a member of the staff who has specialized in this area and this has helped all of us. I see us playing a "catch-up" game in the area of helping the classroom teacher with reading and spelling problems.

CONCLUSION

In this chapter we have looked at various school speech language and hearing programs. Included are speech language improvement and development programs, high-school programs, vocational school programs, summer programs, as well as programs in Arizona, California, Delaware, and Ohio.

The needs of the school and the community, the educational policies of the local school system, the capabilities of the staff—all these matters play a part in determining the kinds of programs that can be included in each school system.

11 | *program maintenance and professional responsibilities*

INTRODUCTION

The time to start preparing for the future is today. This chapter will focus on activities which will affect the future of the programs and the persons involved in them.

Accountability is an important aspect of any school program and maintaining an efficient and effective record and report system is one method by which this can be accomplished.

Research has been a long-neglected aspect of the school speech, language, and hearing program. Today, however, many school clinicians are conducting research in the schools and in the future more will be doing so. The use of computers in both research and record and report systems will be discussed in this chapter.

The school clinician has a professional responsibility to keep abreast of new ideas, new research, and new developments by maintaining professional affiliations, by enrolling in continuing education programs, by participating in workshops, and by reading professional books, journals, and other publications.

Finally, what is the role of the school speech, language, and hearing specialist in teacher organizations? This issue, along with others, will be discussed in this chapter.

RECORD AND REPORT SYSTEMS
AND ACCOUNTABILITY

There are good reasons for maintaining a comprehensive record and report system in the language, speech, and hearing program in the school system. While it has always been done by school clinicians, the reasons today are somewhat more compelling and the goals of such a system are more inclusive.

Public Law 94-142, the Education for all Handicapped Children Act of 1975, places a tremendous emphasis on accountability in the school system. Accountability has made it urgent that special services in the schools develop a method of reliably and accurately reporting data on handicapped children.

Historically, the school clinician maintained written records of the work done in the school in order to inform, to keep track of the services provided, to provide continuity both to the program and to the child's progress in therapy, to serve as a basis for research, to coordinate the child's therapy with the child's school program, and to serve as a basis for program needs and development. These reasons remain valid, however there are additional reasons why an accounting system is needed today. One reason is a legal one. Many states at the present time have licensing for speech pathologists and audiologists. This factor implies a legal responsibility and the need for accountability becomes greater (Caccamo, 1973).

Another reason, according to Caccamo, is in the fiscal area. Several court decisions in education have carried financial damages for failure of the school to teach the child to read. The precedence for money damages in this type of case has already been set. Also in the fiscal area, with the increasing competition for tax dollars, government agencies are requiring statements of accountability prior to fund giving. Local, federal, and state agencies want to know what results are being obtained for the tax money spent.

O'Toole poses some questions for school clinicians in regard to accountability:

How appropriate is speech therapy for each student in your program? Does each one belong in therapy? Have you established goals which, if accomplished, will make a difference? Is therapy time so well used as to justify taking students away from their academic subjects? Do you know how much progress each of your cases is making? Is that recorded? Are you aware of the rate of change? If progress is very slow or nonexistent, are you seeking additional help? How many cases have you followed through either to complete remediation or to the greatest degree of compensation that can be expected? If not very many, why not? Are you using therapy time as efficiently as possible? Is your coordination time justifiable because it is being used for the ultimate benefit of your student? Are you making use of all the knowledge and resources available? Are you moving children along as fast as they can go, or only as fast as is comfortable for you? Are you adapting to student needs, or are they suiting yours? Does your immediate supervisor understand what you do and the type of students you can and should see in therapy? Does he understand that if results are expected, the quality as well as the quantity of therapy is important? (1971, p. 24-25.)

In addition to the impetus added by Public Law 94-142 for record and report keeping, it makes good sense for the clinician to keep an account of a child's progress in therapy simply because the clinician is dealing with a large number of children and it would be impossible to remember all of the facts and details pertinent to each one of them.

PROGRAM RECORDS

In addition to keeping records on each child, the school clinician will need to keep program records related to the program. The American Speech-Language-Hearing Association has developed a prototype system known as the *Comprehensive Assessment and Service Evaluation Information System* (CASE) (Pikus, 1976). The prototype was developed for language, speech, and hearing programs in schools and describes a formal system for collecting, storing, and retrieving essential information categorized under the following processes: referral, screening, diagnostic assessment, placement decisions, intervention programs, coordination of service delivery, and program management. One of the important aspects of the program is that it has computer potential. This would make it important to a large school system or a state or a local educational agency interested in developing a data system which would aid in determining the actions necessary to improve the program, analyze operating costs, facilitate research, furnish information on which to base future program planning, improve record keeping practices, and free the school pathologist for more productive activities.

The CASE system is in the process of being developed and field tested, both as a record keeping system and as a computer-assisted program. Information about the system may be obtained by writing to: The School Services Program, American Speech-Language-Hearing Association, 10801 Rockville Road, Rockville, Maryland 20852.

One of the problems in record and report systems is the quick retrieval of information regarding the status, disposition, and intervention of individual students as well as the collective data that must be recorded in order to report program statistics. Wing (1975) developed a concise form to help itinerant school clinicians who are responsible for managing caseloads of between 75 and 150 children throughout a school year. Wing reports that while the caseloads, exclusive of mass screenings, have been reduced in recent years, there is the increasing demand for accurate record keeping, case management reporting, and statistical data being placed on school clinicians for accountability to school administrators, boards of education, and state departments of education. Figure 11-1 shows the data recording form used in the Great Falls, Montana, school speech, language, and hearing program.

Figure 11-1   Data recording form for speech and hearing services.

Student's Name	Grade	Referral Date and Source	Evaluation Dates	Outside Referral	Classification	Etiology	Severity	Therapy—Dates	Prescriptive	Program—Dates	Resource Room	Ongoing Assessment	Data	No Program	Waiting List	Parent Conferences	Teacher Conferences	Recommendation
						Cases					Disposition							Recommendation
Jones, Johnny	3	9/14 T	9/5 9/21	1	F	II		12/4 3/18 3/2 5/25						10/1 12/4	1	III	Reevaluate in Sept.
Smith, Billy	1	9/16 T	9/18	1	I	I					12/3 2/16 4/7						IIII	
Adams, Nancy	3	9/20 T	9/22 ENT 9/30 10/8 10/6	2	A	II		10/20 1/15							IIII	III	Reevaluate in March.
Monroe, Brian	K	9/20 Cl	9/22 Phys 9/26 10/7 10/5	1 2	B	III		10/15 5/25							IIII	III II	Continue next year.

Referral source: T (teachers), Cl (clinician). *Outside referral:* ENT (ear, nose, and throat specialist), phys. (physician), sch. psyl. (school psychologist), and so on. *Classification:* I, articulation; 2, phonation; 3, rhythm; 4, language; 5, no problem (any appropriate classifications may be used, listed in order of significance). *Etiology:* A, organic pathology; B, cleft palate; C, cerebral palsy; D, mental retardation; E, hearing loss; F, dental anomalies; G, emotional factors; H, environmental factors; I, developmental factors; J, undetermined (any appropriate classifications may be used, listed in order of significance). *Severity:* I, mild, II, moderate; III, severe. *Note:* slash marks are used to indicate change of status in any category. This form can be stenciled on standard 8½x11" paper with spaces to accommodate seven to nine student names.

In addition to assisting in the overall managing of a school program, there are other areas in which a record keeping system can aid the school clinician. One area is the therapy itself. Journot's *A Tabulated Accountability Plan for Speech Therapy Services* (1973) presents four tabulation sheets geared to determining cost of any portion of a specific language and speech program of therapy, pinpointing areas where supervision may be needed, as well as evaluating therapy goals and methods. The amount of time spent each day on direct services and other activities can also be tabulated on one of the monthly report forms. Annual report forms are also presented.

Journot's tabulation forms are designed to be used by clinicians who use Van Riper's traditional steps for articulation therapy, Irwin and Weston's paired stimuli approach, McLean's stimulus control techniques, or any other individual therapy plan for articulation, language, rhythm, or voice therapy.

accountability through cost accounting

One way of looking at accountability is in relation to cost accounting. When the cost of a product or service is known, it is then possible to predict the cost of producing similar products or services. Applying the model to speech-language and hearing services, one might consider this principle in relation to the various aspects of therapy, program management, and the instructional materials used. One of the first persons to apply the cost accounting method to speech therapy services was Mowrer (1972), who used it in an analysis of the cost of correcting speech misarticulations. Mowrer hypothesized that the use of a cost accounting system might make it possible to determine the economic value of different training programs such as programmed instruction, group therapy, and various time-schedule programs of instruction. Mowrer felt that the major goal should not be to provide therapy services at the lowest possible cost, but to provide the highest caliber services for a given amount of money.

Research projects to evaluate several aspects of a school district's program in speech and language (Work, 1975 and 1976) through the process of cost accounting have been reported. The first project dealt with the cost of services provided by an itinerant staff while the second project dealt with an analysis of instructional materials.

An analysis of the data in the first project (Work, 1975) revealed that the itinerant program cost was less than anticipated and less than that of most clinic or private therapy programs in the same geographic area. Another finding indicated that further data are needed for school services utilizing different delivery-of-service models.

The project dealing with the evaluation of materials and their effectiveness in clinical intervention developed a prototype that could be used with phonological disorders as well as other types of disorders. The study was undertaken in order to assist the school clinician who is required to answer questions and seek information on the large amount of commercially developed instructional materials. Questions facing clinicians include: How effective are the materials? Do clinicians choose appropriate materials for the type of therapy planned? Are materials related to performance objectives and therapy goals?

A catalog describing the project and the evaluation procedures is available through the School Board of Broward County, Florida. The catalog contains information on twenty pieces of material analyzed, publishers, costs, descriptions, pictures, effectiveness ratings, relationships to objectives, and applications of descriptor terms (Work, 1976).

setting up and maintaining
a system of records and reports

A school clinician going into a program that has been established will probably find a record and report system already set up and in operation, while a clinician who starts a program will have to develop a system of records and reports. In both instances it will be necessary to continuously evaluate and monitor the system and make the necessary changes in the forms. The confidentiality of information makes it imperative that the storage of records and reports be a major consideration. Security is important and the policies regarding the security measures should be established and in writing. The same is true of the availability of such records and reports to other school personnel, administrators, other clinicians on the staff, and parents of children enrolled. Policies should be in writing and should be adhered to once agreed upon.

The abundance of records and reports essential to a program should be taken into account on the school clinician's weekly schedule. One of the most time-consuming tasks facing the clinician is filling out reports, keeping up to date on information recorded, and filing as well as retrieving material. The task is a daily one for much of the information, and when weekly, monthly, or yearly reports are involved, a large chunk of time is needed. Some of the work can be assigned to an aide and some of it might be given to the school secretary, however there are usually many demands on their time as well. A large program may need some secretarial help, either on a part-time or full-time basis depending on the size and scope of the program. Most of it, however, will be up to the school clinician to do and if this is the case, scheduled time should be allotted for it.

Most school systems provide a central office for the school clinicians and in this way a uniform filing system, retrieval system, recording system, and security system can be utilized. A central office system has another advantage in that secretarial or aide assistance can be pooled.

School clinicians will have to abide by the policies of the school system in regard to how long records and reports on individual children should be retained, which records should be retained, and how records are transferred from school to school as well as from school system to school system. Statistical information in relation to program management and incidence figures can be very useful to clinicians in planning future program trends and serving as a basis for research. The retaining of this type of information might be decided by the school clinical staff. Provisions for the storage of such information would have to be made.

In an effort to improve information systems for the school speech, language, and hearing programs, a Task Force on Data Collection and Information Systems (Healey, 1973) was appointed to study the issue. Among recommendations made to school systems for planning such a system, the following steps were considered essential:

1. Formulate a school-wide policy.
2. Develop a general framework for planning.
3. Determine a policy relating to information gathering and distribution.
4. Provide a clearinghouse and a meaningful circulation system.
5. Assure checks for control of information.
6. Protect individual privacy and insure confidentiality.
7. Develop uniform nomenclature.
8. Select computer language if necessary.
9. Determine what output is desired.
10. Insure accuracy and quality of the data input.
11. Determine the categories of information needed for measurement.
12. Ascertain the action that will be taken once the data have been collected.

The task force also suggested an outline for basic data collection which could be adapted to educational and professional agencies at the local, state, and national levels. (See Figure 11-2.) The school speech, language, and hearing clinician might consider this outline as a framework for developing the record and report forms necessary to the program. An outline such as this also could be used as a framework for evaluating clinician behavior in the clinical process as well as analyzing the total program management data in order to effect changes in program design and practices.

RESEARCH

The need for research related to school programs in speech-language and hearing programs has been clearly established. Pronovost et al. (1961) outlined priorities for future research. The topics of greatest concern were: (1) the collection of longitudinal normative data on articulation, voice, and fluency, (2) comparative studies of program organization, and (3) comparative studies on the use of different remedial procedures with children of various ages presenting various different types of disorders.

Brett (1976), in a report of the Public School Caucus, cited as one of the eleven goals of the caucus attention to research needs in the schools. Fisher (1977), in "An Open Letter to ASHA Members Employed in the Schools," outlined ten critical issues affecting the School Services Program of ASHA. One of the issues was the need to promote research efforts in schools with universities.

Unquestionably a fertile field for possible research studies, the school programs have produced little in the past in the way of research. There are a number of possible reasons given by school clinicians. Among them are the lack of time, the lack of funding, the lack of support by school boards, the lack of cooperation by university staff members, and the lack of interest by journals in publishing research done by school clinicians.

In recent years there has been a change and more research has been produced both by school clinicians and in areas related to school programs and therapy.

In some states, Ohio, for example, Research and Development Units are funded through the State Department of Special Education in an effort to encourage research by school clinicians (Gross, 1972). A school pathologist may apply for a full-time or part-time unit for the purpose of evaluating new instructional methodology and, or, alternative procedures related to speech, language, and hearing services. If a school district wishes to apply for such a unit they must submit a written proposal to the Division of Special Education and the written authorization must be obtained before implementation of the project. An application for an *R and D* unit must include: (1) rationale for the project, (2) definition of the target population, (3) projected staffing ratios, (4) description of facilities to be used, (5) list of materials and equipment, and list of measurable objectives at the administrative, program, therapist, and child levels. A final requirement calls for an annual evaluation of the objectives to be submitted by July 1 in accordance with the format provided by the Division of Special Education.

The R and D units must have the approval of the school administration and many of them are carried on in cooperation with university staff members.

The publication, *Language, Speech and Hearing Services in Schools,* since its inception in 1970, has published numerous articles on research carried on in school systems and related to school programs. Many other articles point out specific needs for research, and as school clinicians and school systems become more aware of the role of research in program improvement, the opportunities

Figure 11-2   Recommended Outline for Data Collection Systems

Demographic Data	Program Planning and Management Data

I. Case
  A. Identification
    1. Vital statistics (social security number; birth data; chronological age; sex; grade; parent's name, address, and telephone number)
    2. History (health history of child and family, type of problem, treatment provided or offered)
    3. Referent (name of referral agency— teacher, parents, others; date of referral; history of evaluations)
  B. Diagnostic information
    1. Type of problem
    2. Test administered
    3. Psychological information

Diagnostic information
  Behavior observed (anecdotal records by teacher/clinician)
  Comparative speech behavior
    Formal
      Normative data
      Test of articulation
      Test of language
    Informal
      Estimate of child's ability based upon clinician's experience and training

  C. Educational
    1. Preschool
    2. Regular
    3. Special
  D. Services needed
    1. Screening
    2. Diagnostic
  E. Treatment
    1. Speech
      a. Articulation
      b. Voice
      c. Rhythm
    2. Hearing
      a. Audiological
      b. Rehabilitation audiology
    3. Language
      a. Phonologic
      b. Auditory discrimination
      c. Auditory sequencing
      d. Memory span
      e. Morphologic
      f. Syntax

Figure 11-2   (continued)

Demographic Data	Program Planning and Management Data
II. Clinician	Clinician
A. Current case load	Effectiveness of treatment
B. Waiting list	techniques
C. Attendance records of children	Behavioral objectives
D. Amount of time spent in travel	Criteria for case selection, therapy techniques based on the needs of the child, individualizing instruction (group or individual session, frequency and length of sessions)
III. Program (supervisory)	Program
A. Number of clinicians	Plan for recording and evaluating
B. Number of children to be served	treatment techniques
	Program objectives
	Assessment of clinician and need for continuing education
	Evaluation of progress
	Planning of research
	Long and short-term objectives
IV. Administration (local, state, federal)	Administration
A. Child-clinician ratio	
B. Statistical summary	Cost benefit analysis
	Pattern of expenditures
C. Dissemination	
D. Conversion to ADP	
E. Projected population growth patterns	Projected need for services
	Projected need for facilities
F. Projected program growth	
G. Facilities available	

From *Language, Speech and Hearing Services in Schools*, April 1973, pp. 62-63.

for research by school clinicians are expanding.

Pronovost (1961) pointed out that research by school clinicians is not the only answer. Some of the research topics are of a scope which would require full-time research workers, research coordinators, and a central agency for reporting research in progress. Through the creation of a *data bank* and the use of standardized forms for reporting details of programs and the children with the disorders, much valuable information could be collected which would be useful in resolving many problems and providing information on the basis of which hypotheses could be formulated and tested.

School speech-language and hearing pathologists in many areas of the United States are cooperating in research projects which are national in scope. Through the Bureau of Education for the Handicapped, the School Services Program of ASHA is engaged in a study entitled, "A Normative Service Cost Analysis Model for Language, Speech and Hearing Programs in the Schools." School personnel are asked to provide information on the percentage of the population that receive the service, personnel who provide the service, number of times the service is provided, and the time needed to provide the service. The information will be computerized and interfaced with budget information obtained from schools in order to obtain a cost analysis of program service in school districts (Healey and Dublinske, 1977).

Another federally funded research project was completed by the Bureau of Education for the Handicapped (BEH) in the Los Angeles Unified School District, and concerned the condition of hearing aids worn by school children. The study indicated that audiological services are necessary for hearing handicapped children to receive appropriate special education and related services (Healey and Dublinske, 1978).

A study of prevalence data was initiated in 1977 with funds provided by BEH. The study has been conducted on information related to major handicapping conditions with specific attention given to the prevalence of communicative handicaps. Information was submitted through various state education agencies. The plans projected the total number of handicapped children in the United States in twelve categorical areas. According to Healey and Dublinske (1978):

> "The information from the literature and the state plans will be analyzed and presented on a prevalence chart that can be used to make comparative studies of the data and determine the future professionals needed in speech pathology and audiology."

The school clinician of the future will undoubtedly be involved in research on the local level, the state level, or as part of a national research project. The questions are everywhere and the need to find answers is urgent. The questions of the school clinician in Mississippi may be the same ones asked by the clinician in Montana. Not only is the search for answers important, but equally important is the need to exchange professional information. By recording data on standardized forms the information can then be computerized and interfaced with data collected and recorded in other geographical areas. The use of computers has already been proven to be effective in speech, language, and hearing, and will undoubtedly continue to grow as a valuable method of storing, retrieving, and displaying data.

THE FUTURE—
AND YOUR PLACE IN IT

The school speech-language and hearing clinician is one of the most visible members of the profession. The implementation of Public Law 94-142 has literally placed the school clinician on the front line in providing speech, language, and hearing services to children and is serving as a catalyst to improve existing programs as well as to initiate new programs from early childhood through early adulthood. The education of the school clinician does not terminate with the granting of a college degree or even with the attainment of a state license or the Certificate of Clinical Competence from the American Speech-Language-Hearing Association. The education continues throughout the professional life of an individual. This is part and parcel of what being a professional means.

How does one keep up to date with all that is going on in the field of communication disorders? To be sure, it is not an easy task but there are ways by which the professional person may continually seek to improve skills and increase knowledge.

organizations

One way is to affiliate with professional organizations. The American Speech-Language-Hearing Association, its state associations as well as local affiliates, hold professional meetings, publish professional journals and newsletters, and provide an opportunity for the speech members of the profession to meet together and discuss, both formally and informally, matters of importance.

Students may wish to affiliate with the National Student Speech-Language-Hearing Association through the many chapters located on university campuses. This organization is an affiliate of ASHA, publishes a journal, holds meetings, and provides professional stimulation.

The national as well as state and local speech, language, and hearing professional organizations are concerned with such things as research, the study of human communication and its disorders, the investigation of therapeutic and diagnostic procedures, and the maintenance of high standards of performance. The professional organizations are also interested in the dissemination of information among its members and the upholding of high ethical standards to protect the consumer. There are other benefits to be derived from affiliating with a professional organization. Such a group can provide a forum for discussion of issues and can speak with a concerted voice on matters of professional interest. If the professional individual wishes to have a voice in decisions and opinions, the best way to do so is through a professional organization on the state, local, or national level.

The American Speech-Language-Hearing Association is the nationally recognized accrediting organization. Through the Education Training Board it accredits university training programs and through the Professional Services Board service programs are accredited. Individual members are also accredited.

There are a number of other organizations with which the school clinician may wish to become acquainted or join. These organizations are listed in Appendix 3.

teacher organizations

A decision faced by many school pathologists is whether or not to join the local teacher organizations which are involved in negotiations with school boards, grievance procedures, and collective bargaining. The question becomes one of identifying with the classroom teachers or negotiating individually with boards of education. Part of the dilemma stems from our own identity crisis which is reflected in part by our indecision as to what we call ourselves.

The issues dealt with by a teachers' organization are not the same as those dealt with by a professional organization such as ASHA or a state speech-language and hearing association. Professional organizations are not collective bargaining units. The decision to join a teachers' organization must be an individual one based on the school clinician's assessment of the local situation. According to Johns (1974):

> A strong local teachers' organization can offer representation before the school board, county board, or state legislature; communications including action reports, news releases, and media coverage for educational problems; professional services and developments such as negotiations with the school board (concerning salary), arbitration of grievances, attainment of better employment conditions, and greater voice in curriculum matters; and such advantages as tax-sheltered annuities, notary service, legal service or legal defense, housing placement, civic representation, and discounts with local merchants.

Gross and Fichter (1970) pointed out that however good the professional organizations are, school speech-language pathologists and audiologists are still employed by boards of education and must work within the framework of the schools. Fichter and Gross posed several questions which school clinicians need to evaluate critically. They are:

1. Who negotiates with boards of education for school clinicians' salaries, working conditions, secretarial help, released time for professional meetings, etc.?
2. Will teacher associations continue to offer membership to school clinicians when in some places they have excluded school psychologists, attendance officers, supervisors and administrators?
3. If the school pathologists are paid more than classroom teachers will teacher associations argue a clinician's cause with zeal even if they accept his membership?
4. Should a clinician honor an administrator's request to man a classroom during a work stoppage if he is not a member of the teacher association? If clinicians ally themselves with the administration, can they expect the future cooperation of teachers?
5. If school clinicians ally themselves with teachers, cannot a school administration realistically expect clinicians to perform such duties as playground or lunchroom assistance?

6. If strikes occur, can state and national associations provide assistance to a clinician in a local school district? Do these organizations have a position concerning strikes? Can they impose sanctions? Do they provide legal assistance? In fact, do they even have a stand on these issues?

The unmistakable trend toward collective bargaining in the public sector makes it clear that the school speech-language pathologists and audiologists need to develop procedures for negotiations.

continuing education

Another way in which the school speech-language and hearing pathologist keeps up to date on professional matters is through continuing education. Continuing education takes the form of workshops, short courses, seminars, mini-seminars, in-service training courses, professional meetings highlighted by competent speakers, university courses, extension courses, televised courses, and presentations via film and videotape. Continuing education can be carried on by a structured program or on a more informal basis. Continuing education is a lifelong process for an individual expecting to remain accountable and qualified. It is a process by which one keeps one's skills and knowledge up to date.

Continuing education is not only necessary to the individual currently practicing, but also helps those persons who interrupt their professional lives and wish to reenter at a later date.

Continuing education is not the responsibility of any one institution or agency but should represent the coordinated efforts of a number of groups. Universities cannot offer extension courses in a geographical area unless there is an expressed need concerning the content area of such a course. In order for the university to plan for such courses, the need should be expressed to the university staff by the school clinicians. By the same token, universities should be willing to offer courses at a time that would be convenient to the school clinicians and in a location that would be accessible to them.

School administrators need to understand that speech-language pathologists and audiologists need to have *professional days* for professional improvement just as classroom teachers do.

The recent emphasis on professional accountability has added much impetus to the increase in continuing education opportunities. Accountability, however, is a two-sided coin. The school pathologist is accountable to the school administration, the children being served and their parents, and to professional colleagues. These individuals, in turn, must allow the school pathologist opportunities to take advantage of the professional enrichment being offered through continuing education. Neither the school pathologist, nor the persons to whom that individual is accountable, must abuse the privileges.

publications and resources

As the roles of the school speech-language pathologist and audiologist expand, there is a need to keep abreast of current information. This is particularly crucial for school clinicians working in remote areas or persons located in areas where there is no access to academic libraries, medical libraries, or even public libraries. School libraries usually do not have publications pertinent to a school pathologist's needs.

Throughout the United States regional resource centers have been established. For example, in Ohio SERRC (Special Education Regional Resource Center) is a statewide network system with regional centers (Instructional Resource Centers) which have among their services the collecting and distributing of special education materials as well as providing information about the materials. (Brickell, 1974) They also help school personnel in creating new materials when commercially produced products are not available. Information is provided by the IRC newsletters concerning the services and materials available.

The publications of the American Speech-Language-Hearing Association are available to the members of the organization. They are the *Journal of Speech and Hearing Disorders,* the *Journal of Speech and Hearing Research, ASHA,* and *Language, Speech and Hearing Services in Schools.* (The latter is sent only upon request to members, and to others by subscription.)

Public libraries in almost all communities have an interlibrary loan service whereby library materials are made available by one library to another for use by an individual. In addition to books, materials may include audiotape, videotape, film, and microfilm. The community public library can be of great assistance to the school clinician and librarians are always helpful in obtaining materials. The school clinician may want to visit the library and find out what kinds of services are available.

There are abstracting and indexing services available to interested speech-language pathologists and educational audiologists. *dsh Abstracts,* a quarterly published by the American Speech-Language-Hearing Association and Gallaudet College, contains abstracts of current articles on deafness, speech, and hearing disorders from over 400 journals. The annual subscription rate is $20.

Language and Language Behavior Abstracts is published quarterly at a subscription rate of $62, and examines the contents of approximately 1,000 publications for articles to be summarized. The subject categories are speech and language pathology, special education, verbal learning, and psycholinguistics. Subscriptions can be obtained by writing to: P.O. Box 22206, San Diego, Calif. 92122.

The Council for Exceptional Children publishes *Exceptional Child Education Resources (ECER),* a quarterly journal which contains abstracts of books, articles, research, and conference proceedings. An additional service is that of offering reprints of selected computer searches from ECER and ERIC (Educational Resources Information Center). *Resources in Education* is published monthly and contains abstracts of research reports and materials with the exception of journal articles.

Rehabilitation Literature is published monthly by the National Easter Seal Society for Crippled Children and Adults. The subscription rate is $12.50 a year. The publication contains articles, special reports, book reviews, abstracts of current literature in all areas of rehabilitation, as well as events and comments.

A more complete discussion of informational resources can be found in the article, "Informational Services for School Speech-Language Pathologists and Educational Audiologists" by Parker and Montague (1978), in *Language, Speech and Hearing Services in Schools,* April 1978.

Following is a list of publications of interest to the school speech-language pathologist and audiologist. The list is by no means complete, and it should be understood that the subscription rates are subject to change. School clinicians may want to examine the publication prior to subscribing. Some publications will be of interest to other school personnel as well and it might be worthwhile for the school system to subscribe for the teachers' library collection.

SPEECH PATHOLOGY AND AUDIOLOGY (Professional)

Journal of Speech and Hearing Disorders (JSHD); quarterly; $33/yr., $9/issue; Interstate Printers & Publishers Inc., North Jackson St., Danville, Ill. 61832. Essential for the SLH pathologist.

Journal of Speech and Hearing Research; quarterly; same publisher and price as above (JSHD). Free to members of American Speech-Language-Hearing Association.

ASHA; monthly; same as *JSHD.*

ASHA Monographs; supplement to *JSHD*; $3-$4/copy.

Language, Speech & Hearing Services in Schools; quarterly; $13/yr., student $6/yr.; ASHA, 10801 Rockville Pike, Rockville, Maryland. Excellent publication for clinicians in the schools.

Journal of the Academy of Rehabilitative Audiology; biannual; $4/yr. or $2/ issue (non-members); *JARA*, Dept. of Audiology, Wayne State Univ., Detroit, Mich. 48201. Good for information and research on aural rehabilitation.

Journal of the Acoustical Society of America; monthly; Acoustical Society of America, 335 E. 45th St., New York, N.Y. 10017. Mainly a research book in audiology.

Journal of Auditory Research; quarterly; J. Donald Harris, Editor, Box N, Groton, Conn. Good research journal for those interested in the scientific study of hearing.

Journal of Auditory Communication; bimonthly; $74/vol.; Albert Phiebig, P.O. Box 352, White Plains, N.Y. 10602. Contains research from different countries.

British Journal of Disorders of Communication; biannual; $7.50/yr., $4.50/ copy. Very similar to *JSHD*, but with a British viewpoint.

Cerebral Palsy Journal; bimonthly; Institute of Logopedics, Wichita, Kansas 67219. Interesting journal especially for the speech pathologist who works with cerebral palsied individuals.

Journal of Childhood Communicative Disorders; quarterly; $7.50/yr. (non-members); Council for Exceptional Children, 1411 South Jefferson Davis Highway, Bldg. 1, Suite 900, Arlington, Va. 22202. Official journal of the Division for Children with Communication Disorders, CEC. Excellent publication for school pathologists.

Cleft Palate Journal; quarterly; $20/yr., $5/copy; American Cleft Palate Assoc., Waverly Press, Mt. Royal and Guilford Aves., Baltimore, Maryland. Reflects research and clinical activities in the study and treatment of cleft lip and cleft palate.

Laryngoscope; monthly; $33/yr.; Laryngoscope, 517 S. Euclid Ave., St. Louis, Mo. A medical journal.

Journal of Communication Disorders; quarterly; $15/volume; North Holland Publishing Co., P.O. Box 3489, Amsterdam, Holland. A journal of research and information from different countries; interesting and informative journal.

Folia Phoniatrica; bimonthly; $60/yr.; Albert Phiebig, P.O. Box 352, White Plains, N.Y. An international research journal.

EDUCATION

Today's Education; quarterly; $4/yr. (members), $7/yr. (non-members); Mildred Fenner, National Educational Assoc. of the U.S., 1201 16th St. N.W., Washington, D.C. 20036. Official journal of the largest educational association in the U.S. Valuable to anyone in the teaching profession.

Journal of General Education; quarterly; $9/yr.; The Journal of General Education, Pennsylvania St., University Park, Pa. 16802. Filled with articles that are informative and interesting to anyone in the field of teaching.

Journal of Education; quarterly; $10/yr.; Adolph Manoil, Boston Univ. School of Education, 765 Commonwealth Ave., Boston, Mass. Devoted to the in-service education of school teachers. Each issue focuses on a particular theme and is concerned with elementary and secondary education.

Elementary School Journal; monthly; $6/ yr.; University of Chicago Press, 5750 S. Ellis Ave., Chicago, Ill. 60636. Keeps elementary school teachers abreast of new developments and provides them with practical in-service education.

Childhood Education; monthly; $12/yr.; Assoc. for Childhood Education, 3615 Wisconsin Ave., N.W., Washington, D.C. 20016. Directed to both parent and teacher of the child from prenursery through the elementary grades. An all-around education/childhood magazine.

Instructor; monthly; $8/yr.; Ernest Hilton, Instructor Park, Dansville, N.Y. Primarily for elementary school teachers and special staff.

Grade Teacher; monthly; $8/yr.; Harold Littledale, Professional Magazines, 22 W. Putnam Ave., Greenwich, Conn. Provides practical how-to articles for the elementary school teacher. Covers all subjects and activities of the elementary school program.

Reading Teacher; monthly; $15/yr.; Lloyd Kline, International Reading Assoc., Tyre Ave., Newark, Delaware. Deals with all aspects of the teaching of elementary and secondary reading—useful for the teacher who is searching for new methods of improving reading.

Journal of Reading Behavior; quarterly; $12.50/yr.; National Reading Conference, Clemson Univ., Clemson, S.C. 29150. Includes articles of research on reading skills. Some articles pertinent to the field of communication disorders.

Learning; monthly; $10/yr.; Education Today Co., 530 University Ave., Palo Alto, Calif. Directed to elementary and junior-high-school teachers looking for new ideas on how to teach more effectively.

Education Digest; monthly; $6/yr.; Lawrence Prakken Publications, 416 Longshore Dr., Ann Arbor, Mich. Has a broad scope of new information from the elementary grades to graduate school.

Resources in Education; monthly; $22/yr.; Educational Resources Information Center, Supt. of Documents, U.S. Govt. Printing Office, Washington, D.C. 20402. Important for the speech pathologist to keep abreast of the current research in the field of education, speech, and language pathology.

PTA Magazine; monthly; $2.50/yr.; Eva Grant, 700 N. Rush St., Chicago, Ill. 60611. Although not a source of educational information, it is useful and beneficial for parents and teachers.

Journal of Educational Psychology; bimonthly; $12/yr. (member); American Psychological Assoc., 1200 17th St. N.W., Washington, D.C. 20036. Interesting but not pertinent for speech and language pathologists in schools.

SPECIAL EDUCATION

Mental Retardation Journal; bimonthly; $22/yr. (non-members); available to members of American Association on Mental Deficiency; Boyd Printing Co., 49 Sheridan Ave., Albany, N.Y. 12210. Interesting journal, especially for those who will work with the mentally retarded.

Education and Training of the Mentally Retarded; quarterly; $7.50/yr. (non-members); Council for Exceptional Children, 1411 S. Jefferson Davis Highway, Bldg. 1, Suite 900, Arlington, Va. 22202. Journal of the Council for Exceptional Children's Division on Mental Retardation. A combination of theory and practical advice. Could be beneficial to school pathologists, especially in regard to mainstreaming.

Journal of Special Education; quarterly; $12/yr. (students $8.00); Editorial Board, Buttonwood Farms, Inc., 3515 Woodhaven Road, Philadelphia, Pa. 19154. Good for keeping on top of issues pertaining to special education.

Special Children; 10/yr.; P.O. Box 168, Fryeburg, Maine 04037. Covers wide areas from development to fitness to toys, games, and other recreational activities. Excellent for parents of retarded children.

dsh Abstracts (Deafness, Speech and Hearing Abstracts); annually; $13/yr.; Deafness, Speech and Hearing Publications, Gallaudet College, Washington, D.C. 20002. Abstracted periodical literature on deafness and speech disorders.

Volta Review; bimonthly; $25/yr.; The Volta Review, 3417 Volta Place N.W., Washington, D.C. 20007. Helpful articles on teaching communication skills to hearing-impaired children.

Education of the Visually Handicapped; quarterly; $6/yr.; Association for Education of the Visually Handicapped, 1604 Spruce Street, Philadelphia, Pa. 19103. Interesting journal; has a broad scope from research to practice.

May be interesting and helpful to the school pathologist who has a visually handicapped child on caseload.

Exceptional Children; 8/yr.; $12.50; Grace T. Warfield, Council for Exceptional Children, 1411 S. Jefferson Davis Highway, Jefferson Plaza Bldg., Suite 900, Arlington, Va. 22202. Includes articles on curriculum planning, organization of programs and classroom hints, research, mainstreaming, current topics, etc.

Exceptional Parents; bimonthly; $12/yr.; Editorial Board, Box 101, Back Bay Annex, Boston, Mass. 02117. Information bulletin to parents of exceptional children.

Journal of Learning Disabilities; bimonthly; $10/yr.; P. E. Lane Professional Press, 5 N. Wabash Ave., Chicago, Ill. 60602. Represents twenty-four disciplines from anthropology to speech. Each is supported by a member of a large editorial advisory board. For the professional educator and specialist, yet will have interest for the elementary school teacher through college teacher.

SPEECH AND LANGUAGE

Language and Speech; quarterly; $27/yr.; Robert Draper, Kerbihan House, 85 Udney Pk. Road, Teddington, Middlesex, England. A British journal that covers such things as transmission, perception, and patterns of speech. Also includes articles on abnormalities of language and speech.

Journal of Linguistics; semi-annually; $8/yr.; F. R. Palmer, Cambridge University Press, 32 E. 57th Street, New York, N.Y. 10022. Concerned with all branches of linguistics including phonetics. May be useful.

Today's Speech; quarterly; $10/yr.; Eugene Vasilew, State University of New York, Binghamton, N.Y. 13401. Touches on all phases of speech communication, including speech therapy. Also one of the best in its field, but geared more toward speech departments on high-school level.

Journal of Child Language; 3/yr.; $36/yr.; Cambridge University Press, Bentley House, 200 Euston Road, London, England. International research regarding development and usage of language by children.

American Speech; quarterly; $6/yr.; Columbia University Press, 440 W. 110th St., New York, N.Y. 10025. Concerned with language and linguistics. Majority of articles concentrate on pronunciation, dialects, current usage, new words, and phonetics. It could be useful to a speech pathologist who works with dialectical differences.

CHILDREN'S PERIODICALS

Children's Digest; 10/yr.; $6.95; Elizabeth R. Mattheos, Parents' Magazine Enterprises, Inc., 52 Vanderbilt Avenue, New York, N.Y. 10017. A magazine for children ages seven to twelve presented in a format of 100 pages of material. Activities could be utilized in therapy.

Highlights; 11/yr.; $8.50; Dr. and Mrs. Garry C. Myers and Dr. Walter B. Barbe, 2300 W. Fifth Avenue, Columbus, Ohio 43216. Edited to assist the preschool and elementary child to "gain in creativeness, ability to think and reason, and to learn worthy ways of living." Would be good to stimulate language-delayed child.

Child Life; 10/yr.; $6.95; B. R. SerVaas, 1100 Waterway Blvd., Indianapolis, Ind. 46202. For children from prereaders to sixth graders. Equally divided among fiction, arts, crafts, and miscellaneous. The activity pages could be used by a speech pathologist in therapy.

Humpty Dumpty Magazine for Little Children; 10/yr.; $6.95; Thomas Roberts, Parents' Magazine Enterprises, 52 Vanderbilt Avenue, New York, N.Y. 10017. Written and illustrated for children from three to seven years of age. Stories, articles, and features are written to develop reading and vocabulary.

Jack and Jill; 10/yr.; $6.95; Nelle K. Bell, Jack and Jill Publishing Co., 1100 Waterway Blvd., Indianapolis, Ind. 46202. A variety magazine to suit the reading ability and interests of children ages five to twelve. The games, projects, recipes, and picture features could be used by speech pathologists in therapy.

Sesame Street; monthly; $3/yr.; Jane O'Connor, Children's Television Workshop, 1 Lincoln Plaza, New York, N.Y. 10023. Intended for the preschool child. Each issue has four posters, activities, stories, and a parent's guide section. Would be excellent for visual and auditory discrimination and language therapy.

Children's Playmate; 10/yr.; $6.95; Rita A. Cooper, Children's Playmate Magazine, 1100 Waterway Blvd., Indianapolis, Ind. 46207. Directed to ages three to eight, features games and things to make and do.

Kids; 10/yr.; $5.00; Valentine Smith Co., Dept. TB-1, 777 Third Avenue, New York, N.Y. 10017. A magazine written and illustrated by children aged five to thirteen for each other. There are sections on things to make and do. Could give clinician activity ideas for therapy.

Golden Magazine; monthly; $6/yr.; Beth Thomas, Review Publishing Co., 1100 Waterway Blvd., Indianapolis, Ind. 46202. A special form of reading matter for boys and girls from ages nine to thirteen. Includes a "things to do" section which would be helpful to a clinician with older children in therapy.

CONCLUSION

In this chapter we have looked at record and report systems for school programs. Research by the school clinician and about the school program as well as the use of computers in assisting both data systems and research were discussed.

Professional growth and enrichment is an important facet of the individual's responsibility to himself, to the people he or she serves, and to colleagues. Ways in which this can be accomplished were discussed in this chapter. The role of the school speech, language and hearing specialist in teacher organizations was also discussed.

A list of periodicals of interest to the school clinician is included. Sources of information are also pointed out.

12 | *taking the first step— student teaching*

INTRODUCTION

The next step on the road to becoming a speech-language clinician in the schools is student teaching. It is sometimes regarded with trepidation by the student, probably because, like all new experiences, it contains the element of the unknown. The unknown is usually anticipated with a mixture of fear, curiosity, and excitement. The actual experience may bear out what was anticipated and it may also contain some surprises.

Selecting at random, the comments from self-evaluations made by student teachers at the conclusion of the internship experience reveals a realistic picture of the situation.

The thought that occupied my mind as I drove home after my first day of being a student teacher, was, "How will I ever make it?" I had come face to face with part of my "Sammy Snakes," "quiet sounds," "growling sounds," "frog sounds," and I foresaw ten weeks of writing lesson plans and thinking up activities. And now, here I am ten weeks later. I can look back to that first day and laugh when I think of how my ideas have changed. It doesn't seem possible that I could have experienced all that I did. My student teaching was in all aspects a total learning situation.

Student teaching has been a great experience and has been more of a benefit, not only from the professional point of view, but also from the personal point of view, than I ever imagined it would be. It has been a lot of hard work and a lot of time invested, but the satisfaction, rewards, and learning that this has created has made it all worthwhile.

Without having had the opportunity to student teach, the answers would have taken a long time coming.

I suddenly realized that I didn't need to be unsure, for I could handle the situation that I feared, adequately and surprisingly well.

I have met with many new experiences as a member of a school system. I have met many teachers, talked with them and have gotten to know them as fellow educators. I feel much more confident being out in the schools since I am no longer regarded as a "student." When the teachers ask my professional opinion about various children, their confidence in me boosts my confidence in myself.

I feel the most important things I learned from my student teaching experience were learned through my own mistakes. I had a very intelligent school supervisor who allowed me to experiment and try new things on my own. When I failed, I learned a great deal. Instead of telling me my ideas were inappropriate, she allowed me to find out for myself through my own mistakes.

As a student teacher I have grown to understand the daily routine, unexpected problems and hassles a school clinician must go through and accept. I have also experienced the rewards a therapist obtains when a child achieves progress and success. Being able to take over many of the responsibilities has opened my eyes and allowed me to see how fulfilling it is to be able to help children improve in their speech communication.

One fact which cannot go without mentioning is that in this field we are all professionals and must uphold a certain dignity and respect for our position while complying with ethical standards. Through my student teaching experience I have had a taste of the professional dignity and hope in the future I will be able to combine the professional and personal components for a complementary balance.

My student teaching experience was the most rewarding one of my college career and I owe most of this to my school supervisor, who allowed me to experiment with my own ideas while watching me with a critical eye.

One mistake I feel that I made at the beginning of student teaching was in failure to ask questions about everything that was going on around me. I don't know if I was afraid to ask them or if I didn't know which questions to ask but either way it was a mistake. I think I went in with the attitude that I was "supposed" to know everything. This is, of course, the wrong attitude to take. The whole purpose of student teaching is to learn and what better way to learn than by asking questions?

The seminars during student teaching have been very helpful. The discussions were relaxed, free, and very relevant.

My supervising clinician was very helpful when I asked questions. She gave me her professional opinions and, or, referred me to other professional sources. Although she informed me of reasons why some therapy sessions were less successful, she did not fail to commend the progress she saw and my success in therapy.

Student teaching has shown me how a school can function, how to deal with faculty, staff, and parents, and possible procedures to follow in making referrals and recommendations.

Another thing I've learned is that the activity is not terribly important. I've wasted a lot of time trying to be like Milton-Bradley or some of the other games and toy makers. What is important is getting the child to use his good speech and language as much as possible during the session.

The most valuable information I obtained was how to schedule clients and set up a therapy program.

Mrs. Harms maintained an atmosphere of organization, responsibility, cordiality and resourcefulness throughout the entire ten weeks. Because of such outstanding qualities in my supervising school clinician, I had a very fulfilling and rewarding student teaching experience.

I consider the practical experience that student teaching afforded me to be the most effective learning device in my college education. It was a positive and growing experience. Student teaching has started a growing in me, and a desire to grow more which I can continue for the rest of my life.

These comments, from student teachers fresh from the experience of student teaching in speech pathology and audiology, provide insights and food for thought, not only for prospective student teachers, but for school and university supervisors as well.

According to Anderson (1972):

The purpose of the school practicum as a part of the training program of the speech, language and hearing pathologist is to provide certain learning experiences which the university or clinic setting cannot provide. If the practicum is to be meaningful there must be a careful delineation of those learning experiences which can and/or should be provided in each of those settings. It must be recognized that the student who begins his practicum in the schools is not a "finished" clinician but a student who needs certain types of experiences before he is ready to assume the responsibility of a job of his own.

THE STUDENT TEACHING TRIAD

Basically, there are three persons directly involved in the process of student teaching. The first one is the student teacher who is doing his or her practicum in an off-campus school system. The second person is the pathologist employed by the school system, who is directly responsible for the day-to-day supervision of the student intern. The third person involved is the university supervisor.

Too often the roles and responsibilities of the various participants in the student teaching process are not clearly defined and these individuals are put in a situation of not knowing what is expected of them, what to do, or how to do it. Following is a list of the roles, qualifications, and responsibilities of the persons involved in the clinical practicum in the schools. This is by no means a complete list and others may wish to add to it or delete from it. (Neidecker, 1976)

I. *Qualifications of the University Supervisor:*
  A. Shall have a master's degree in speech pathology and, or, audiology.
  B. Shall have ASHA Certificate of Clinical Competence in speech pathology and, or, audiology.
  C. Shall have had experience as a full-time public school pathologist for a minimum of three years.
  D. Shall be a competent speech-language pathologist.
  E. Shall have had experience in teaching on a university speech pathology and audiology staff.
  F. Shall demonstrate ability in supervision techniques, evaluation methods, counseling, and in-service training.
  G. Shall have knowledge of school administration; general and special education policies and laws; physical planning of speech-language and hearing facilities; the process of developing programs for speech, language, and hearing handicapped children; available social and welfare agencies and services; and the practice and psychology of management techniques.
  H. Shall be aware of the current issues facing educators and contemporary trends in education.
  I. Shall have the following personal characteristics:
    1. Shall be an effective communicator.
    2. Shall be objective and flexible and able to adapt to change.
    3. Shall have the capacity for self-evaluation and the ability to profit from mistakes.

II. *Responsibilities of the University Supervisor:*
  A. Shall be responsible for establishing criteria in regard to the time when a student is ready for practicum in the public schools.
  B. Shall be responsible, in part, for selection of the cooperating pathologist.
  C. Shall assume that the university still has the ultimate responsibility for the student's practicum experience.
  D. Shall be responsible for conducting in-service training for co-operating pathologists.
  E. Shall act as consultant to the cooperating pathologist.
    1. Shall provide time for conferences to keep the cooperating pathologist informed of the university program and policies.
    2. Shall provide written materials concerning the university policies and procedures.
    3. Shall provide information on the background of the student teacher, both general and specific.

4. Shall be able to provide a wide variety of resource materials, approaches, and techniques which are based on sound theory, successful therapy, or documented research.
F. Shall establish goals with the student teacher which are realistic and easily understandable.
1. Shall prepare informational material about the expectations of the student teacher and policies of the university regarding the school practicum.
2. Shall observe the student teacher during the practicum.
3. Shall confer with the student teacher each time a visit is made to the school.
4. Shall provide opportunity for the students to give feedback on their practicum experiences both during and after the practicum experience, either in writing or through conferences.
G. Shall promote communication between the university and the public school setting.
H. Shall act as mediator between the student teacher and school administration.
I. Shall act as mediator between the cooperating pathologist and the student teacher.
J. Shall participate in conferences with the student teacher and the cooperating pathologist individually and collectively.
K. Shall establish that the responsibility for the student teacher's practicum is shared equally by the university supervisor and the cooperating clinician, but that the daily supervision of the student is the responsibility of the cooperating pathologist.
L. Shall be able to demonstrate therapy for both the student and the cooperating pathologist during the therapy session.
M. Shall share with the cooperating clinician in making the final evaluation of the student teacher.

III. *Qualifications of the Cooperating Clinician:*
A. Shall have had at least three years experience in the public schools as a speech, language, and hearing pathologist.
B. Shall have the appropriate credentials as a speech-language pathologist in the schools.
C. Shall be recognized by colleagues as a competent professional person.
D. Shall be willing to have a student teacher.

IV. *Responsibilities of the Cooperating Clinician to the Student Teacher:*
A. Shall be responsible for the day-to-day supervision of the student teacher.
B. Shall acquaint the student teacher with available materials and equipment for screening and diagnostic procedures.
C. Shall acquaint the student teacher with materials available for therapy.
D. Shall encourage the student teacher to create and develop his or her own materials.
E. Shall supplement the student teacher's background information through reading lists and other references.

F. Shall provide the student teacher with information regarding the school system in reference to school policy, location of schools, the community, dismissal and fire drill procedures, and other appropriate information.

G. Shall provide the student teacher with opportunities to:
    1. Observe the cooperating pathologist doing therapy.
    2. Assist in screening and diagnostic programs.
    3. Plan for and evaluate therapy sessions.
    4. Visit classrooms where speech, hearing, and language handicapped children are enrolled.
    5. Meet other school personnel informally and also confer with them about specific children.
    6. Write progress reports, case history reports, letters, therapy logs, and Individual educational programs.
    7. Become familiar with the reporting, recording, filing and retrieval systems used by the cooperating pathologist.

H. Shall provide feedback to the student teacher regarding strengths and weaknesses. The feedback shall be done on a regular basis and may take the form of verbal communication, written communication, tape recordings, video taping and, or, demonstration therapy.

I. Shall encourage the student to develop behavioral objectives regarding himself and the children with whom he works.

J. Shall encourage and assist the student to utilize supportive personnel and aides when available.

K. Shall encourage the student to become increasingly independent in thinking and problem solving.

V. *Responsibilities of the Cooperating Clinician to the University Supervisor:*
    A. Shall inform the university supervisor immediately of any problems that arise.
    B. Shall be aware of and assist the student in fulfilling university requirements.
    C. Shall provide the university supervisor with feedback concerning the student's progress.

VI. *Qualifications of the Student Teacher:*
    A. Shall, after completion of practicum, be no more than one quarter or semester away from completing the degree program in speech-language pathology and, or, audiology at an accredited university.
    B. Shall have completed the required clinical practicum.
    C. Shall have had observation experience in a school setting prior to school practicum.
    D. Shall demonstrate physical, mental, and emotional stability.
    E. Shall possess acceptable speech and language patterns and adequate hearing.

VII. *Responsibilities of the Student Teacher:*
    A. Shall be aware of and adhere to the Code of Ethics of the American Speech-Language-Hearing Association.

B. Shall be aware of and carry out the university requirements during school practicum.
C. Shall adhere to the policies and practices of the school to which assigned.
D. Shall comply with the directives of the cooperating pathologist as to working in the school therapy program.
E. Shall expect to be treated as a professional person and act accordingly.
F. Shall demonstrate ability to be dependable and assume responsibility while realizing that the cooperating clinician is legally responsible for the children being treated.
G. Shall contribute to the fullest extent to the school therapy program based on academic background and university clinical practice.
H. Shall demonstrate ability to establish and maintain appropriate interpersonal relationships with school personnel.
I. Shall demonstrate ability to establish and maintain appropriate rapport with children.
J. Shall demonstrate ability to evaluate self in therapy and a willingness to accept and utilize constructive criticism.
K. Shall be aware of the criteria for evaluating the practicum experience.
L. Shall recognize status as a learner and regard the practicum as a learning situation from which much is to be gained.
M. Shall expect the practicum experience to assist in the development of skills enabling one to function as an independent professional person.
N. Shall demonstrate interest in continued professional growth by making use of resource centers, attending in-service meetings, workshops, and professional meetings.

THE STUDENT TEACHING PROGRAM

Universities have many ways of carrying out the student teaching program in speech-language and hearing. Obviously, there are many different patterns that are followed successfully depending upon conditions and factors present in local areas and upon the philosophy of the university concerned. There are, however, some commonalities which we will consider.

Schedules. It is important that the student teacher submit a day-by-day schedule to the university supervisor. Because many school therapy programs are on intermittent program schedules, several centers may be involved in the student teacher's assignment. Important also is the obligation of the student teacher to keep the university supervisor informed of the hours he or she will be at his schools, as well as times when therapy may not be going on as a result of interruptions to the school's daily schedule.

Log of Clinical Clock Hours. In addition to fulfilling the university's requirements for daily attendance, the student clinician must also consider the future possibility of verification of clinical clock hours for certification by the American Speech-Language-Hearing Association, licensing in various states, and verification of hours for certification by state departments of education. Most universities use a weekly reporting system and the forms used to record this information vary. Besides the identifying information, the forms should include places to record the age range of the children; the various types of communication problems; the amount of time actually spent in diagnosis, in audiometric testing, in screening, and in group and individual therapy sessions. The student teacher and the cooperating pathologist should affix their signatures to the completed form. A summary form may be filled out at the conclusion of student teaching.

Lesson Plans. A daily written plan of intervention for each child with whom the student teacher works is a necessary tool of therapy. The plan should include both long and short-range goals for each child, procedures, materials used, and the evaluation of the therapy session. The evaluation is done by both the co-operating pathologist and the student teacher and may include an evaluation of the progress of each child, the effectiveness of the procedures and the materials used, and the effectiveness of the approach used by the student teacher. There is no one universally accepted form for a lesson plan but most forms include the same basic elements. A more complete discussion of lesson plans is found in chapter 8.

Seminars. It is common practice to hold seminars for the student teachers on a periodic basis. These seminars may be held weekly or less often, depending on the philosophy of the university. Frequently, the seminar time may be used for discussions and sharing of information and problems, speakers may be invited to discuss pertinent issues, panels may be utilized to familiarize student teachers with current information, demonstration therapy or diagnosis may be carried out, visits may be made to agencies or centers, and one seminar may be devoted to an explanation of school policies and practices. It is valuable for student teachers in speech, language, and hearing pathology to attend at least several seminars which include all student teachers in a school system.

Evaluations. Assuming that self-evaluation and evaluation by supervisors is an on-going procedure, it also may be useful to have a more formal type of written evaluation at the mid-way point and at the conclusion of student teaching. The form used for these evaluative procedures should be in the hands of the student teachers during the first week of student teaching, or even prior to it, so that they know exactly what will be expected of them.

The mid-point evaluation should let the student teacher know what his or her weak points are, where strengths lie, which areas need improvement, and how these improvements may come about. The student teacher then has the responsibility to act upon the suggestions for improvement.

The final evaluation may be an evaluation of the student teacher during that experience and it may also contain the perceived professional potential of that individual. It is important to differentiate between these two items. No student teacher emerges from the student teaching experience a "finished product" and this should be conveyed in the final evaluation report.

If a competency-based evaluation system is used, the student teacher may be expected to:

Demonstrate clear articulation, adequate hearing, and good voice quality,

Communicate with pupils through appropriate word choices, sentence length, and quantity of speech,

Maintain a low level of manifest anxiety in stress situations,

Maintain a low level of defensiveness in accepting suggestions and criticisms from supervisors and peers,

Maintain a high level of consistency and stability in managing specific behavior problems,

Maintain a high level of personality adjustment in establishing rapport with pupils,

Maintain a high degree of creativity to meet individual needs and interests of children in a learning situation,

Maintain a high level of enthusiasm and energy,

Maintain a high degree of warmth with pupils,

Organize and utilize time, energy, materials, and experience,

Maintain a high degree of sensitivity to pupils and their needs,

Demonstrate a high degree of coping ability,

Secure teacher referrals,

Carry out speech-language and, or, hearing screening programs,

Determine realistic goals for therapy,

Work toward goals through effective lesson planning and case management,

Keep accurate and up-to-date records and reports,

Adapt to group therapy,

Adapt to individual therapy,

Objectively evaluate the therapy situation,

Evoke motivation in pupils,

Maintain order and discipline by maintaining an effective working situation,

Keep professional confidences,

Show evidence of awareness of research needs,

Show evidence of awareness of professional ethics,

Show evidence of professional bearing through grooming, cleanliness, appropriateness of attire.

As a supplement to a formal standardized evaluation some universities ask student teachers for a narrative self-evaluation at the conclusion of the student teaching experience.

additional requirements
for student teaching

There are additional requirements for student teaching that many university training centers have found productive and valuable in assisting student teachers to become full-fledged, competent professional persons. One such requirement is a checklist of experiences the prospective student teacher has had before the student teaching experience. Such a checklist submitted to the cooperating pathologist is helpful in acquainting that person with the student teacher's capabilities. It might include information on any experience in childcare such as baby-sitting or teaching church school, observational experience, clinical practicum experience, diagnostic experience, academic experience, and experience with tape recorders, audiometers, auditory training units, video tape machines, duplicating machines and typewriters.

Student clinicians should know something about the community in which they are doing their student teaching. Knowing the socioeconomic backgrounds of the families in the school districts helps student teachers to better understand the children with whom they will be working. This may be especially important for student teachers whose own backgrounds are different from those of their prospective clients.

This is but a partial list of possible requirements for the student teaching experience, and, understandably, each university training center will develop its own set.

a word of advice to student teachers

Are you ready to start your student teaching? Here are some suggestions which might be helpful to you:

1. Work in harmony with your cooperating pathologist and your university supervisor. Their job is to help you become a better speech-language and hearing pathologist.
2. Be enthusiastic about your work and sincerely interested in the children with whom you will be working.
3. Keep healthy; get plenty of rest and eat the right foods.
4. Take advantage of every opportunity to become involved in the unique experiences a school has to offer.
5. Ask questions when you aren't sure, and ask questions even if you *are* sure.
6. Know what you can expect of children at various age and ability levels.
7. Be firm, fair, consistent, and compassionate in all your dealings with children. Every human being deserves respect.
8. Know the ground rules of the various schools and adhere to them.
9. When making professional decisions always ask yourself, "Is this in the best interests of the child?"
10. Enjoy your student teaching experience!

GUIDELINES FOR THE
COOPERATING CLINICIAN

In a chapter dealing with student teaching it is appropriate to include information useful to the person who plans and directs the student internship. That person is the cooperating clinician in the schools.

An article entitled "Guidelines for a Cooperating Clinician in Working With a Student Clinician in the Schools" by Rhoda Hess (1976) contains many excellent suggestions. According to Hess:

> It is vital for the cooperating clinician working with a student clinician to realize the importance of student teaching. The student deserves the chance to be involved in a worthwhile program, and it will be worthwhile if he is met with leadership, an opportunity for growth, and a well-planned program.

Hess discusses the responsibilities of the cooperating clinician in the first week of student teaching. They are:

1. Communicate with the student clinician before the first week, by telephone call or letter, or an invitation to visit the school ahead of time.
2. On the first day provide orientation for the student by having him meet with the program director and other school pathologists and student teachers to discuss school policies, complete necessary forms, map out routes to the schools, and generally to minimize anxieties. He could also be informed of time schedules of the various schools, as well as the school calendar.
3. During the first week the student teacher should be given a tour of the school buildings and should be introduced to the principal and secretary of each building to which he has been assigned, as well as the teachers, school counselor, nurse, and psychologist.
4. The cooperating pathologist should prepare the children enrolled in therapy for the arrival of the student teacher in such a way that they understand his role in relation to them.
5. The cooperating pathologist and the student teacher should discuss the university's materials, requirements, and suggestions so they are mutually understood.
6. The major goals for the student teaching program, as well as assignments and weekly goals, should be discussed. The cooperating pathologist should discuss his expectations of the student teacher and encourage the student to express his own expectations.
7. The student teacher should be made aware of rules, regulations and policies of individual schools, the school system as a whole, and of the speech-language and hearing program in the state.
8. The first week of student teaching should include the opportunity to observe therapy sessions and to become acquainted with the children. During the first week the student teacher may assist with segments of the therapy sessions.

9. If the student teacher is assigned at the beginning of the school year he may assist in the screening programs.

According to Hess, the assigned weeks of student teaching should be utilized effectively and efficiently but the student teacher should not be overloaded.

There are numerous school activities the student clinician can take part in during the weeks of student teaching. It is important for the cooperating clinician to have a list of priorities or activities that seem most valuable for the student. The list can be compiled from various sources: from university information, other clinicians, published articles, and from discussions with the student clinician. The student should have the opportunity to take part in as many phases as possible of the school therapy program. Besides learning to organize and carry out a therapy program, the student clinician will want to become familiar with related activities. For instance, it is helpful for the student to attend meetings of the clinicians as well as those meetings held in the individual schools.

The cooperating clinician should discuss with the student clinician how to begin and how to terminate the school year. The clinician will want to include the student in obtaining referrals for therapy and in conferences with teachers and parents. Furthermore, the cooperating clinician can discuss with the student clinician bulletin board ideas, newsletters for parents, parent conferences, and special therapy ideas that have proven successful. The student should learn to use the ditto machine and any other office equipment that is applicable to the therapy program. Also the student clinician will want to have information about the many sources of therapy materials.

CONCLUSION

The purpose of this chapter has been to provide the prospective student teacher with some information on student teaching in the schools, including his or her roles and responsibilities, as well as the tasks of the other two persons in the triad: the cooperating clinician and the university supervisor. Another purpose is to assist the pathologist in the schools who may sometime have a student teacher assigned to him.

Student teaching in speech-language pathology and audiology can be a stimulating experience in which everyone involved is a teacher as well as a learner.

The publication, *Introduction to Clinical Supervision in Speech Pathology* by George W. Schubert (1978), contains much information that would be of interest to the supervisor of the student teacher in the school. In addition, there are numerous articles on supervision in professional journals.

appenaix

code of ethics of the American speech-language-hearing association

1

(Effective January 1, 1979)

PREAMBLE

The preservation of the highest standards of integrity and ethical principles is vital to the successful discharge of the professional responsibilities of all speech-language pathologists and audiologists. This Code of Ethics has been promulgated by the Association in an effort to stress the fundamental rules considered essential to this basic purpose. Any action that is in violation of the spirit and purpose of this Code shall be considered unethical. Failure to specify any particular responsibility or practice in this Code of Ethics should not be construed as denial of the existence of other responsibilities or practices.

The fundamental rules of ethical conduct are described in three categories: Principles of Ethics, Ethical Proscriptions, Matters of Professional Propriety.

1. Principles of Ethics. Six Principles serve as a basis for the ethical evaluation of professional conduct and form the underlying moral basis for the Code of Ethics. Individuals[1] subscribing to this Code shall observe these principles as affirmative obligations under all conditions of professional activity.

---

[1] "Individuals" refers to all Members of the American Speech-Language-Hearing Association and non-members who hold Certificates of Clinical Competence from this Association.

2. *Ethical Proscriptions.* Ethical Proscriptions are formal statements of prohibitions that are derived from the Principles of Ethics.

3. *Matters of Professional Propriety.* Matters of Professional Propriety represent guidelines of conduct designed to promote the public interest and thereby better inform the public and particularly the persons in need of speech-language pathology and audiology services as to the availability and the rules regarding the delivery of those services.

PRINCIPLE OF ETHICS I

Individuals shall hold paramount the welfare of persons served professionally.
A. Individuals shall use every resource available, including referral to other specialists as needed, to provide the best service possible.
B. Individuals shall fully inform persons served of the nature and possible effects of the services.
C. Individuals shall fully inform subjects participating in research or teaching activities of the nature and possible effects of these activities.
D. Individuals' fees shall be commensurate with services rendered.
E. Individuals shall provide appropriate access to records of persons served professionally.
F. Individuals shall take all reasonable precautions to avoid injuring persons in the delivery of professional services.
G. Individuals shall evaluate services rendered to determine effectiveness.

Ethical Proscriptions

1. Individuals must not exploit persons in the delivery of professional services, including accepting persons for treatment when benefit cannot reasonably be expected or continuing treatment unnecessarily.
2. Individuals must not guarantee the results of any therapeutic procedures, directly or by implication. A reasonable statement of prognosis may be made, but caution must be exercised not to mislead persons served professionally to expect results that cannot be predicted from sound evidence.
3. Individuals must not use persons for teaching or research in a manner that constitutes invasion of privacy or fails to afford informed free choice to participate.
4. Individuals must not evaluate or treat speech, language or hearing disorders except in a professional relationship. They must not evaluate or treat solely by correspondence. This does not preclude follow-up correspondence with persons previously seen, nor providing them with general information of an educational nature.
5. Individuals must not reveal to unauthorized persons any professional or personal information obtained from the person served professionally, unless required by law or unless necessary to protect the welfare of the person or the community.
6. Individuals must not discriminate in the delivery of professional services on any basis that is unjustifiable or irrelevant to the need for and potential benefit from such services, such as race, sex or religion.
7. Individuals must not charge for services not rendered.

PRINCIPLE OF ETHICS II

Individuals shall maintain high standards of professional competence.
A. Individuals engaging in clinical practice shall possess appropriate qualifications which are provided by the Association's program for certification of clinical competence.
B. Individuals shall continue their professional development throughout their careers.

C. Individuals shall identify competent, dependable referral sources for persons served professionally.
D. Individuals shall maintain adequate records of professional services rendered.

Ethical Proscriptions

1. Individuals must neither provide services nor supervision of services for which they have not been properly prepared, nor permit services to be provided by any of their staff who are not properly prepared.
2. Individuals must not provide clinical services by prescription of anyone who does not hold the Certificate of Clinical Competence.
3. Individuals must not delegate any service requiring the professional competence of a certified clinician to anyone unqualified.
4. Individuals must not offer clinical services by supportive personnel for whom they do not provide appropriate supervision and assume full responsibility.
5. Individuals must not require anyone under their supervision to engage in any practice that is a violation of the Code of Ethics.

PRINCIPLE OF ETHICS III

Individuals' statements to persons served professionally and to the public shall provide accurate information about the nature and management of communicative disorders, and about the profession and services rendered by its practitioners.

Ethical Proscriptions

1. Individuals must not misrepresent their training or competence.
2. Individuals' public statements providing information about professional services and products must not contain representations or claims that are false, deceptive or misleading.
3. Individuals must not use professional or commercial affiliations in any way that would mislead or limit services to persons served professionally.

Matters of Professional Propriety

1. Individuals should announce services in a manner consonant with highest professional standards in the community.

PRINCIPLE OF ETHICS IV

Individuals shall maintain objectivity in all matters concerning the welfare of persons served professionally.
A. Individuals who dispense products to persons served professionally shall observe the following standards:
   (1) Products associated with professional practice must be dispensed to the person served as a part of a program of comprehensive rehabilitative care.
   (2) Fees established for professional services must be independent of whether a product is dispensed.
   (3) Persons served must be provided freedom of choice for the source of services and products.
   (4) Price information about professional services rendered and products dispensed must be disclosed by providing to or posting for persons served a

complete schedule of fees and charges in advance of rendering services, which schedule differentiates between fees for professional services and charges for products dispensed.

(5) Products dispensed to the person served must be evaluated to determine effectiveness.

Ethical Proscriptions

1. Individuals must not participate in activities that constitute a conflict of professional interest.

Matters of Professional Propriety

1. Individuals should not accept compensation for supervision or sponsorship from the clinician being supervised or sponsored.
2. Individuals should present products they have developed to their colleagues in a manner consonant with highest professional standards.

PRINCIPLE OF ETHICS V

Individuals shall honor their responsibilities to the public, their profession, and their relationships with colleagues and members of allied professions.

Matters of Professional Propriety

1. Individuals should seek to provide and expand services to persons with speech, language and hearing handicaps as well as to assist in establishing high professional standards for such programs.
2. Individuals should educate the public about speech, language and hearing processes, speech, language and hearing problems, and matters related to professional competence.
3. Individuals should strive to increase knowledge within the profession and share research with colleagues.
4. Individuals should establish harmonious relations with colleagues and members of other professions, and endeavor to inform members of related professions of services provided by speech-language pathologists and audiologists, as well as seek information from them.
5. Individuals should assign credit to those who have contributed to a publication in proportion to their contribution.

PRINCIPLE OF ETHICS VI

Individuals shall uphold the dignity of the profession and freely accept the profession's self-imposed standards.
A. Individuals shall inform the Ethical Practice Board of violations of this Code of Ethics.
B. Individuals shall cooperate fully with the Ethical Practice Board inquiries into matters of professional conduct related to this Code of Ethics.

appendix

2

requirements for the certificate of clinical competence

(Effective July 1, 1977)

The American Speech-Language-Hearing Association issues Certificates of Clinical Competence to individuals who present satisfactory evidence of their ability to provide independent clinical services to persons who have disorders of communication (speech, language, and/or hearing). An individual who meets these requirements may be awarded a Certificate in Speech Pathology or in Audiology, depending upon the emphasis of his preparation; a person who meets the requirements for both professional areas may be awarded both Certificates.

I. STANDARDS

The individual who is awarded either, or both, of the Certificates of Clinical Competence must hold a master's degree or equivalent with major emphasis in speech pathology, audiology, or speech and hearing science. The individual must also meet the following qualifications:

I,A. General Background Education

As stipulated below, applicants for a certificate should have completed specialized academic training and preparatory professional experience that provides an in-depth knowledge of normal communication processes, development and disorders thereof, evaluation procedures to assess the bases of such disorders, and clinical techniques that have been shown to improve or eradicate them. It is expected that the applicant will have obtained a broad general education to serve as a background prior to such study and experience. The specific content of this general background education is left to the discretion of the applicant and to the training program which he attends. However, it is highly desirable that it include study in the areas of human psychology, sociology, psychological and physical development, the physical sciences (especially those that pertain to acoustic and biological phenomena) and human anatomy and physiology, including neuroanatomy and neurophysiology.

I,B. Required Education

A total of 60 semester hours[1] of academic credit must have been accumulated from accredited colleges or universities that demonstrate that the applicant has obtained a well-integrated program of course study dealing with the normal aspects of human communication, development thereof, disorders thereof, and clinical techniques for evaluation and management of such disorders.

Twelve (12) of these 60 semester hours must be obtained in courses that provide information that pertains to normal development and use of speech, language, and hearing.

Thirty (30) of these 60 semester hours must be in courses that provide (1) information relative to communication disorders, and (2) information about and training in evaluation and management of speech, language, and hearing disorders. At least 24 of these 30 semester hours must be in courses in the professional area (speech-language pathology or audiology) for which the certificate is requested, and no less than six (6) semester hours may be in audiology for the certificate in speech-language pathology or in speech-language pathology for the certificate in audiology. Moreover, no more than six (6) semester hours may be in courses that provide credit for clinical practice obtained during academic training.

Credit for study of information pertaining to related fields that augment the work of the clinical practitioner of speech-language pathology and/or audiology may also apply toward the total 60 semester hours.

Thirty (30) of the total 60 semester hours that are required for a certificate must be in courses that are acceptable toward a graduate degree by the college or university in which they are taken. Moreover, 21 of those 30 semester hours must be within the 24 semester hours required in the professional area (speech-language pathology or audiology) for which the certificate is requested or within the six (6) semester hours required in the other area.[2]

---

[1] In evaluation of credits, one quarter hour will be considered the equivalent of two-thirds of a semester hour. Transcripts that do not report credit in terms of semester or quarter hours should be submitted for special evaluation.

[2] This requirement may be met by courses completed as an undergraduate providing the college or university in which they are taken specifies that these courses would be acceptable toward a graduate degree if they were taken at the graduate level.

I,C. Academic Clinical Practicum

The applicant must have completed a minimum of 300 clock hours of supervised clinical experience with individuals who present a variety of communication disorders, and this experience must have been obtained within his training institution or in one of its cooperating programs.

I,D. The Clinical Fellowship Year

The applicant must have obtained the equivalent of nine (9) months of full-time professional experience (the Clinical Fellowship Year) in which bona fide clinical work has been accomplished in the major professional area (speech-language pathology or audiology) in which the certificate is being sought. The Clinical Fellowship Year must have begun after completion of the academic and clinical practicum experiences specified in Standards I,A., I,B., and I,C. above.

I,E. The National Examinations in Speech Pathology and Audiology

The applicant must have passed one of the National Examinations in Speech Pathology and Audiology, either the National Examination in Speech Pathology or the National Examination in Audiology.

II. EXPLANATORY NOTES

II,A. General Background Education

While the broadest possible general educational background for the future clinical practitioner of speech-language pathology and/or audiology is encouraged, the nature of the clinician's professional endeavors suggests the necessity for some emphasis in his general education. For example, elementary courses in general psychology and sociology are desirable as are studies in mathematics, general physics, zoology, as well as human anatomy and physiology. Those areas of introductory study that do not deal specifically with communication processes are not to be credited to the minimum 60 semester hours of education specified in Standard I,B.

II,B. Required Education

II,B,1. Basic Communication Processes Area. The 12 semester hours in courses that provide information applicable to the normal development and use of speech, language, and hearing should be selected with emphasis on the normal aspects of human communication in order that the applicant has a wide exposure to the diverse kinds of information suggested by the content areas given under the three broad categories that follow: (1) anatomic and physiologic bases for the normal development and use of speech, language, and hearing, such as anatomy, neurology, and physiology of speech, language, and hearing mechanisms; (2) physical bases and processes of the production and perception of speech and hearing, such as (a) acoustics or physics of sound, (b) phonology, (c) physiologic and acoustic phonetics, (d) perceptual processes, and (3) psychoacoustics; and (3) linguistic and psycholinguistic variables related to normal development and use of speech, language, and hearing, such as (a) linguistics (historical, descriptive, sociolinguistics, urban language), (b) psychology of language, (c) psycholinguistics, (d) language and speech acquisition, and (e) verbal learning or verbal behavior.

It is emphasized that the three broad categories of required education given above, and the examples of areas of study within these classifications, are not meant to be analogous with, nor imply, specific course titles. Neither are the examples of areas of study within these categories meant to be exhaustive.

At least two (2) semester hours of credit must be earned in each of the three categories.

Obviously, some of these 12 semester hours may be obtained in courses that are taught in departments other than those offering speech-language pathology and audiology programs. Courses designed to improve the speaking and writing ability of the student will not be credited.

II,B,2. Major Professional Area, Certificate in Speech Pathology. The 24 semester hours of professional education required for the Certificate of Clinical Competence in Speech Pathology should include mastery of information pertaining to speech and language disorders as follows: (1) understanding of speech and language disorders, such as (a) various types of disorders of communication, (b) their manifestations, and (c) their classifications and causes; (2) evaluation skills, such as procedures, techniques, and instrumentation used to assess (a) the speech and language status of children and adults, and (b) the bases of disorders of speech and language, and (3) management procedures, such as principles in remedial methods used in habilitation and rehabilitation for children and adults with various disorders of communication.

Within these categories at least six (6) semester hours must deal with speech disorders and at least six (6) hours must deal with language disorders.

II,B,3. Minor Professional Area, Certificate in Speech Pathology. For the individual to obtain the Certificate in Speech Pathology, he must have not less than six (6) semester hours of academic credit in audiology. Where only this minimum requirement of six (6) semester hours is met, three (3) semester hours must be in habilitative/rehabilitative procedures with speech and language problems associated with hearing impairment, and three (3) semester hours must be in study of the pathologies of the auditory system and assessment of auditory disorders. However, when more than the minimum six (6) semester hours is met, study of habilitative/rehabilitative procedures may be counted in the *Major Professional Area for the Certificate in Speech Pathology (Section II,B,8).*

II,B,4. Major Professional Area, Certificate in Audiology. The 24 semester hours of professional education required for the Certificate of Clinical Competence in Audiology should be in the broad, but not necessarily exclusive, categories of study as follows: (1) auditory disorders, such as (a) pathologies of the auditory system, and (b) assessment of auditory disorders and their effect on communication; (2) habilitative/rehabilitative procedures, such as (a) selection and use of appropriate amplification instrumentation for the hearing impaired, both wearable and group, (b) evaluation of speech and language problems of the hearing impaired, and (c) management procedures for speech and language habilitation and/or rehabilitation of the hearing impaired (that may include manual communication); (3) conservation of hearing, such as (a) environmental noise control, and (b) identification audiometry (school, military, industry); and (4) instrumentation, such as (a) electronics, (b) calibration techniques, and (c) characteristics of amplifying systems.

Not less than six (6) semester hours must be in the auditory pathology category, and not less than six (6) semester hours must be in the habilitation/rehabilitation category.

II,B,5. Minor Professional Area, Certificate in Audiology. For the individual to obtain the Certificate in Audiology, not less than six (6) semester hours must be obtained in the areas of speech and language pathology, of these three (3) hours must be in the area of speech pathology and three (3) hours in the area of language pathology. It is suggested that where only this minimum requirement of six (6) semester hours is met, such study be in the areas of evaluation procedures and management of speech and language problems that are not associated with hearing impairment.

II,B,6. *Related Areas.* In addition to the 12 semester hours of course study in the Basic Communication Processes Area, the 24 semester hours in the Major Professional Area and the six (6) semester hours in the Minor Professional Area, the applicant may receive credit toward the minimum requirement of 60 semester hours of required education through advanced study in a variety of related areas. Such study should pertain to the understanding of human behavior, both normal and abnormal, as well as services available from related professions, and that, in general should augment his background for a professional career. Examples of such areas of study are as follows: (a) theories of learning and behavior, (b) services available from related professions that also deal with persons who have disorders of communication, and (c) information from these professions about the sensory, physical, emotional, social, and/or intellectual status of a child or an adult.

Academic credit that is obtained for practice teaching or practicum work in other professions will not be counted toward the minimum requirements.

In order that the future applicant for one of the certificates will be capable of critically reviewing scientific matters dealing with clinical issues relative to speech-language pathology and audiology, credit for study in the area of statistics, beyond an introductory course, will be allowed to a maximum of three (3) semester hours. Academic study of the administrative organization of speech-language pathology and audiology programs also may be applied to a maximum of three (3) semester hours.

II,B,7. *Education Applicable to All Areas.* Certain types of course work may be acceptable among more than one of the areas of study specified above, depending upon the emphasis. For example, courses that provide an overview of research, e.g., introduction to graduate study or introduction to research, that consist primarily of a critical review of research in communication sciences, disorders, or management thereof, and/or a more general presentation of research procedures and techniques that will permit the clinician to read and evaluate literature critically will be acceptable to a maximum of three (3) semester hours. Such courses may be credited to the Basic Communication Processes Area, or one of the Professional Areas or the Related Areas, if substantive content of the course(s) covers material in those areas. Academic credit for a thesis or dissertation may be acceptable to a maximum of three (3) semester hours in the appropriate area. An abstract of the study must be submitted with the application if such credit is requested. In order to be acceptable, the thesis or dissertation must have been an experimental or descriptive investigation in the areas of speech and hearing science, speech-language pathology or audiology; that is, credit will not be allowed if the project was a survey of opinions, a study of professional issues, an annotated bibliography, biography, or a study of curricular design.

As implied by the above, the academic credit hours obtained for one course or one enrollment, may, and should be, in some instances divided among the Basic Communication Processes Area, one of the Professional Areas, and/or the Related Areas. In such cases, a description of the content of that course should accompany the application. This description should be extensive enough to provide the Clinical Certification Board with information necessary to evaluate the validity of the request to apply the content to more than one of the areas.

II,B,8. *Major Professional Education Applicable to Both Certificates.* Study in the area of understanding, evaluation, and management of speech and language disorders associated with hearing impairment may apply to the 24 semester hours of Major Professional Area required for either certificate (speech-language pathology or audiology). However, no more than six (6) semester hours of that study will be allowed in that manner for the certificate in speech pathology.

II,C. Academic Clinical Practicum

It is highly desirable that students who anticipate applying for one of the Certificates of Clinical Competence have the opportunity, relatively early in their training program, to observe the various procedures involved in a clinical program in speech-language pathology and audiology, but this passive participation is not to be construed as direct clinical practicum during academic training. The student should participate in supervised, direct clinical experience during that training only after the student has had sufficient course work to qualify for work as a student clinician and only after the student has sufficient background to undertake clinical practice under direct supervision. A minimum of 150 clock hours of the supervised clinical experience must be obtained during graduate study. Once this experience is undertaken, a substantial period of time may be spent in writing reports, in preparation for clinical sessions, in conferences with supervisors, and in class attendance to discuss clinical procedures, and experiences; such time may not be credited toward the 300 minimum clock hours of supervised clinical experience required.

All student clinicians are expected to obtain direct clinical experience with both children and adults, and it is recommended that some of their direct clinical experience be conducted with groups. Although the student clinician should have experience with both speech and hearing disorders, at least 200 clock hours of this supervised experience must be obtained in the major professional area (speech-language pathology or audiology) in which he will seek certification and not less than 35 clock hours must be obtained in the minor area.

For certification in speech-language pathology, the student clinician is expected to have experience in both the evaluation and management of a variety of speech and language problems. The student must have no less than 50 clock hours of experience in evaluation of speech and language problems. The applicant must also have no less than 75 clock hours of experience in management of language disorders of children and adults, and no less than 25 clock hours each of experience in management of children and adults with whom disorders of (1) voice, (2) articulation, and (3) fluency are significant aspects of the communication handicap.[3]

Where only the minimum 35 clock hours of clinical practicum in audiology is met that is required for the persons seeking certification in speech-language pathology, that practicum must include 15 clock hours in assessment and/or management of speech and language problems associated with hearing impairment, and 15 clock hours must be in assessment of auditory disorders. However, where more than this minimum requirement is met, clinical practicum in assessment and/or management of speech and language problems associated with hearing impairment may be counted toward the minimum clock hours obtained with language and/or speech disorders.

For the student clinician who is preparing for certification in audiology, 50 clock hours of direct supervised experience must be obtained in identification and evaluation of hearing impairment, and 50 clock hours must be obtained in habilitation or rehabilitation of the communication handicaps of the hearing impaired. It is suggested that the 35 clock hours of clinical practicum in speech-

---

[3] Work with multiple problems may be credited among these types of disorders. For example, a child with an articulation problem may also have a voice disorder. The clock hours of work with that child may be credited to experience with either articulation or voice disorders, whichever is most appropriate.

language pathology required for certification in audiology be in evaluation and management of speech and language problems that are not related to a hearing impairment.

Supervisors of clinical practicum must be competent professional workers who hold a Certificate of Clinical Competence, or equivalent[4] in the professional area (speech-language pathology or audiology) in which supervision is provided. This supervision must entail the personal and direct involvement of the supervisor in any and all ways that will permit him to attest to the adequacy of the student's performance in the clinical training experience. Knowledge of the student's clinical work may be obtained through a variety of ways such as conferences, audio- and videotape recordings, written reports, staffings, discussions with other persons who have participated in the student's clinical training, and must include direct observation of the student in clinical sessions.

II,D. The Clinical Fellowship Year

Upon completion of his professional and clinical practicum education, the applicant must complete his Clinical Fellowship Year under the supervision of one who holds the Certificate of Clinical Competence or equivalent[4] in the professional area (speech-language pathology or audiology) in which that applicant is working (and seeking certification).

Professional experience is construed to mean direct clinical work with patients, consultations, record keeping, or any other duties relevant to a bona fide program of clinical work. It is expected, however, that a significant amount of clinical experience will be in direct clinical contact with persons who have communication handicaps. Time spent in supervision of students, academic teaching, and research, as well as administrative activity that does not deal directly with management programs of specific patients or clients will not be counted as professional experience in this context.

The Clinical Fellowship Year is defined as no less than nine months of full-time professional employment with full-time employment defined as a minimum of 30 hours of work a week. This requirement also may be fulfilled by part-time employment as follows: (1) work of 15-19 hours per week over 18 months; (2) work of 20-24 hours per week over 15 months; or, (3) work of 25-29 hours per week over 12 months. In the event that part-time employment is used to fulfill a part of the Clinical Fellowship Year, 100% of the minimum hours of the part-time work per week requirement must be spent in direct professional experience as defined above. The Clinical Fellowship Year must be completed within a maximum period of 36 consecutive months. Professional employment of less than 15 hours per week will not fulfill any part of this requirement. If the CFY is not initiated within two years of the date the academic and practicum education is completed, the applicant must meet the academic and practicum requirements current when the CFY is begun.

CFY supervision must entail the personal and direct involvement of the supervisor in any and all ways that will permit him to monitor, improve, and evaluate the applicant's performance in professional clinical employment. The supervision must include on-site observations of the applicant. Other monitoring activities such as conferences with the applicant, evaluation of written reports, evaluations by professional colleagues, and so on may be executed by correspondence. The CFY supervisor must base his total evaluation on no less

[4] The American Boards of Examiners in Speech Pathology and Audiology define "equivalent" as meeting academic course work, clinical practicum, Clinical Fellowship Year and examination requirements equivalent to those stipulated for the Certificate of Clinical Competence.

than 36 occasions of monitoring activities (a minimum of four hours each month). The monitoring activities must include at least 18 on-site observations (a minimum of two hours each month). Should any supervisor suspect that at any time during the Clinical Fellowship Year an applicant under his supervision will not meet requirements, he must counsel the applicant both orally and in writing and maintain careful written records of all contacts and conferences in the ensuing months.[5]

II,E. The National Examinations in
Speech Pathology and Audiology

The National Examinations in Speech Pathology and Audiology are designed to assess, in a comprehensive fashion, the applicant's mastery of professional concepts as outlined above to which the applicant has been exposed throughout professional education and clinical practicum.[6] The applicant must pass the National Examination, in either Speech Pathology or Audiology, that is appropriate to the certificate being sought. An applicant will be declared eligible for the National Examination on notification of the acceptable completion of the educational and clinical practicum requirements. The Examination must be passed within three years after the first administration for which an applicant is notified of eligibility.

In the event the applicant fails the examination, it may be retaken. If the examination is not successfully completed within the above mentioned three years, the person's application for certification will lapse. If the examination is passed at a later date, the person may reapply for clinical certification.[7]

III. PROCEDURES FOR OBTAINING
THE CERTIFICATES

III,A. Application for membership in the American Speech and Hearing Association and the initial application for certification may be made simultaneously and applicants are urged to follow this procedure.[8] However, applications for certification will not be evaluated until membership is approved and validated by the payment of dues.

III,B. The applicant must submit to the Clinical Certification Board, a description of professional education and academic clinical practicum on forms provided for that purpose. The applicant should recognize that it is highly desirable to list upon this application form the entire professional education and academic clinical practicum training.

No credit may be allowed for courses listed on the application unless satisfactory completion is verified by an official transcript. *Satisfactory completion* is defined as the applicant's having received academic credit (i.e., semester hours, quarter hours, or other unit of credit) with a passing grade as defined by the

---

[5] Further requirements for the Clinical Fellowship Year are available, and, moreover, such requirements are provided with application material for certification.

[6] An applicant whose application has been rejected may reapply if changes in the requirements make his application acceptable as a result of such changes. However, if the Clinical Fellowship Year is not initiated within two years of the time academic and practicum requirements are completed, the applicant must meet academic and practicum requirements that are current when the Clinical Fellowship Year is begun.

[7] Upon such reapplication, the individual's application will be reviewed and current requirements will be applied. Appropriate fees will be charged for this review.

[8] Application material for membership and certification, including a schedule of fees, may be obtained by writing to Director, Professional Services Office, American Speech and Hearing Association, 10801 Rockville Pike, Rockville, Maryland 20852.

training institution. If the majority of an applicant's professional training is received at a program accredited by the Education and Training Board (ETB) of the American Boards of Examiners in Speech Pathology and Audiology (ABESPA), approval of educational and academic clinical practicum requirements will be automatic.

The applicant must request that the director of the training program where the majority of graduate training was obtained sign the application. In the case where that training program is not accredited by the ETB of ABESPA, that director, by signature, (1) certifies that the application is correct, and (2) recommends that the applicant receive the certificate upon completion of all the requirements. In the case where the training program is accredited by the ETB of ABESPA that director (1) certifies that the applicant has met the educational and clinical practicum requirements, and (2) recommends that the applicant receive the certificate upon completion of all the requirements.

In the event that the applicant cannot obtain the recommendation of the director of the training program, the applicant should send with the application a letter giving in detail the reasons for the inability to do so. In such an instance letters of recommendations from other faculty members may be submitted.

Application for approval of educational requirements and academic clinical practicum experiences should be made (1) as soon as possible after completion of these experiences, and (2) either before or shortly after the Clinical Fellowship Year is begun.

III,C. Upon completion of educational and academic clinical practicum training, the applicant should proceed to obtain professional employment and a supervisor for the Clinical Fellowship Year. The applicant and supervisor must then submit to the Clinical Certification Board, prior to the end of the first month of employment, a plan outlining how supervision of the Clinical Fellowship Year will be carried out. Assuming that this plan is approved, the applicant should then proceed to complete the Clinical Fellowship Year, after which an appropriate report should be submitted to the Clinical Certification Board.

III,D. Upon notification by the Clinical Certification Board of approval of the academic course work and clinical practicum requirements the applicant will be sent registration material for the National Examinations in Speech Pathology and Audiology. Upon approval of the Clinical Fellowship Year, achieving a passing score on the National Examination, and payment of all fees and current dues the applicant will become certified.

III,E. As mentioned in Footnote 8, a schedule of fees for certification may be obtained, and payment of these fees is requisite for the various steps involved in obtaining a certificate. Checks should be made payable to the American Speech-Language-Hearing Association.

IV. APPEALS

In the event that at any stage the Clinical Certification Board informs the applicant that the application has been rejected, the applicant has the right of formal appeal. In order to initiate such an appeal, the applicant must write to the Chairman of the Clinical Certification Board and specifically request a formal review of the application. If that review results, again, in rejection, the applicant has the right to request a review of the case by the American Boards of Examiners in Speech Pathology and Audiology (ABESPA) by writing to the Chairman of ABESPA at the National Office of the American Speech and Hearing Association.

organizations

Following is a list of organizations and their addresses, which the school speech-language pathologist and audiologist may want to join or know more about. All of them represent sources of information for the school pathologist.

In addition to the organizations listed, there are other sources of professional assistance and information. These agencies are in existence in each state and in most communities. The school clinician will want to obtain their addresses and keep the information on file. They are:

State education department

State and local health agencies

State bureau of crippled children services

State and local bureau of vocational rehabilitation

Universities with speech, language, and hearing clinics and diagnostic facilities

Community hearing, speech, and language agencies with service and diagnostic facilities

State speech, language, and hearing associations

Local and regional speech and hearing associations
Local welfare department
Local mental hygiene clinic
Local child welfare organizations
Local medical society
Interested civic organizations

AMERICAN SPEECH-LANGUAGE-HEARING
ASSOCIATION (ASHA)
10801 Rockville Pike
Rockville, Maryland 20852
Exec. Sec.

Founded: 1925. *Members*: 20,500. Professional society of specialists in speech pathology and audiology. Presents annual awards. *Publications*: (1) *ASHA*, monthly; (2) *Journal of Speech and Hearing Disorders*, quarterly; (3) *Journal of Speech and Hearing Research*, quarterly; (4) *Language, Speech and Hearing Services in Schools,* quarterly; (5) *Directory,* annual; (6) Reports, irregular; and published monographs. *Convention/Meeting*; annual—always November. *Membership*: Requirements include a master's degree or equivalent with major emphasis in speech pathology, audiology, or speech and hearing science, plus a willingness to abide by the Code of Ethics of the association.

ASHA lobbies for needed legislature in the field and provides a body of trained people to whom the government can turn when questions arise. The organization protects the public by maintaining a Code of Ethics for its membership. The ethical code also serves to protect the reputation of the professional membership from any unethical or questionable conduct of persons professing to be professionals.

NATIONAL STUDENT SPEECH AND HEARING
ASSOCIATION (NSSHA)
10801 Rockville Pike
Rockville, Maryland 20852
Dr. Nicholas W. Bankson, Adm. Consultant

Founded: 1972. *Members*: 10,000. *Local Groups*: 100. Preprofessional organization for undergraduate and premaster's level graduate students in speech pathology and audiology. Compiles annual survey of students in speech pathology and audiology. *Publications*: (1) *Journal*, annual; (2) *Clinical Series*, irregular; (3) *Newsletter*, irregular. *Convention/Meeting*: annual—always November. *Benefits*: (1) Become part of a growing number of students who are finding that involvement in NSSHA leads to a fuller appreciation of the professions and a greater awareness of the issues affecting the field; (2) Receive three ASHA publications: the quarterly *Journal of Speech and Hearing Disorders*, the quarterly *Journal of Speech and Hearing Research*, and the monthly journal, *ASHA*; (3) Receive two NSSHA publications: the annual *Journal of the National Student Speech and Hearing Association* and one issue of the *Clinical Series*; (4) Register at a reduced fee for the ASHA/NSSHA Convention; (5) Order other ASHA publications at special student rates; (6) Receive assistance from the Graduate

Information Center at the convention; (7) Become eligible for NSSHA Regional Project funding; (8) Purchase or rent the NSSHA videoclinical series of films at reduced rates; (9) Become eligible to join ASHA via the credit plan.

ACOUSTICAL SOCIETY OF AMERICA
335 E. 45th Street
New York, N.Y. 10017
Phone: (212) 685-1940

Founded: 1929. *Members*: 5,000. *Staff*: 4. *Local Groups*: 15. *Membership*: physicists, engineers covering fields of electroacoustics, ultrasonics, architectural acoustics, physiological and psychological acoustics, music, noise, and vibration control. *Committees*: Architectural Acoustics, Engineering Acoustics, Musical Acoustics, Noise, Physical Acoustics, Psychological and Physiological Acoustics, Shock and Vibration, Speech Communication, Underwater Acoustics. *Publications*: *Journal of the Acoustical Society of America*, monthly. *Convention/ Meeting*: semiannual.

ALEXANDER GRAHAM BELL
ASSOCIATION FOR THE DEAF (AGBA)
3417 Volta Pl. N.W.
Washington, D.C. 20007
Sara E. Conlon, Exec. Dir.

Founded: 1890. *Members*: 7,000. *Staff*: 18. *Local Groups*: 250. Teachers of the deaf, speech and hearing therapists, physicians, hearing aid dealers, and all others interested in the problems of hearing impairment. *Affiliate members*: organized groups (250) of parents of deaf children. To promote the teaching of speech, lipreading, and use of residual hearing to the deaf, encourage research on deafness, and assist schools and agencies working for better educational facilities for deaf children. Offers educational consultation and scholarships for oral deaf students; conducts research on expanding opportunities for employment of the deaf. Serves as information center and maintains library on speech and hearing. *Sections*: American Organization for Education of the Hearing Impaired, International Parents Organization; Oral Deaf Adults. *Publications*: (1) *World Traveler*, 10/year; (2) *The Volta Review* (journal), 9/year; also publishes bibliographies, teachers' and clinicians' handbooks, several lipreading books, references and children's books. *Convention/Meeting*: biennial.

CONVENTION OF AMERICAN INSTRUCTORS
OF THE DEAF (CAID)
5034 Wisconsin Ave. N.W.
Washington, D.C. 20016
Phone: (202) 363-1327
Howard M. Quigley, Exec. Dir.

Founded: 1850. *Members*: 4,000. Professional organization of teachers, administrators and professionals in allied fields in the education of the deaf. To provide opportunities for a free interchange of views concerning methods and means of educating the deaf; to promote that education by the publication of reports, essays, and other information; to seek to develop more effective methods of teaching hearing-impaired children. *Committees*: Auditing; Council on Education of the Deaf; Council of Organizations of Children and Youth; Interpreters; Joint Advisory-American Annals of the Deaf; Necrology; Parents, Resolutions. *Publications*: (1) *American Annals of the Deaf*, 5/year; (2) *Directory of Services for the Deaf in the United States*, annual; (3) *Proceedings of the Convention of American Instructors of the Deaf*, biennial; (4) News Releases, irregular. Also known as: American Instructors of the Deaf. *Convention/Meeting*: biennial.

JUNIOR NATIONAL ASSOCIATION
FOR THE DEAF (JrNAD)
Gallaudet College
Washington, D.C. 20002
Phone: (202) 447-0741
Frank R. Turk, Natl. Dir.

Founded: 1961. *Members*: 5,000. *Local Groups*: 70. Hearing-impaired teenagers. *Purposes are*: to provide deaf students with unlimited opportunities to reach the highest individual potentials and to contribute to community growth and development; to provide deaf students with the knowledge and understanding necessary to safeguard and promote the independent living and self-determinism of all deaf individuals; to assist the Jr. NAD and Collegiate NAD groups in every way possible. Maintains Deaf Youth Leadership Camp in Minnesota. Bestows National Volunteer Award Citation. Maintains biographical archives. Sponsors competitions. Compiles statistics. *Publications*: (1) *Newsletter*, monthly; (2) *Junior Deaf American Publication*, quarterly; (3) *Silent Voice*, biennial. *Convention/Meeting*: annual.

AMERICAN CLEFT PALATE ASSOCIATION
(ACPA)
Administrative Office
331 Salk Hall
University of Pittsburgh
Pittsburgh, Pa. 15261
Phone: (412) 681-9620

Founded: 1943. *Members*: 12,000. Physicians, dentists, speech pathologists, audiologists, psychologists, and others actively engaged in the care of individuals with cleft lips, palates, and other associated deformities of the mouth and face. Presents Honors Award and Service Award, irregularly. *Committees:* Educational Materials, International Relations Nomenclature. *Publications*: (1) *Cleft Palate Journal,* quarterly; (2) *Directory,* biennial. *Convention/Meeting:* annual.

NATIONAL EASTER SEAL SOCIETY
FOR CRIPPLED CHILDREN
AND ADULTS (HANDICAPPED)
2023 W. Ogden Ave.
Chicago, Ill. 60612
Phone: (312) 243-8400

Founded: 1921. *State Groups*: 52. *Local Groups*: 2,000. Federation of state units and their affiliated local societies. To establish and conduct programs that serve the physically handicapped; work with other voluntary and governmental agencies to support services for the handicapped; publish and disseminate information on the needs of the crippled, on existing services for them, and on medical and professional activities related to rehabilitation. Maintains Information Center, operates Easter Seal Research Foundation. *Publications*: (1) *Rehabilitation Literature*, monthly; (2) *Easter Seal Communicator*, 10/yr. Also known as Easter Seal Society. *Convention/Meeting*: annual—always November.

UNITED CEREBRAL PALSY ASSOCIATIONS (UCPA)
66 E. 34th St.
New York, N.Y. 10016
Phone: (212) 889-6655
Earl H. Cunerd, Exec. Dir.

Founded: 1949. *Members*: 308. *Staff*: 100. Federation of state (44) and local (232) affiliates aiding the cerebral palsied. Membership is held by affiliates which designate their representatives from among civic and philanthropic leaders. The national association supports research; provides traineeships for medical and allied personnel; sponsors professional and public education in the interest of the prevention and management of cerebral palsy; cooperates with governmental and other agencies concerned with the welfare of the handicapped; undertakes demonstration projects to establish models of exemplary community services for persons with cerebral palsy and other disabilities; offers guidance to the programs and activities of affiliates. At the state level supports governmental activities; coordinates local affiliates; provides services in areas not served by local affiliates. Local affiliates provide medical treatment, therapy and social service aid; conduct vocational training; sponsor special education for children; arrange for home instruction; maintain recreational facilities for children and adults; offer psychological guidance to parents of cerebral palsied children. Presents awards. *Committees*: Awards; Campaign, Concerned Youth for Cerebral Palsy; Consumer Activities; Governmental Activities; Legal Advocacy; Professional Program Services; Public Relations; Women's. *Departments*: Campaign; Field Services; General Services; Legal and Legislative; Medical; Professional Services; Public Relations; Women's Activities; Youth Activities. *Publications*: *Work from Washington*, monthly; *UCP Crusader*, bimonthly; *Annual Report*. Affiliated with: American Academy for Cerebral Palsy; National Committee on Research in Neurological Disorders (member). *Convention/Meeting*: annual conference.

NATIONAL ASSOCIATION FOR RETARDED CITIZENS (MENTAL RETARDATION) (NARC)
2709 Avenue E. East
Arlington, Va. 76011
Phone: (817) 261-4961
Philip Roos, Exec. Dir.

Founded: 1950. *Members*: 275,000. *Staff*: 65. *State Groups*: 60. *Local Groups*: 1,800. Parents, professional workers, and others interested in mentally retarded individuals. Works on local, state, and national levels to promote treatment, research, public understanding, and legislation for mentally retarded persons and counseling of parents. Maintains library of 2,000 volumes. *Committees*: Community Services; Education; Government Affairs; International Relations; Legal Advocacy; Poverty; Prevention and Public Health; Public Information; Research Advisory Board; Residential Services and Facilities. *Publications*: *Mental Retardation News*, 10/yr. *Convention/Meeting*: annual.

COUNCIL FOR EXCEPTIONAL CHILDREN
(SPECIAL EDUCATION) (CEC)
1520 Association Dr.
Reston, Va. 22091
Phone: (703) 620-3660
William C. Geer, Exec. Dir.

Founded: 1922. *Members*: 65,000. *Staff*: 75. *State and Provincial Groups*: 53. *Local Groups*: 950. A professional association of teachers, school administrators, and teacher educators. "An organization with major concern for those children and youth whose instructional needs differ sufficiently from the average to require special services and teachers with specialized qualifications." Types of children with which the council is concerned include the mentally gifted, mentally retarded, visually handicapped, auditorily handicapped, physically handicapped, and those with behavioral disorders, learning disabilities, and speech defects. *Committees*: Canadian Affairs; International Relations; Minority Groups; Professional Standards; Research. *Divisions*: Association for the Gifted; Children with Learning Disabilities; Communication Disorders; Council of Administrators of Special Education; Council for Children with Behavioral Disorders; Diagnostic Services; Early Childhood; Mental Retardation; Partially Seeing and Blind; Physically Handicapped; Homebound, and Hospitalized; Teacher Education; Visually Handicapped. *Publications*: (1) *Exceptional Children,* 8/yr.; (2) *Abstracts*, quarterly; (3) *Teaching Exceptional Children*, quarterly; (4) *Update*, quarterly; also publishes reprints, produces microfilms, films, books, and other materials relevant to teaching exceptional children. *Convention/Meeting*: annual.

appendix

4 | commercial materials, equipment, publishers, and prices

Following is a partial list of commercial materials, equipment, and prices as of 1976, along with the names and addresses of the publishers or manufacturers. The prices listed here should be considered only as a guide and the school clinician should write to the company in order to obtain the current prices.

Equipment	Publisher/Manufacturer	Price
Beltone Portable Audiometer (Model 10-D)	Beltone Electronics Corp. 4201 West Victoria Chicago, Illinois 60646	$485.00
Portable Cassette Tape Recorder (Superscope C-103)	Local Dealer in Sound Equipment	89.95
Phonic Mirror (HC-500)	HC Electronics P.O. Box 201 Dayton, Ohio 45405	500.00
DAF Unit	HC Electronics	650.00

Equipment	Publisher/Manufacturer	Price
Language Master (Model 717)	Bell & Howell Audio Visual Products Div. 7100 McCormick Road Chicago, Illinois	250.00
Voxcom	Gordon Stowe & Associates 1728 Chapel Court Northbrook, Illinois 60062	199.50
Auditory Trainer EB-41CA with Circumaural Headsets	Guinta Associates 13 East Fort Lee Rd. Bogota, New Jersey 07603	270.00
Talk Time (Voice Feedback & Programming)	Voice Identifications P.O. Box 714 Sommerville, N.J. 08876	675.00
Electrolarynx (Model 5-A)	Ohio Bell Telephone Company	45.00
Floxite Mirror Lamp (Set No.2)	Floxite Co., Inc. Box 1094 Niagara Falls, N.Y. 14303	16.75

Tests	Publisher/Manufacturer	Price
Photo Articulation Test	The Interstate Publishers 19-27 N. Jackson Danville, Illinois	14.75
Goldman-Fristoe Test of Articulation	AGS, Inc. Publisher's Bldg. Circle Pines, Minn. 55014	22.60
Templin-Darley Tests of Articulation	Bureau of Educ. Research & Service Ext. Division-C-20 East Hall University of Iowa Iowa City, Iowa 52240	5.40
McDonald Deep Test (Combination)	Stanwix House, Inc. 3020 Chartiers Ave. Pittsburgh, Pa. 15204	17.00
McDonald Screening Test (Combination)	Stanwix House, Inc.	9.50
Peabody Picture Vocabulary Test	AGS, Inc. Publisher's Bldg. Circle Pines, Minn. 55014	18.50
Assessment of Children's Language Comprehension	Consulting Psychologist's Press 577 College Ave. Palo Alto, Calif. 94306	15.75
Test for Auditory Comprehension of Language (Carrow)	Learning Concepts 2501 N. Lamar Austin, Texas	34.95
Carrow Elicited Language Inventory	Learning Concepts	39.95

Utah Test of Language Development	Communication Research Assoc. P.O. Box 11012 Salt Lake City, Utah 84111	15.00
Illinois Test of Psycholinguistic Abilities	Western Psychological Services Order Dept. 12031 Wilshire Blvd. Los Angeles, Calif. 90025	57.50
Verbal Language Development Scale	AGS, Inc. Publisher's Bldg. Circle Pines, Minn. 55014	3.25
Porch Index of Communicative Ability	Consulting Psychologists' Press 577 College Ave. Palo Alto, Calif. 94306	62.70
Porch Index of Communicative Ability for Children	Consulting Psychologists' Press	52.50
Minnesota Test for Differential Diagnosis of Aphasia	Western Psychological Services 12031 Wilshire Blvd. Los Angeles, Calif. 90025	21.00
Lincoln-Oseretsky Motor Development Scale	Western Psychological Services	47.50
Wepman Auditory Discrimination Test	Western Psychological Services	8.50
Auditory Memory Span Test	Western Psychological Services	9.50
Auditory Sequential Memory Test	Western Psychological Services	9.50
Vineland Social Maturity Scale	Western Psychological Services	22.50
Columbia Mental Maturity Scale	Western Psychological Services	64.50
Goldman-Fristoe-Woodcock Test for Auditory Discrimination with Cassette	AGS, Inc. Publisher's Bldg. Circle Pines, Minn. 55014	23.00
Goldman-Fristoe-Woodcock Auditory Skills Test Battery with Cassettes	AGS, Inc.	98.00
Full Range Picture Vocabulary Test (Ammons & Ammons) with Form A and Form B	Psychological Test Specialists Box 1441 Missoula, Montana 58801	20.00
Boehm Test of Basic Concepts	The Psychological Corporation 304 East 45th St. New York, N.Y. 10017	7.95
Basic Concepts Inventory	Follett Educational Corp. 1010 W. Washington Blvd. Chicago, Illinois 60607 ·	11.55
Bzoch-League Receptive-Expressive Language Scale	Anhinga Press P.O. Box 13501 Gainesville, Fla. 32604	14.50

Auditory Discrimination In Depth	Teaching Resources Corp. 100 Boylston St. Boston, Mass. 02116	59.50
Sequenced Inventory of Communication Development	University of Washington Press Seattle, Washington 98195	57.00
Hannah-Gardner Pre-School Language Screening Test	Joyce Publications, Inc. 18702 Bryant St. P.O. Box 458 Northridge, Calif. 91324	43.50
Yellow Brick Road Test Battery	Learning Concepts 2501 N. Lamar Austin, Texas 78705	29.95

Sample Stimulus Material

Peabody Articulation Deck	AGS, Inc. Publisher's Bldg. Circle Pines, Minn. 55014	26.00
Peabody Articulation Cards	AGS, Inc.	44.00
Goldman-Lynch Sounds & Symbols Kit	AGS, Inc.	140.00
Peabody Language Development Kits:	AGS, Inc.	
Level P—Ages 3-5		192.00
Level 1—Ages 4½-6½		74.00
Level 2—Ages 6-8		88.00
Level 3—Ages 7½-9½		66.00
Early Experiences Kit		260.00
Therapy Kit	Modern Education Corp. P.O. Box 721 Tulsa, Oklahoma 74101	24.00
Fokes Sentence Builders	Teaching Resources Corp. 100 Boylston St. Boston, Mass. 02116	39.00
Parts of Speech (5 sets of cards)	Teaching Resources Corp.	29.95
Word Families (5 sets of cards)	Teaching Resources Corp.	26.75
Written Language Cards	Developmental Learning Materials 7440 Natchez Niles, Illinois 60648	6.00
Sequential Picture Cards IV	Developmental Learning Materials	2.75
Category Cards		2.75
Photo Sequential Cards		3.00
Open Sequence Cards		3.25
Many Faces of Youth Posters		3.25
Colored Plastic Chips		1.50
APT Auditory Discrim. Program		74.00

Auditory Familiar Sounds Tape		4.75
Spatial Relations Picture Cards		1.40
Same/Different Size Cards		1.40
Same/Different Proportion Cards		1.75
Visual Memory Cards—Set I-IV		10.50
Size Sequencing Cards		2.50
Buzzer Board		9.00
Same/Different Color Cards		1.40
Color Assoc. Picture Cards		1.40
Homonyn Cards		2.75
Antonym Cards		2.75
Language Making Action Cards	Word Making Productions 70 West Louise Ave. Salt Lake City, Utah 84115	25.00
Word Making Cards	Word Making Productions	27.50
Paired-Stimulus Kit	Memphis State University Press Memphis, Tenn. 38152	45.00
GOAL: Language Development Program	CLEO Living Aids 3957 Mayfield Cleveland, Ohio 44121	125.00
Play & Say Cards (Set A,B,C,D)	Stanwix House 3020 Chartiers Ave. Pittsburgh, Pa. 15204	32.00
Teach Your Child to Talk	CEBCO Standard Publishing Co. 104 Fifth Ave. New York, N.Y. 10011	2.25
Hand Counter	Local Dealer	5.00
Visually Cued Language Cards (Series 1,2,3)	Consulting Psychologists Press 577 College Ave. Palo Alto, Calif. 94306	60.75
Language Building Cards (Color & Form and Serial Speech)	Interstate Publishers 19-27 N. Jackson Danville, Illinois 61832	19.50
Workbook for Neurologically Impaired	Interstate Publishers	5.95
Geometric Form Frames	Ideal School Supplies Oak Lawn, Illinois 60453	7.00
Size Form Frames	Ideal School Supplies	7.00
Directionality Form Frames	Ideal School Supplies	7.00
Aphasia Rehab. Manual & Therapy Kit	Western Psychological Services Order Dept. 12031 Wilshire Blvd. Los Angeles, Calif. 90025	20.50
Developmental Syntax Program	Learning Concepts 2501 N. Lamar Austin, Texas 78705	29.95

Stuttering Therapy: A Total Approach	Learning Concepts	49.95
Materials for Expressive Syntax Therapy	Specialized Services P.O. Box 526 San Rafael, Calif. 94902	65.00
Karnes Early Language Activities	Young World Products P.O. Box 433 Clinton, Tenn. 37716	52.00

appendix

5 | **record and report forms**

School speech-language and hearing clinicians have developed and utilized record and report forms which can be used in the school systems in which they are employed. The variations among them reflect the needs and policies of each individual school system. In order to acquaint beginning school clinicians with a few of the most frequently used forms, the Fremont, Ohio, speech-language and hearing staff members have allowed us to include a few selected forms in this book. They have indicated that the forms should not be regarded as a finished product inasmuch as they are continually reevaluated and brought up to date.

For the inclusion of these forms we are indebted to Karen Heldt, Lois Easley, Karen Middleswarth, speech, language, and hearing clinicians; and Kent Watkins, coordinator of Pupil Personnel Services, all of the Fremont, Ohio, schools.

Continuation, Alteration, or Termination in the
Speech-Language and Hearing Program

Dear Dr. Branson,

    I understand that the placement of_____ in the Fremont City Schools Speech and Hearing Program is being

_____ Continued

_____ Altered

_____ Terminated

Reasons for the course of action above have been communicated to me.

    In view of all factors, permission is granted to hereby commence with the decision as specified above.

_____

Parent Signature

_____

Date

Parental Permission for Placement in the
Speech-Language and Hearing Program

Dear Dr. Branson,

    I know that the Fremont City Schools provide special assistance for children with speech and hearing problems and that_____ is eligible for this more individualized help. I appreciate the fact that the placement committee has chosen my child for this opportunity.

    After evaluating all factors, it is my decision that one of the following will be complied with by school officials until such time that a new written directive is given.

_____ Please permit my son/daughter to be enrolled in the Speech-Language and Hearing Program as soon as there is room for him/her.

_____ It is requested that my son/daughter not be placed in the Speech-Language and Hearing Program even though he/she is eligible.

    I certify that the decision reached has been my own and that I have not been coerced in reaching this decision.

_____

Parent Signature

_____

Date

Permission for Testing
Speech, Hearing, Language

Dear Parents:

During the Kindergarten Pre-School Screening, it was found that _____
should be re-tested in one or all of the following areas as marked. Results have been shared
with you.

_____   Speech
_____   Hearing
_____   Language

This form grants permission for further testing (re-testing) of your child, in the areas
noted above, in the fall.

_____   Permission is granted for further testing.

_____   Permission is denied for further testing.

_____
Parent's Signature

_____
Date

Parental Permission for Speech-Language-Hearing Evaluation

Student's Name _____ Date _____

Teacher's Name _____ School _____

Dear Parents:

Your child falls into one of the following criteria.

_____ A. recently received speech and hearing screening evaluation

_____ B. previously placed on waiting list for therapy

_____ C. new student to Fremont City Schools

_____ D. has been dismissed from therapy

_____ E. referred by_____for (a) speech (b) hearing (c) language evaluation

Further evaluation of your child is needed to determine if speech, hearing and/or language therapy is presently needed. Therefore parental permission is required to complete the testing.

If a conference is desired to discuss these matters, please notify me at your child's school.

_____

Speech-Language and Hearing Clinician

Please *sign* and *return* this form to me as soon as possible.

Yes _____ permission is granted for testing

No _____ permission denied for testing

_____

Parent's Signature

Progress Report

Name _____ School _____ Grade_____

Dear Parent:

This is a report of progress being made by your child in speech therapy class. Only the checked items apply to your child — Satisfactory Progress

Unsatisfactory Progress

I. RESULTS OF THERAPY
   A. Description of Difficulty
      1. Therapy has been completed on the _____ sounds.
      2. The_____ sounds are being worked on presently.
      3. Therapy will be needed on the _____ sounds.
   B. Ear Training
      1. Can identify his/her sound. _____
      2. Can tell correct and incorrect sound apart in speech of others. _____
   C. Production
      1. Can produce the sound in isolation. _____
      2. Can produce the sound in syllables. _____
      3. Can produce the sound in words and sentences. _____
      4. Can produce the sound in reading._____
      5. Can produce the sound in speaking situations. _____
   D. Self-Evaluation
      1. Can tell correct and incorrect sound apart in own speech._____
      2. Remembers to correct himself/herself if necessary during most speaking situations. _____

II. RECOMMENDATIONS
   A. Continued Therapy   _____
   B. Clinical Vacation   _____
   C. Conditionally Dismissed   _____
   D. Dismissed _____ Date _____

III. REMARKS:

Note: Complete in Triplicate
   1 — Parent
   2 — Child's Permanent Record
   3 — Speech & Hearing Folder

Thank you for your cooperation,

_____
Speech-Language-Hearing Clinician

Medical Referral Form

Date _____

Child's Name _____ Grade _____ Age_____

Dear Parent,

Your child's score in the screening test seems to indicate that an ear, nose and throat examination would be advisable. We are, therefore, suggesting that you take him/her to your doctor for an examination.

Please give these forms to your doctor and ask him to fill out and return this form to us with the information we need for your child's welfare.

1. Was treatment for the hearing problem necessary?   Yes _____ No _____
2. Did you treat the child?   Yes _____ No _____
3. Was the child sent to an ear specialist?   Yes _____ No _____
4. Summary of hearing problem:

5. Recommendations for school: (seating, speech therapy, avoid swimming, etc.)

6. Would you like the child to be retested at any specific interval of time?
    Yes ____ No ____ When _____
7. Comments:

_____ M.D.

_____
            (address)
_____

Return to:

_____, Speech Clinician

_____ School

_____
(address)
_____

Dismissal Notification Speech-Language Program

Dear Parent:

This is to inform you that _____ has been dismissed from the Speech-Language Program which is offered at his/her school.

The reason for dismissal is:

_____ Correction of speech pattern
_____ Maximum improvement of speech pattern
_____ Lack of cooperation or interest in therapy
_____ Conditional Dismissal

If you have any questions, you may contact me at school.

Thank you,

_____
Speech-Language-Hearing Clinician

Hearing Screening Report

Dear Parent:

_____ was given a Hearing Screening evaluation as part of the continuing hearing conservation program in the Fremont City Schools.

The following results were obtained:

_____ Hearing appears to be within normal limits.
_____ Further diagnostic evaluation is indicated and will be accomplished at a later date. You will be notified of the results when completed.

Comments:

Date _____   Screened by: _____
                                                      Speech-Language-Hearing Clinician

Placement Team Conference Report

Date _____

Parents Name_____

RE: _____   Birth Date _____

Address _____   Phone Number _____

Voting
Team Members:_____ , Position_____

_____ , Position_____

_____ , Position_____

_____ , Position_____

_____ , Position_____

Support Personnel Present: Name	Position or Relationship To Child
1. _____	_____
2. _____	_____
3. _____	_____
4. _____	_____
5. _____	_____
6. _____	_____
7. _____	_____
8. _____	_____
9. _____	_____

Current Educational Placement of the Child:_____
_____

Discussion and Recommendation: Upon review of the recommendation and findings of the speech-language and hearing clinician to the Placement Committee,_____ is hereby recommended for _____ enrollment, _____ continuation, ____ alteration, _____ dismissal in/to/from the speech-language and hearing program for the reason(s) as checked below:

PROBLEM   Statement of Specific Reason:

____ articulation

____ language   _____

____ voice

____ fluency   _____

____ hearing

_____
Placement Committee Chairperson

Speech-Language Evaluation and Progress Report

Name _____ Date _____

School_____ Age _____ Grade _____

Teacher _____ Speech-Language Clinician _____

This pupil has been in the Speech-Language Program _____ years, _____ mos. and has received _____ group and/or _____ individual therapy.

Tests and Results (Speech Clinicians, clinic services, hospitals _____)

Clinical Impression:

Progress reports and summary of therapy techniques utilized:

(Use reverse side and attach additional sheets if necessary)

Conference Report

Name _____ Age _____

Grade _____ Teacher _____ Room No. _____

Clinician _____

Report:

Hearing Screening Check Sheet

School_____ Date____ Grade_____ Room/Teacher_____

_____

Student	250	500	1000	2000	4000	6000	8000
1.							
2.							
3.							
4.							
5.							
6.							
7.							
8.							
9.							
10.							
11.							
12.							
13.							
14.							
15.							

Hearing Follow-up Report

School   Principal   Grade   Date

Names of children needing threshold tests	Date given	Teacher & Room	Parents notified	Audiogram sent to Nurse	Remarks	Follow-up	Remarks

Speech and Language Screening Report

			To be filled out by Therapist							Remarks
School_____ Clinician_____ Date _____			Articulation	Voice	Delayed speech	Hard of hearing	Dysfluency	Corrected	No problem	
Name	*Gr.*	*Rm.*								
1.										
2.										
3.										
4.										
5.										
6.										
7.										
8.										
9.										
10.										

Parent Permission for Speech, Language, and/or Hearing Assessment

School _____   School Year _____

Speech & Hearing Therapist _____

Grade	Name	Reason for Referral	Date Tested	Results of Assessment

Students Scheduled for Speech-Language Therapy

School_____

Year _____

Time	Student	Teacher	Grade	Room	Comments

_____

Speech & Hearing Clinician

INDIVIDUALIZED EDUCATION PLAN (IEP)

Name _____ School Year _____ Age (Oct. 1) _____ Birthdate _____

Parents _____ Address _____ County _____ Phone No. _____

Recommended District or Educational Agency _____

I. Evaluations Completed and Information Gathered
   (See attached IIP checklist)

II. Statement of Present Levels of Educational Performance

	Mild	Moderate	Severe
Articulation			
Language			
Voice			
Stuttering			
Hearing			

III. Statement of the Specific Educational Services

Program Placement and Services:	Needed	Date Initiated	Anticipated Duration	Comments
Regular Class				
Special Class Part-time				
Special Class Full time				
Special School				
Institution				
Home Instruction				
Related Services:				
Tutoring				
Speech Therapy				
Occupational Therapy				
Physical Therapy				
Transportation				
Orientation & Mobility				
Counseling				
Vocational				
Work Experience				

ANNUAL GOALS

IV. Objectives
V. Results of Mid-term Retesting
VI. Status at the End of Therapy
VII. Criteria and Dates for Annual Review
     (See attached IIP Checklist for above information)

VIII. Recommendations:

A. ____ Conditional Dismissal
B. ____ Dismissal
C. ____ Recheck
D. ____ Continued
E. ____ Clinical Vacation
F. ____ Referral to other agency

IX. Provisions for Short Term Instructional Objectives:
    (Responsibility for by Title or Position)

    _____
    (Speech, Language, and Hearing Therapist)

The signed below agree to be fully knowledgeable with the contents of this form and thereby affix our signatures.

_____ _____
Signature of Placement Committee Chairperson   Date

_____ _____
Signature of Superintendent or Designee   Date

_____ _____
Signature of Parent   Date

REFERENCES

Ainsworth, Stanley. "The Speech Clinician in Public Schools: 'Participant' or 'Separatist'?" *Asha*, 7, no. 12 (December, 1965), pp. 495-503.

Alpiner, Jerome G. "Public School Hearing Conservation." *Audiological Assessment*, 2nd ed. Darrell E. Rose, ed. Englewood Cliffs, N.J.: Prentice-Hall, Inc., 1978.

_____, John A. Ogden, and James E. Wiggins. "The Utilization of Supportive Personnel in Speech Correction in the Public Schools: A Pilot Project," *Asha*, 12, no. 12 (December, 1970), pp. 599-604.

American Speech and Hearing Association (ASHA), Committee on Definitions of Public School Speech and Hearing Services, "Services and Functions of Speech and Hearing Specialists in Public Schools, *Asha*, 4, no. 4 (April, 1962), pp. 99-100.

ASHA, Committee on Legislation, "The Need for Adequately Trained Speech Pathologists and Audiologists." *Asha*, 1, no. 4 (December, 1959), p. 138.

ASHA, Committee on Speech and Hearing Services in Schools, "The Speech Clinician's Role in the Public School." *Asha*, 6, no. 6 (June, 1964), pp. 189-91.

ASHA, Committee on Supportive Personnel, "Guidelines on the Role and Training and Supervision of the Communication Aide." *Asha*, 12, no. 2 (February, 1970), pp. 78-80.

Anderson, Jean L., ed. *Conference on Supervision of Speech and Hearing Programs in Schools.* Bloomington, Indiana: Indiana University Publications, 1970.

_____. *Handbook for Supervisors of School Practicum in Speech, Hearing, and Language.* Bloomington, Indiana: Indiana University Publications, 1972.

Backus, Ollie. "Group Structure in Speech Therapy." *Handbook of Speech Pathology*, 1st ed. Lee Edward Travis, ed. Englewood Cliffs, N.J.: Prentice-Hall, Inc., 1957.

_____. "The Use of Group Structure in Speech Therapy." *Journal of Speech and Hearing Disorders*, 17, no. 2 (June 1952), pp. 116-22.

_____ and Ruth Coffman. "Group Therapy with Preschool Children Having Cerebral Palsy." *Journal of Speech and Hearing Disorders*, 18, vol. 4 (December 1953), pp. 350-54.

Bankson, Nicholas W. *Bankson Language Screening Test.* Baltimore, Md.: University Park Press, 1978.

Barrett, Mark D., and John W. Welsh. "Predictive Articulation Screening." *Language, Speech and Hearing Services in Schools.* VI, No. 2 (April 1975), pp. 91-95.

Beall, Adelaide. *Communication Disorders Program for Adolescents and Adults.* Scottsdale, Ga.: De Kalb County School System, Dept. of Special Education, 1977.

Beasley, Jane. "Development of Social Skills as an Instrument in Speech Therapy." *Journal of Speech and Hearing Disorders*, 16, no. 3 (September 1951), pp. 241-45.

Bender, Ruth E. *The Conquest of Deafness.* Cleveland, Ohio: The Press of Western Reserve University, 1960.

Berg, Fredrick S. *Educational Audiology: Hearing and Speech Management.* New York: Grune and Stratton, 1976.

Bergman, Moe. "Screening the Hearing of Preschool Children." *Maico Audiological Library Series*, III, report 4 (1964), Maico Electronics, Inc.

Blanchard, Marjorie M., and E. Harris Nober. "The Impact of State and Federal Legislation on Public School Speech, Language and Hearing Clinicians." *Language, Speech and Hearing Services in Schools*, IX, no. 2 (April 1978), pp. 77-84.

Braunstein, Muriel Sue. "Communication Aide: A Pilot Project." *Language, Speech and Hearing Services in Schools*, III, no. 3 (July 1972), pp. 32-35.

Brett, Richard J. "The Public School Caucus: A Progress Report." *Language, Speech and Hearing Services in Schools*, VII, no. 3 (July 1976), pp. 197-98.

Brickell, Henry M., et al. *A Study of the Ohio Special Education Instructional Resource Centers: Progress and Prospects.* New York: Policy Studies in Education, 1974.

Brunson, W. Joshlin. *A Progress Report on the Communications Aide Training Program.* Baltimore, Md.: The Community College of Baltimore, 1975.

_____. *Special Education Assistant's Program.* Baltimore, Md.: The Community College of Baltimore, 1978.

Byrne, Margaret C. *The Child Speaks: A Speech Improvement Program for Kindergarten and First Grade.* New York: Harper & Row, Pub., 1965.

_____. "A Speech Improvement Program for Kindergarten and First Grade Children," *The Instructor,* 75 (1966), pp. 75-82.

Caccamo, James M. "Accountability—A Matter of Ethics?" *Asha,* 15, no. 8 (August 1973), pp. 411-12.

Carrow, Elizabeth. *Screening Test for Auditory Comprehension of Language; Test Manual.* Austin, Tex.: Urban Research Group, 1973.

Cartwright, Dorwin, and Alvin Zander. *Group Dynamics: Research and Theory.* New York: Harper & Row, Pub., 1960.

C.E.C. Policies Commission, Maynard Reynolds, Chairman, "Policy Statements: Call for Response. Basic Commitments and Responsibilities to Exceptional Children." *Exceptional Children,* 37, no. 6 (February 1971), pp. 421-33.

Cody, Robert C. "Hearing Screening in the Schools: The Tympano-Audiometric Approach." Paper presented at the West Virginia Speech and Hearing Association Convention. Charleston, April, 1976.

Conlon, Sara, et al. "Task Force Report on School Speech, Hearing and Language Screening Procedures." *Language, Speech and Hearing Services in Schools,* IV, no. 3 (July 1973), pp. 109-19.

Connell, Phil J., Joseph E. Spradlin, and Leija V. McReynolds. "Some Suggested Criteria for Evaluation of Language Programs." *Journal of Speech and Hearing Disorders,* 42. no. 4 (November 1977), 563-67.

Costello, Janis, and Judith Schoen. "The Effectiveness of Paraprofessionals and a Speech Clinician as Agents of Articulation Intervention using Programmed Instruction." *Language, Speech and Hearing Services in Schools,* IX, no. 2 (April 1978), pp. 118-28.

Coventry, W. F. and Irving Burstiner. *Management: A Basic Handbook.* Englewood Cliffs, N.J.: Prentice-Hall, Inc., 1977.

Crabtree, Margaret, and Elizabeth Peterson. "The Speech Pathologist as a Resource Teacher for Language/Learning Disabilities." *Language, Speech and Hearing Services in Schools,* V, no. 4 (October 1974), pp. 194-97.

Curry, E. Thayer. "The Efficiency of Teacher Referrals in a School Hearing Testing Program." *Journal of Speech and Hearing Disorders,* 15, no. 3 (September 1950), pp. 211-14.

Diehl, Charles F., and Charles D. Stinnett. "Efficiency of Teacher Referrals in a School Speech Testing Program." *Journal of Speech and Hearing Disorders,* 24, no. 1 (February 1959), pp. 34-36.

Dopheide, William R., and Jane R. Dallinger. "Improving Remedial Speech and Language Services Through Clinician-Teacher In-Service Interaction." *Language, Speech and Hearing Services in Schools,* VI, no. 4 (October 1975), pp. 196-205.

Dublinske, Stan. "Special Reports: PL 94-142: Developing the Individualized Education Program (IEP). *Asha,* 20, no. 5 (May 1978), pp. 393-97.

_____, and William C. Healey. "PL 94-142: Questions and Answers for the Speech-Language Pathologist and Audiologist." *Asha,* 20, no. 3 (March 1978), pp. 188-205.

Dunn, Harriet M. "A Speech and Hearing Program for Children in a Rural Area." *Journal of Speech and Hearing Disorders,* 14 (June 1949), pp. 166-70.

Dunn, Lloyd. *Peabody Picture Vocabulary Test.* Minneapolis: American Guidance Service, Inc., 1965.

_____, and J. Smith. *Peabody Language Development Kits, Level 1 and Level 2.* Circle Pines, Minn.: American Guidance Service, Inc., 1965 and 1967.

_____, K. Horton, and J. Smith. *Peabody Language Development Kits, Level P.* Circle Pines, Minn.: American Guidance Service, Inc., 1968.

Engelmann, S., J. Osborn, and T. Englemann. *Distar Language—An Instructional System.* Chicago: Science Research Associates, 1969.

Engnoth, Gloria, et al. "Recommendations for Housing of Speech Services Schools." Subcommittee on Housing, Committee on Speech and Hearing Services in Schools, *Asha,* 11, no. 4 (April 1969), pp. 181-82.

Ervin, Jean E. "A Study of the Effectiveness of Block Scheduling Versus Cycle Scheduling for Articulation Therapy for Grades Two and Three in the Public Schools." *Journal of the Speech and Hearing Association of Virginia.* 6, no. 2 (Spring 1965).

Fairbanks, Grant. *Voice and Articulation Drillbook* 2nd ed., New York: Harper & Row, Pub., 1960.

Fisher, Hilda B., and Jerilyn A. Logemann. *Fisher-Logemann Test of Articulation Competence.* Boston, Mass.: Houghton Mifflin Co., 1971.

Fisher, Lee J. "An Open Letter to ASHA Members Employed in the Schools." *Language, Speech and Hearing Services in Schools,* VIII, no. 2 (April 1977), pp. 72-75.

Foster, C., J. Giddan, and J. Stark. *ACLC: Assessment of Children's Language Comprehension,* Palo Alto, Calif.: Consulting Psychologists Press, 1969.

Freeman, Gerald G. "The Speech Clinician—as a Consultant." *Clinicial Speech In The Schools* 1st ed. Roland J. Van Hattum, ed. Springfield, Ill.: Chas. C. Thomas Publishers, 1969.

_____, *Speech and Language Services and the Classroom Teacher.* Reston, Va.: The Council for Exceptional Children, 1977.

_____, and Jean Lukens. "A Speech and Language Program for Educable Mentally Retarded Children." *Journal of Speech and Hearing Disorders,* 27, no. 3 (August 1962), pp. 285-87.

Galloway, Herbert F. and C. Milton Blue. "Paraprofessionals in Articulation Therapy." *Language, Speech and Hearing Services in Schools,* VI, no. 3 (July 1975), pp. 125-30.

Garbee, Frederick E. "Legal and Professional Foundations for a Speech and Hearing Program." *The California Program for Speech and Hearing Handicapped School Children,* California State Department of Education Bulletin, XXXIII, no. 4 (December 1964) p. 8.

Garrison, Geraldine, et al. "Speech Improvement." *Journal of Speech and Hearing Disorders,* Monograph Supplement 8 (June 1961), p. 80.

Gerstenslager Company. *Speech and Hearing Testing Gets Right to the Problems.* Wooster, Ohio: Gerstenslager Company.

Goldman, R., and M. Fristoe. *Goldman-Fristoe Test for Articulation.* Circle Pines, Minn.: American Guidance Service, Inc. 1969.

Goldman, R., and M. Lynch. *Goldman-Lynch Sounds and Symbols Development Kit.* Circle Pines, Minn.: American Guidance Service, Inc., 1971.

Greenberg, Herbert J. "Fundamentals of Acoustic Impedance or Admittance Measurement— A Tutorial Presentation." *Asha,* 17, no. 10 (October 1975), pp. 729-32.

Gross, Frank P., and George Fichter. "Professional Negotiations and the School Speech and Hearing Clinician." *Asha,* 12, no. 3 (March 1970), pp. 124-26.

_____. "State Board of Education Program Standards." *Ohio School Speech and Hearing Services.* Worthington, Ohio: Ohio Division of Special Education, 1972.

Gruenewald, Lee J., and Sara A. Pollak. "The Speech Clinician's Role in Auditory Learning and Reading Readiness." *Language, Speech and Hearing Services in Schools,* IV, no. 3 (July 1973), pp. 120-26.

Haines, Harold H. "Trends in Public School Therapy." *Asha,* 7, no. 6 (June 1965), pp. 166-70.

Healey, William C. "Notes from the Associate Secretary for School Affairs, Task Force Report on Data Collection and Information Systems." *Language, Speech and Hearing Services in Schools,* IV, no. 2 (April 1973), pp. 57-65.

_____. *Standards and Guidelines for Comprehensive Language, Speech and Hearing Programs in the Schools.* Rockville, Md.: American Speech and Hearing Association, 1973-1974.

_____. "Notes from the Director, School Services Program." *Language, Speech and Hearing Services in Schools,* VIII, no. 1 (January 1977), p. 4.

_____, and Stan Dublinske. "Notes from the School Services Program Official Title: Speech-Language Pathologist." *Language, Speech and Hearing Services in Schools,* VIII, no. 2 (April 1977), p. 67.

_____. "Notes From the School Services Program." *Language, Speech and Hearing Services in Schools,* VIII, no. 3 (July 1977), p. 139.

_____. "Notes from the School Services Program." *Language, Speech and Hearing Services in Schools,* IX, no. 1 (January 1978), p. 3.

Hess, Rhoda. "Guidelines for a Cooperating Clinician in Working with a Student Clinician in the Schools." *Ohio Journal of Speech and Hearing,* 11, no. 2 (Spring 1976), pp. 83-89.

Howerton, Gerald E. "What Can Be Done About Substandard Space for Speech Correction Programs." *Language, Speech and Hearing Services in Schools,* IV, no. 2 (April 1973), pp. 95-96.

Hull, F. M., et al. *National Speech and Hearing Survey Interim Report.* (Project No. 50978.) Washington, D.C.: Department of Health, Education, and Welfare, Office of Education, Bureau of Education for the Handicapped, 1969.

Irwin, Ruth Beckey. "Speech Therapy in the Public Schools: State Legislation and Certification." *Journal of Speech and Hearing Disorders,* 24, no. 2 (May 1959), p. 127.

_____. "Speech and Hearing Therapy in the Public Schools of Ohio." *Journal of Speech and Hearing Disorders,* 14, no. 1 (March 1949), pp. 63-68.

Jelinek, Janis A. "A Pilot Program for Training and Utilization of Paraprofessionals in Pre-Schools." *Language, Speech and Hearing Services in Schools,* VII, no. 2 (April 1976), pp. 119-23.

Johns, Elizabeth Lambert. "Teacher Organizations and the School Clinician." *Language, Speech and Hearing Services in Schools,* 5, no. 3 (July 1974), pp. 171-73.

Johnson, Wendell. *Children With Speech and Hearing Impairment: Preparing To Work With Them in the Schools.* U. S. Dept. of Health, Education and Welfare, Bulletin No. 5, 1959.

Jones, Shirley A., and William C. Healey. *Project UPGRADE: Model Regulations for School Language, Speech and Hearing Programs and Services.* Washington, D.C.: The American Speech and Hearing Association, 1973.

_____. *Essentials of Program Planning, Development, Management, Evaluation: A Manual for School Speech, Hearing and Language Programs.* Wash., D.C.: American Speech and Hearing Association, 1973.

Journot, Vida M. *A Tabulated Accountability Plan for Speech Therapy Services.* Hurst, Tex.: Tabulated Accountability Plan, 1973.

Kindred, Leslie W. *School Public Relations.* Englewood Cliffs, N.J.: Prentice-Hall, Inc., 1957.

Knight, Helen Sullivan. "Functions of the School Clinician." *Speech and Hearing Services in Schools.* no. 3 (1970), pp. 12-23.

Kodman, Frank, Jr. "Identification of Hearing Loss by the Classroom Teacher." *Laryngoscope.* 66 (August 1950), pp. 1346-49.

Lynch, John. "Operation: Moving Ahead." *Language, Speech and Hearing Services in Schools,* III, no. 4 (October 1972), pp. 82-87.

MacLearie, Elizabeth, and F. P. Gross. *Experimental Programs for Intensive Cycle Scheduling of Speech and Hearing Therapy Classes.* Columbus, Ohio: Ohio Dept. of Education, 1966.

Martin, Edwin W. "The Right to Education: Issues Facing the Speech and Hearing Profession." *Asha,* 17, no. 6 (June 1975), p. 384-87.

McCandless, G. A. "Screening for Middle Ear Disease on the Wind River Indian Reservation." *Hearing Instruments* (April 1975), pp. 19-20.

McDonald, Eugene. *A Deep Test of Articulation.* Pittsburgh: Stanwix House, 1964.

Melnick, William, Eldon L. Eagles, and Herbert S. Levine. "Evaluation of a Recommended Program of Identification Audiometry with School-Age Children." *Journal of Speech and Hearing Disorders,* 29, no. 1 (February 1964), pp. 3-13.

Milisen, Robert. "The Incidence of Speech Disorders." *Handbook of Speech Pathology and Audiology,* ed. Lee Edward Travis. Englewood Cliffs, N.J.: Prentice-Hall, Inc., 1971.

Miner, Ray, Donna Hibbard, and Diane Carmean. *Wood County Audiological Services,* 1977-1978 School Year Report. Wood County, Ohio: Office of Education, 1978.

Moll, Kenneth L. "Issues Facing Us—Supportive Personnel." *Asha,* 16, no. 7 (July 1974).

Moore, G. Paul, and Dorothy Kester. "Historical Notes on Speech Correction in the Pre-association Era." *Journal of Speech and Hearing Disorders*, 18, no. 1 (March 1953), pp. 48-53.

Mowrer, Donald E. "Accountability and Speech Therapy in the Public Schools." *Asha*, 14, no. 3 (March 1972), pp. 111-15.

Muma, John. *Language Handbook: Concepts, Assessment, Intervention.* Englewood Cliffs, N.J.: Prentice-Hall, Inc., 1978.

National Conference on Identification Audiometry: Identification Audiometry. *Journal of Speech and Hearing Disorders, Monograph Supplement 9,* 1961.

National Institute of Neurological Diseases and Stroke. *NINDS Research Profile: No. 4, Hearing, Language and Speech Disorders.* Washington, D.C.: U.S. Government Printing Office, 1967.

Navarro, M. Richard, and David A. Klodd. "Impedance Audiometry for the School Clinician." *Language, Speech and Hearing Services in Schools*, IX, no. 1 (January 1978), pp. 50-56.

Neal, W. R., Jr. "Speech Pathology Services in the Secondary Schools." *Language, Speech and Hearing Services in Schools*, VII, no. 1 (January 1976), pp. 6-16.

Neidecker, Elizabeth A. "Supervision in the School Clinical Practicum Situation: Roles and Responsibilities." *Ohio Journal of Speech and Hearing*, 10, no. 2 (Spring 1976), pp. 83-89.

Nemoy, Elizabeth, and S. F. Davis. *Correction of Defective Consonant Sounds.* Magnolia, Mass.: The Expression Company, 1945.

Nigro, Louis J. *Carteret Public Schools Speech and Hearing Services.* Wooster, Ohio: The Gerstenslager Company.

Nodar, Richard H. "Teacher Identification of Elementary School Children with Hearing Loss." *Language, Speech and Hearing Services in Schools*, IX, no. 1 (January 1978), pp. 24-28.

Northcott, Winifred H. "The Hearing-Impaired Child: A Speech Clinician as an Interdisciplinary Team Member." *Language, Speech and Hearing Services in Schools*, III, no. 2 (April 1972), pp. 7-19.

O'Toole, Thomas J. "Accountability and the Clinician in the Schools." *Speech and Hearing Service in Schools*, no. 3, pp. 24-25.

_____, and Elinor Zaslow. "Public School Speech and Hearing Programs: Things Are Changing." *Asha*, 11, no. 11 (November 1969), pp. 499-501.

Paden, Elaine Pagel. *A History of the American Speech and Hearing Association 1925-1958.* Washington, D.C.: American Speech and Hearing Association, 1970.

Parker, Barbara L. "The Speech and Language Clinician on a Learning Center Team." *Language, Speech and Hearing Services in Schools*, III, no. 3 (July 1972), pp. 18-23.

Parker, Steve, and J. Montague. "Information Services for School Speech-Language Pathologists and Educational Audiologists." *Language, Speech and Hearing Services in Schools*, IX, no. 2 (April 1978), pp. 103-8.

Pendergast, Kathleen, Stanley Dickey, John Selmar, and Anton Soder. *Photo Articulation Test.* Danville, Ill.: The Interstate Printers and Publishers, 1966.

Phelps, Richard A., and Roy A. Koenigsknecht. "Attitudes of Classroom Teachers, Learning Disabilities Specialists, and School Principals toward Speech and Language Programs in Public Elementary Schools." *Language, Speech and Hearing Services in Schools*, VIII, no. 1 (January 1977), pp. 33-42.

Phillips, Phyllis. *Speech and Hearing Problems in the Classroom.* Lincoln, Nebraska: Cliff Notes, Inc., 1975.

_____. "Variables Affecting Classroom Teachers' Understanding of Speech Disorders." *Language, Speech and Hearing Services in Schools*, VIII, no. 3 (July 1976), pp. 142-49.

Pickering, Marisue, and William R. Dopheide. "Training Aides to Screen Children for Speech and Language Problems." *Language, Speech and Hearing Services in Schools*, VII, no. 4 (October 1976), pp. 236-41.

Pikus, Anita, Project Director. *Comprehensive Assessment and Service Evaluation Information System for Language, Speech and Hearing Programs in Schools*, NEEDS II Project. Rockville, Md.: American Speech and Hearing Association, 1976.

Prahl, Harriett M., and Eugene B. Cooper. "Accuracy of Teacher Referrals of Speech-Handicapped School Children." *Asha*, 6, no. 10 (October 1964), Convention Abstracts, p. 392.

Pronovost, Wilbert L., C. G. Wells, D. L. Gray, R. K. Sommers. "Research: Current Status and Needs." *Journal of Speech and Hearing Disorders, Monograph Supplement 8,* (June 1961), pp. 114-23.

Raia, Anthony P. *Managing By Objectives.* Glenview, Illinois: Scott, Foresman, 1974.

Raph, June Beasley. "Determinants of Motivation in Speech Therapy." *Journal of Speech. and Hearing Disorders*, 25, no. 1 (February 1960).

Rees, Norma S. "The Speech Pathologist and the Reading Process." *Asha*, 16, no. 5 (May 1974), p. 258.

Reynolds, Maynard C., and Sylvia W. Rosen. "Special Education: Past, Present, and Future." *The Educational Forum.* XL, no. 4 (May 1976), pp. 551-62.

Rodgers, William C. *Picture Articulation and Language Screening Test.* Salt Lake City, Utah: Word-Making Productions, 1976.

Roe, Vivian I., et al. "Clinical Practice: Diagnosis and Measurement." *Journal of Speech and Hearing Disorders, Monograph Supplement 8* (June 1961), pp. 51-57.

Sanders, Derek A. *Auditory Perception of Speech: An Introduction to Principles and Problems.* Englewood Cliffs, N.J.: Prentice-Hall, Inc., 1977.

Sayre, Joan, and James Mack. *Think, Listen and Say.* Jamaica, N.Y.: Eye Gate House, 1967.

Scalero, Angela M., and Constance Eskenazi. "The Use of Supportive Personnel in a Public School Speech and Hearing Program." *Language, Speech and Hearing Services in Schools*, VII, no. 3 (July 1976), pp. 150-8.

Scarvel, Lucia D. "Standardizing Criteria for Evaluating Physical Facilities and Organizational Patterns of Speech, Language and Hearing Programs." *The Journal of the Pennsylvania Speech and Hearing Association*, X, no. 2 (June 1977) pp. 17-19.

Schoolfield, Lucille. *Better Speech and Better Reading.* Magnolia, Mass.: The Expression Co., 1937.

Schubert, George W. *Introduction to Clinical Supervision in Speech Pathology.* St. Louis, Missouri: Warren H. Green, Inc., 1978.

Schultz, Martin. *An Analysis of Clinical Behavior in Speech and Hearing.* Englewood Cliffs, N.J.: Prentice-Hall, Inc., 1972.

Sherr, Richard. "Meeting to Develop the Individualized Education Program." *A Primer on Individualized Education Programs for Handicapped Children.* ed. Scottie Torres. Reston, Va.: The Foundation for Exceptional Children, 1977.

Simon, Charlann S. "Cooperative Communication Programming: A Partnership Between the Learning Disabilities Teacher and the Speech-Language Pathologist." *Language, Speech and Hearing in Schools*, VIII, no. 3 (July 1977), pp. 188-98.

Sommers, Ronald K., et al. "Effects of Speech Therapy and Speech Improvement on Articulation and Reading." *Journal of Speech and Hearing Disorders*, 26, no. 1 (February 1961), pp. 27-38.

Sommers, Ronald K. "Case Finding, Case Selection, Case Loan." *Clinical Speech in the Schools*, ed. Rolland Van Hattum. Springfield, Ill.: Chas. C. Thomas, 1969.

Stark, Joel. "Reading Failure: A Language-Based Problem." *Asha*, 17, no. 12 (December 1975), pp. 832-34.

Steer, Mark D., and Hazel G. Drexler. "Predicting Later Articulation Abilities from Kindergarten Tests." *Journal of Speech and Hearing Disorders*, 25, no. 4 (November 1960), pp. 391-97.

Steer, Mark D., et al. "Public School Speech and Hearing Services. A Special Report Prepared with Support of the United States Office of Education and Purdue University." *Journal of Speech and Hearing Disorders, Monograph Supplement 8.* U.S. Office of Education Cooperative Research Project No. 649 (8191), July 1961.

Stephens, I. *The Stephens Oral Language Screening Test.* Peninsula, Ohio: Interim Publishers, 1977.

Strong, Beverly. "Public School Speech Technicians in Minnesota." *Language, Speech and Hearing Services in Schools,* III, no. 1 (January 1972), pp. 53-56.

Task Force Report on Traditional Scheduling Procedures in Schools." *Language, Speech and Hearing Services in Schools,* IV, no. 3 (July 1973), pp. 100-9.

Templin, Mildred and Frederic Darley. *Templin-Darley Tests of Articulation: 2nd ed.* Iowa City, Iowa: Bureau of Educational Research and Services, 1969.

Toffler, Alvin. *Future Shock.* "Education in the Future Tense." New York: Random House, 1970.

Van Hattum, Rolland. "The Defensive Speech Clinician in the Schools." *Journal of Speech and Hearing Disorders,* 31, no. 3 (August 1966), pp. 234-40.

Van Riper, Charles. "My Grandfather." *Speech Correction: Principles and Methods.* Englewood Cliffs, N.J.: Prentice-Hall, Inc., 1954.

_____, and Robert L. Erickson. *Predictive Screening Test of Articulation* 3rd ed. Kalamazoo, Mich.: Continuing Education Office, Western Michigan University, 1973.

Waters, Betty J., Marilyn D. Bill, and Elizabeth L. Lowell. "Precision Therapy—An Interpretation." *Journal of Speech and Hearing Disorders,* VIII, no. 4 (October 1977), pp. 234-44.

Wechsler, D. *Wechsler Intelligence Scale for Children.* New York: Psychological Corp., 1949.

Weintraub, Frederick, et al. *State Law and Education of Handicapped Children: Issues and Recommendations.* Arlington, Va.: Council for Exceptional Children, 1971.

Wepman, Joseph. *Auditory Discrimination Test.* Chicago: Language Research Associates, 1958.

Wiig, Elizabeth H., and Eleanor M. Semel. "Wiig-Semel Test of Linguistic Concepts," *Language Disabilities in Children and Adolescents.* Columbus, Ohio: Chas. E. Merrill, 1976.

_____. *Language Disabilities in Children and Adolescents.* Columbus, Ohio: Chas. E. Merrill, 1976.

Wilson, Betty A. "The Development and Evaluation of a Speech Improvement Program for Kindergarten Children." *Journal of Speech and Hearing Disorders,* no. 1 (March 1954), pp. 4-13.

Wing, Douglas M. "A Data Recording Form for Case Management And Accountability." *Language, Speech and Hearing Services in Schools,* VI, no. 1 (January 1975), pp. 38-40.

Work, Rhonda S., E. C. Hutchinson, W. C. Healey, R. K. Sommers, E. I. Stevens. "Accountability in a School Speech and Language Program: Part 1: Cost Accounting." *Language, Speech and Hearing Services in Schools,* VI, no. 1 (January 1975), pp. 7-13.

_____. "Accountability in a School Speech and Language Program: Part II: Instructional Materials Analysis." *Language, Speech and Hearing Services in Schools,* VII, no. 4 (October 1976), pp. 259-70.

Zemmol, Caroline S. "A Priority System of Case-Load Selection." *Language, Speech and Hearing Services in Schools,* VIII, no. 2 (April 1977), pp. 85-98.

Zimmerman, J., V. Steiner, and R. Evatt. *Preschool Language Manual.* Columbus, Ohio: Chas. E. Merrill, 1969.

index

American Speech-Language-Hearing Association, 4, 23, 24, 27, 33, 179. *See also* American Speech and Hearing Association
Analysis of Clinical Behavior in Speech and Hearing, An, 29
Anderson, Jean, 56, 190
Appraisal and diagnosis, 97
  clinicians' responsibility in, 98
  steps in, 98-99
Articulation disorders, 28
  screening for, 88-91
Assessment of Children's Language Comprehension, 160, 162
Audiologist. *See* Educational audiologist
Auditory Comprehension of Language, 162
Auditory Perception of Speech, 138
Auditory Test for Language Comprehension, 161
Average Daily Attendance (ADA), 45
Average Daily Membership (ADM), 45

Backus, Ollie, 123
Bankson Language Screening Test, 90
Barrett, Mark D., 88
Beall, Adelaide, 152
Beasley, Jane, 123
Bender, Ruth E., 5
Benevolent and Protective Order of Elks, 94
Berg, Frederick S., 94
Bergman, Moe, 95
Bill, Marilyn D., 123
Blanchard, Marjorie M., 141
Block system. *See* Intensive cycle model
Blue, C. Milton, 144
Boehm Test of Basic Concepts, 162
Braunstein, Muriel Sue, 142
Brett, Richard J., 175
Brickell, Henry M., 182
Brown v. Board of Education, 10
Burkland, Marjorie, 153, 154
Burstiner, Irving, 57
Byrne, Margaret C., 149, 151

Caccamo, James M., 170
Camp, Pauline, 4
Carrow, Elizabeth, 161, 162
Carry-over, 117
Cartwright, Dorwin, 123

Case finding, 82
Carteret, New Jersey school district, 69
Certificate of Clinical Competence, 24, 158, 179
  requirements for, 204-12
Chicago Teachers' College, 3
Child Find Program, 46-47
Children's periodicals, 186-87
Child Speaks, The, 151
Classroom teacher, 131-34
Clinical impressions, 126
Clinical vacation, 122
Clinician(s)
  adequate room for, 65
  duties of, 76
  effective use of time, 79
Code of Ethics, 14, 22, 200-203
Cody, Robert C., 95
Coffman, Ruth, 123
Colorado Evaluation Conference (1975), 45
Commercial materials
  equipment, publishers, and prices, 219-24
  list of, 72
Communicately impaired children
  receiving educational services, 34
Communication differences, 29
Communication disorders, 28
  among school-age children, 8
  incidence of, in children, 46
Communication Disorders, Department of, 94
Communication problems, incidence of, 6-9
Communicative development program, 33
Community College of Baltimore, 145
Community information program, 145
Community resources required, knowledge of, 38
Comprehensive Assessment and Service Evaluation Information System (CASE), 171
Comprehensive Assessment and Service Evaluation Information System for Language, Speech and Hearing Programs in Schools, 28
Conlon, Sara, 85
Connell, Phil J., 74
Continuing education, 181
Continuum-of-services model, 30-36
  uses of, 33
Cooper, Eugene B., 82

Generalization, 117
Gerstenslager Company, 69
Goal-setting, 57-58
Goldman-Fristoe Test of Articulation, 89, 161, 162
Goldman-Fristoe-Woodcock Auditory Selective Attention Test, 162
Goldman-Fristoe-Woodcock Sound/ Symbol Test, 162
Goldman-Fristoe-Woodcock Test of Auditory Discrimination, 161
Goldman-Lynch Sounds and Symbols Development Kit, 150
Goldman-Woodcock-Fristoe Auditory Memory Test, 162
Greenberg, Herbert J., 95
Gross, Frank P., 112, 175, 180
Group Dynamics: Research and Theory, 123
Group screening program, consent for, 86
Group therapy, 122-24
Gruenewald, Lee J., 138, 139
Guidance counselor, 136

Haines, Harold H., 4
Handbook of Speech Pathology, 123
Handicap, defined, 11-12
Head Start programs, 18, 144, 145
Healey, William C., 7, 8, 52, 53, 56, 92, 93, 97, 111, 174, 178
Health, Education and Welfare, Department of (HEW), 7
Health and Social Development, Department of, 94
Hearing-impaired, 18-19, 29, 116
development of programs for, 5
Hearing testing facilities, 93
Hess, Rhoda, 198, 199
High school programs, 151-56
Home and/or hospital services, 36
Houston Test of Language Development, 161
Howerton, Gerald E., 67
Hull, F. M., 7

Identification audiometry, 91-93
Illinois Test of Psycholinguistic Abilities, 160, 161, 162
Impedance audiometry, 94-95
disadvantage of, 95

Indiana University, 56
Individualized Educational Programs (IEPs), 81, 99
form, 101-7
In-service program, 133-34
Intensive cycle model, 112
problems of, 112-13
Intermediate units, 65
Irwin, Ruth Beckey, 4, 172
Ithaca College Mobile Audiology Unit, 94
Itinerant model, 111-12

Jelinek, Janis A., 144
Johns, Elizabeth L., 180
Johnson, Wendell, 7
Jones, Shirley A., 7, 8, 52, 56, 92, 93
Journal of Speech and Hearing Disorders, 16-17, 182
Journal of Speech and Hearing Research, 182
Journot, Vida M., 172

Kester, Dorothy, 2, 3
Kindred, Leslie W., 124
Klodd, David A., 94
Knight, Helen Sullivan, 153
Kodman, Frank, Jr., 83
Koenigsknecht, Roy A., 131

Language and Language Behavior Abstracts, 182
Language Disabilities in Children and Adolescents, 138
Language disorders, 6, 28
Language Handbook: Concepts, Assessment, Intervention, 138
Language, Speech and Hearing Services in Schools, 10, 18, 21, 36, 175, 182, 183
Legislation, impact of, 37
Lesson planning, 119-21
Letter and report writing, 124-25
Levine, Herbert S., 93
Licensing, 23-24
Litigation, 39
Logemann, Jerilyn A., 162
Lowell, Elizabeth L., 123
Lukens, Jean, 19
Lynch, M., 143